The Motor Routes of England

Western Section

Gordon Home

(Contributor: Charles Henry Ashdown)

Alpha Editions

This edition published in 2023

ISBN : 9789357950626

Design and Setting By
Alpha Editions
www.alphaedis.com
Email - info@alphaedis.com

Contents

PREFACE

There have been many inquiries for this new volume of the 'Motor Routes of England,' which I should have been glad to publish a year ago had the necessary time been at my disposal. Finding that there was little chance of getting the book out even this year, I obtained the help of Mr. Charles H. Ashdown, who has written a considerable portion of the letterpress under my supervision. We motored over a great part of the routes together last year, and part of North Wales, which I had no time to visit, Mr. Ashdown motored through in my car without me. Although he knew the country intimately, I thought it better, from the motorist's point of view, that he should go through the district afresh. I hope, therefore, that, having taken great pains to give the latest available information, this book will prove of use to all who take their cars into Wales and those parts of England which are included.

As in the previous volumes of this series, I am greatly indebted to the Secretary of the Touring Department of the Royal Automobile Club for his exceedingly kind assistance in working out the routes. They are planned on the accumulated experience of a great many members of the club, who have placed their knowledge at the disposal of their fellow-members.

My experience of the Daimler 38 h.-p. car in which we toured through the greater part of Wales and the adjoining English counties was, as before, entirely satisfactory. We never had to give a thought to the running of the car in the hundreds of miles of mountainous roads we traversed.

Although the route maps accompanying the text are generally sufficient for all the ordinary needs of the touring motorist, I do not think it desirable to travel without the sheets of Bartholomew's half-an-inch-to-the-mile reduced survey maps. The coloured contours are of such service in showing the chief features of the surrounding country that I always feel happier with them. The sheets required for this book are numbered 8, 11, 12, 16, 17, 18, 21, 22, 23, 24, 25, 28, 29, 30.

I have been asked by those who have used the previous volumes of this series to give a list of hotels, and in that printed at the end of this book I give the names of those hotels I can recommend. I shall be exceedingly grateful to any reader who discovers any inaccuracies in this book if he will be kind enough to let me hear of them.

GORDON HOME.

43, GLOUCESTER STREET,
Warwick Square,
London, S.W.
May 1, 1911.

SECTION I
(TRUNK ROUTE)

THE HOLYHEAD ROAD

LONDON TO DUNSTABLE, 32 MILES

DISTANCES ALONG THE ROUTE

Miles.		
London—Marble Arch to Elstree	11	½
Elstree to St. Albans	8	
St. Albans to Dunstable	12	½

NOTES FOR DRIVERS

From the **Marble Arch** to **Elstree** the surface is very good, in spite of trams for part of the way.

Elstree to **St. Albans**.—A hilly but good road.

St. Albans.—Speed limit, 10 miles per hour; dangerous cross-roads in centre of town.

St. Albans to **Dunstable**.—Excellent surface, almost level.

PLACES OF INTEREST ON THE ROUTE

Edgware.—An old-fashioned village.

Elstree.—A charmingly situated village, overlooking Aldenham Park.

The road through Highgate, Finchley, and Barnet passes the following places on the way to St. Albans:

Chipping Barnet.—A growing town, much modernized; church, Perpendicular style, but recently almost entirely rebuilt.

Monken Hadley.—A pretty village; interesting church with cradle beacon affixed to tower; obelisk of Battle of Barnet.

South Mimms.—Small village; Perpendicular church, with traces of Early English; the Frowyke Chapel, with effigy.

Salisbury Hall.—A sixteenth-century moated grange.

St. Albans.—Cathedral, Early Norman (1077) to Decorated, of exceptional interest; great gateway of the monastery; Roman walls of *Verulamium* and British causeway; medieval clock-tower; sites of the two battles; St. Michael's Church, Saxon, with monument of Bacon; old timbered houses.

Redbourne.—Small village; church, Norman and Early English; fine chancel screen.

Dunstable.—Ancient town, with earthworks; Priory Church, Transition Norman, impressive west front.

THE STARTING-POINT

The best and most direct route from London to the finest scenery in Wales, as well as to many of the most picturesque towns and districts in the western half of the central or midland portion of England, is the Holyhead Road. The older route books invariably give the General Post Office as the best starting-point, and this has been indicated on the route map on this page, and that road beyond Barnet is described, but as the Edgware Road is so much preferable in many ways, the distances by that way are given at the head of this section. From the Marble Arch the road goes as straight as an arrow, passing through Maida Vale, Brondesbury, and Cricklewood. The Welsh Harp Reservoir is crossed, and the villages of Edgware and Elstree passed through, and the road from Barnet is joined at St. Albans.

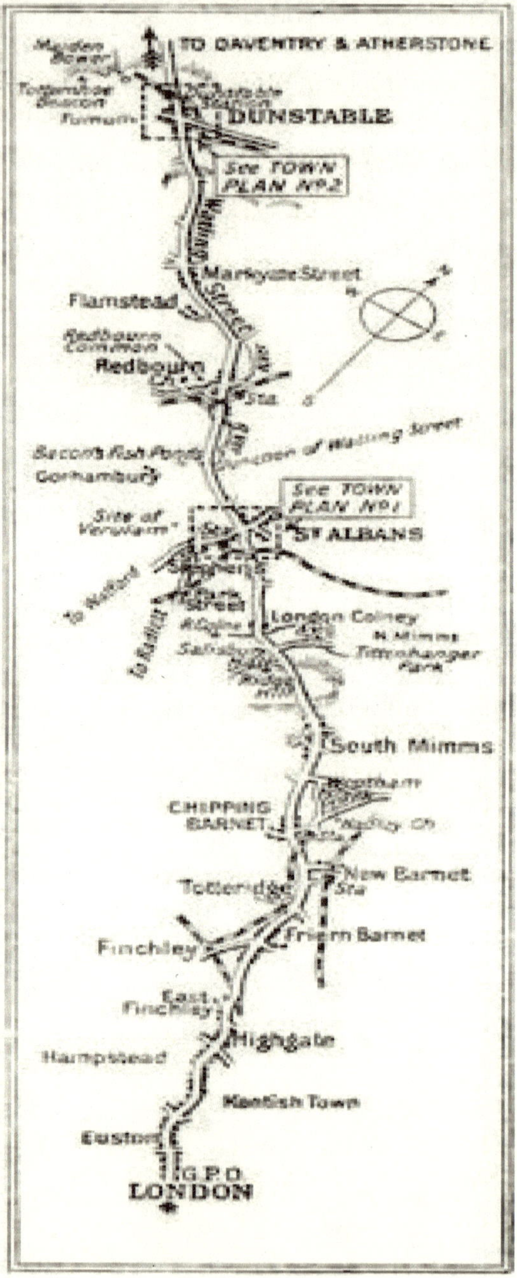

(TRUNK) No. 1.
LONDON TO DUNSTABLE.

By the older route shown in the map the first open country is not reached until Barnet is passed. Barnet itself is now a suburban town without any interest.

MONKEN HADLEY

Upon leaving Barnet, a slight detour to the right, occupying a few minutes, leads to Monken Hadley Church, of varied styles of architecture. It stands upon high ground near the road, and is picturesquely surrounded by trees and pleasantly situated old houses on a village green. The iron cradle beacon affixed to the tower is an object of great rarity. It was used in past times to signal the approach of disturbers of the peace. A tall obelisk near the church was erected early in the eighteenth century to mark the site of the battlefield of Barnet, 1471, immortalized in Bulwer Lytton's 'Last of the Barons,' and memorable for the death of the great King-maker. A road with a few easy turns in it leads back to the main route. It passes Wrotham Park, the seat of the Rev. the Earl of Strafford, whose family name is Byng. Within one of the rooms the oak cabin of the flag-ship once occupied by Admiral Byng has been erected, conveyed thither when the vessel was broken up. Since 1757, when the Admiral was shot upon his own quarter-deck, *pour encourager les autres*, no Byng has entered the navy, the family having transferred its allegiance to the army as a mild protest.

SOUTH MIMMS

The church contains traces of Early English architecture, but the main features are Perpendicular. In the Frowyke Chapel, separated from the church by a Perpendicular parclose screen, is a well-preserved effigy of the Transition period and an interesting brass let in the floor. The door to the vanished rood-loft is in good condition, and a low-side window may be found in the chancel. Thomas de Frowyke, died 1448, is buried under the tower; the inscription states that six sons and twelve daughters furnished the matrimonial quiver. The ecclesiologist with time upon his hands will find an interesting church at North Mimms, about two miles across country (see map), standing in the grounds of an Elizabethan mansion. From South Mimms a long and easy ascent leads to the summit of Ridge Hill, where the massive tower of St. Alban's fane comes into view in the midst of a beautiful landscape. An equally long and easy descent leads to a turn, where a cottage stands upon the left, at some white gates. This is the entrance to Salisbury Hall, a picturesque moated grange of exceptional interest, with quaint gables, twisted chimneys, and beautiful surroundings. Originally built in the time of Henry VIII. by Sir John Cutts, Treasurer of England, it subsequently was occupied by the well-known Sir Jeremy Snow. Nell Gwynn was often here, recouping from Court revels, and tradition asserts that Prince Charles sought refuge within its walls after the Battle of Worcester. Visitors are generally permitted to walk up to the farmyard to see the front of the house. At London Colney a piece of water is crossed. Tyttenhanger lies to the right, at a distance of about two miles; it was the country house of the Abbots of St. Albans, and has been adapted to modern requirements. The road from here to St. Albans is easy, but care should be exercised at the cross-roads in the centre of the town, where a policeman generally regulates traffic.

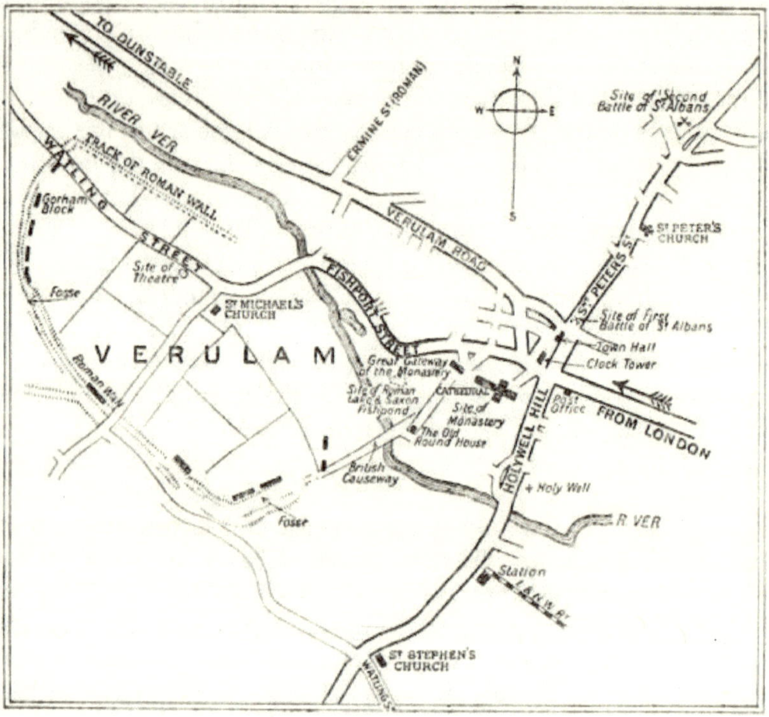

TOWN PLAN NO. 1—ST. ALBANS.

ST. ALBANS

A walk through the cloisters opposite the Great Red Lion Hotel affords a striking view of a considerable part of the vast Abbey Church, the most ancient of the great churches in England. It stands upon higher ground than any other cathedral in the British Isles, and is the longest next to Winchester. It possesses, moreover, the longest Gothic nave in the world. The Norman tower, dating from 1077, is composed of Roman bricks from the neighbouring *Verulamium*, and flints, bricks, and stone from the same site may be detected in the walls. The walk leads round to the southern part of the church, through the ancient sumpter-yard, with its fine old cedar, and thence to the west front, the site of the demolished monastery showing in irregular heaps upon the left.

The nave is open to the public free of charge. Sixpence is charged for entrance to the eastern portions (threepence each for a party of ten). Open from—

November 1 to February 28	*10 a.m. to 4 p.m.*
March 1 to April 30 *September 16 to October 31*	*10 a.m. to 5 p.m.*
May 1 to September 15	*10 a.m. to 6 p.m.*

Building Dates.

Roman Period.—St. Alban was executed upon this spot, presumably in the amphitheatre, in 303, and a church was erected to his memory by the Christians of Verulam in 313, which was still standing in Bede's time.

793. Offa the Great, King of Mercia, founded the monastery, and either repaired and enlarged the Romano-British church or built a new one.

1077. Shortly after the Conquest, Paul de Caen, a relative of Lanfranc, was appointed the first Norman abbot, and proceeded to demolish the church, subsequently erecting a great Norman building in its place, the remains of which—viz., the tower, transepts, parts of the nave and the presbytery—still remain.

On entering by the west front, which has been rebuilt by Lord Grimthorpe, the first part of the nave is Early English, dating from *c.* 1214, and one of the best examples in England. Farther on Norman bays, dating from 1077, are upon the north, while opposite them are Decorated Gothic bays, built *c.* 1323 to replace the Norman work which had fallen. The screen has been despoiled; it was erected in 1350. Passing through the door, the abbot's entrance from the cloisters is seen upon the right, and the south transept is reached, having a curious feature, the slype of Transition Norman work at the south end. The tower dates from 1077, and is the largest and heaviest of the Norman towers now remaining in England. Eight of the baluster columns round the triforia are from the former Saxon church, and date from 793. The choir-stalls are new, and above them is a remarkable ceiling, the panels dating from 1368 to 1450. The north transept is the reputed site of St. Alban's martyrdom. In the presbytery is the high-altar screen, only rivalled by that at Winchester, and dating from 1484. It is the work of Abbot Wallingford, was despoiled at the Reformation, and recently restored by the late Lord Aldenham. South of it lies the chantry tomb of Abbot Wheathampstead, and north that of Abbot Ramryge. Leaving by the north door, the presbytery aisle is reached, partly Norman and partly Early English. The old doors from the west front preserved here date from the time of Henry VI. Proceeding eastwards, the entrance to the Saint's Chapel is on the right. Here is the far-famed shrine of St. Alban, or rather the pedestal of the shrine, since the shrine itself was portable, and rested upon the top of the structure. It dates from 1306, was demolished in 1539, and built up in the three lancets at the east end of the chapel. When the arches were opened some time since, the fragments were recovered and put together. The tomb of Humphrey, Duke of Gloucester (died, or murdered, 1447; see Shakespeare, *Henry VI.*, Part II.), stands on the south of the chapel; the coffin may be seen by raising the trap-door. On the north side is the Watching Gallery, where a monk sat to guard the shrine and its treasures. It dates from *c.* 1400. There is only one other in England.

Leaving by the north door again, the shrine of St. Amphibalus, dating from 1350, is seen. It was likewise demolished at the Reformation. The Lady Chapel and its ante-chapel were erected between 1260 and 1320, and exhibit Early English and Decorated architecture. They have been restored under Lord Grimthorpe. Forty nobles who fell in the first Battle of St. Albans are interred here. At the Reformation the chapels were converted into school premises for St. Albans Grammar School, and used as such for 300 years. The stone carving is particularly beautiful. Passing out by the south door, an altar slab is seen, with its five crosses; a grille, dating from *c.* 1270, which is the only trellis screen in England; and upon the south the openings to former external chapels. In the Wheathampstead Chapel may be seen the brass of Abbot de la Mare (1349 to 1396), reputed to be the finest ecclesiastical brass in existence.

The Great Gateway of the Monastery, opposite to the west front of the Abbey Church, dates from 1361, and now forms part of St. Albans Grammar School, one of the oldest, if not *the* oldest, scholastic foundations in the kingdom. It was probably founded in the reign of King Edred, about 948, and among the eminent personages attending it have been Alexander Nequam, foster-brother of Richard I.; Matthew Paris, who left the school in 1217 and entered the monastery; Sir John Mandeville, the famous writer of his supposed travels, who lies buried in the abbey; and Nicholas Breakspere, born in 1090, who subsequently became Pope of Rome, the only Englishman who has attained to that dignity. In 1195 the school was the largest in England. In 1381 the gates were forced by the rioters in Wat Tyler's rebellion and the precincts of the monastery invaded; and in 1480 the third printing-press in England was set up in the building. Among post-Reformation scholars one of the most distinguished was Francis Bacon.

At the bottom of the lane leading from the monastery gateway is the well-known Fighting Cocks Inn, reputed to be the oldest inhabited house in

Britain, and a few steps from it the River Ver. Crossing the stream, the British causeway is reached, one of the most ancient earthworks in Great Britain, and the Roman walls lie just beyond. The visitor here stands upon soil which recalls memories of the earliest period in the chronology of English history.

Verulamium.—At the time of Cæsar's invasion, 54 B.C., Cassivelaunus was ruling over a great tract of country, with his capital at *Verulamium*, the home of a long line of ancestors. The Roman general captured the city and exacted tribute. In A.D. 42 the town submitted to the Romans under Aulus Plautius, but was sacked and burnt by Boadicea and her followers in A.D. 61. Rebuilt and fortified with walls and towers, it was the first Roman city built in Britain. Its area is 203 acres. In A.D. 58 Nero made it a *municipium*, or free city, York being the only other town so honoured. It was essentially a trading and residential city, and became the capital of Southern Britain. In 303 St. Alban was led out of the gates and martyred upon Holmhurst, where the Abbey Church was subsequently erected. By 436 the Roman occupation had ceased, and swarms of Picts and Scots, Irish pirates, and Northmen overran the district. Many battles were fought, and in 516 *Verulamium* was sacked and burnt. It served as a quarry for many hundreds of years, yielding building materials for the monastery and town. The only Roman theatre as yet discovered in Britain came to light about fifty years since, and the foundations of the largest building as yet unearthed in our islands were revealed a few years ago. The thorough excavation of the whole site is being mooted at the present time.

St. Michael's Church is of Saxon architecture, dating from 948. It contains an Elizabethan pulpit with hour-glass stand, and the tomb and statue of Francis Bacon, Viscount St. Albans.

The Two Battles of St. Albans were fought in 1455 and 1461, the first chiefly in St. Peter's Street and its byways, and the second upon Bernard's Heath, lying to the north of St. Peter's Church, in whose churchyard many thousands of the slain were interred.

The Clock Tower in the High Street dates from 1410, and contains a medieval bell of beautiful workmanship, *c.* 1403, the curfew bell.

Other objects of interest in St. Albans are Sopwell Ruins, St. Stephen's Church, and Gorhambury, two miles distant, the house of the Bacons.

Shortly after leaving St. Albans by the Redbourn road, the River Ver is crossed at Bow Bridge, and here the Watling Street from London, which has passed through the centre of Verulam, joins the road, and from this point until Chester is reached the way lies almost entirely upon this great Roman artery. It is intact from London to St. Stephen's Church, St. Albans, and, with a few gaps, from near Bow Bridge to Chester.

At Redbourn a few quaint old houses still linger in the long, narrow street. To reach the church, which is Norman and Early English, a turn to the left is taken at the entrance to the village. It contains a very fine chancel screen.

Flamstead lies half a mile off the main road, at the summit of a steep hill. The church has recently been restored—a restoration in the true sense of the word.

A long, steady rise through beautiful country eventually leads to

DUNSTABLE

The modern town is successor to the ancient station of *Durocobrivæ* and a great Roman market, the *Forum Dianæ*.

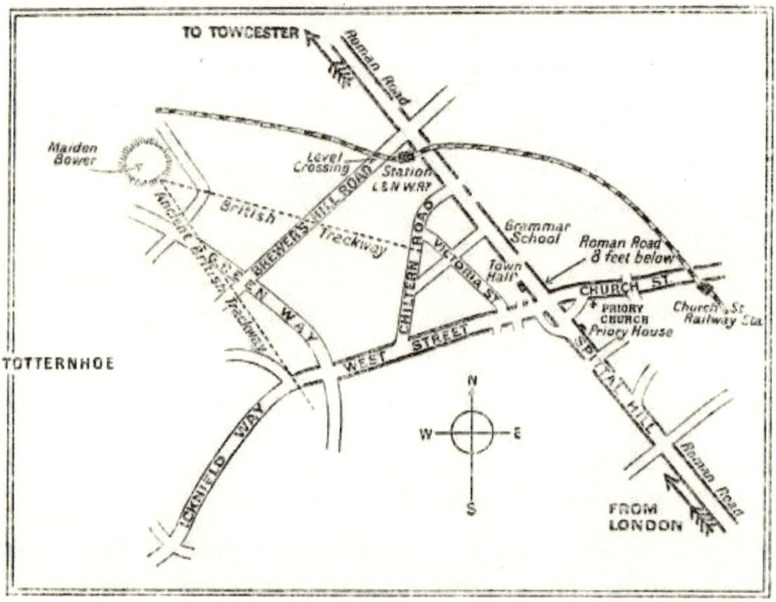

TOWN PLAN NO. 2—DUNSTABLE.

The district is remarkably rich in British and Roman remains: Maiden Bower, a circular British earthwork, and Totternhoe, a combined British and Roman fort, lie at short distances from the town (see Map). The Watling Street is crossed here in the centre of the town by the Icknield Way, and a piece of the Roman road was exposed near this spot, which was 9 inches thick and intensely hard, of cemented flints and sandstone.

Turning to the right, along Church Street (part of the Icknield Way), the priory church, with its beautiful west front, is seen upon the right.

Dunstable Priory Church.—Founded 1131, the church is but a fragment of that which formerly stood here. Tower, transepts, chancel, and Lady Chapel have disappeared, and even the nave, which remains, has been curtailed. The body of Queen Eleanor rested here in 1290 upon its progress to London; and in 1533 Archbishop Cranmer held his court in the church, and formally divorced Queen Catherine of Aragon from the King. The priory was dissolved in 1534. The greater part of the building is Transition Norman, the chevron and billet ornamentation being of excellent workmanship. The north aisle is Perpendicular. In the chancel are ten balusters of Flemish design and execution. Undoubtedly the great feature of the building is the exquisite west front, which, though suffering in parts from recent restoration, still delights the ecclesiologist. It contains four orders of architecture, which effectually harmonize with one another.

Mr. Worthington G. Smith, the eminent local antiquary, has written a most admirable handbook to the town, which will supplement these brief particulars.

SECTION II
(TRUNK ROUTE)

DUNSTABLE TO ATHERSTONE, 72½ MILES

DISTANCES ALONG THE ROUTE

Miles.		
Dunstable to Hockliffe	4	½
Hockliffe to Fenny Stratford	7	¼
Fenny Stratford to Stony Stratford	7	
Stony Stratford to Towcester	8	
Towcester to Daventry	12	¼
Daventry to Kilsby	5	½
Kilsby to Lutterworth	9	¾
Lutterworth to Cross-in-Hand	2	½
Cross-in-Hand to High Cross	3	¾
High Cross to Atherstone	12	

NOTES FOR DRIVERS

Dunstable to Daventry.—Undulating in places, but with good surface to Daventry.

Daventry to Lutterworth.—Poor road to Kilsby; 4 miles from Kilsby an ascent of 1 in 14, followed by a descent of 1 in 12; then a gradually improving road to Lutterworth.

Kilsby to Atherstone.—Undulating road, with good surface.

PLACES OF INTEREST ON THE ROUTE

Fenny Stratford.—A small town with a Georgian church.

Stony Stratford.—A small town with no great interest.

Towcester.—Easton Neston House and Park.

Daventry.—Small town; historic inn.

Lutterworth.—Quiet country town; associations with Wycliffe, especially in the Perpendicular church, where the great Protestant's pulpit is still to be seen.

Cross-in-Hand.—Roman centre for roads.

Nuneaton.—Two miles off the main road to the south-west; the George Eliot country.

Hartshill.—Two miles off route; remains of Norman castle.

Mancetter.—Church, Roman camp, and manor-house.

Atherstone.—A small manufacturing town on the Watling Street, without any interesting features.

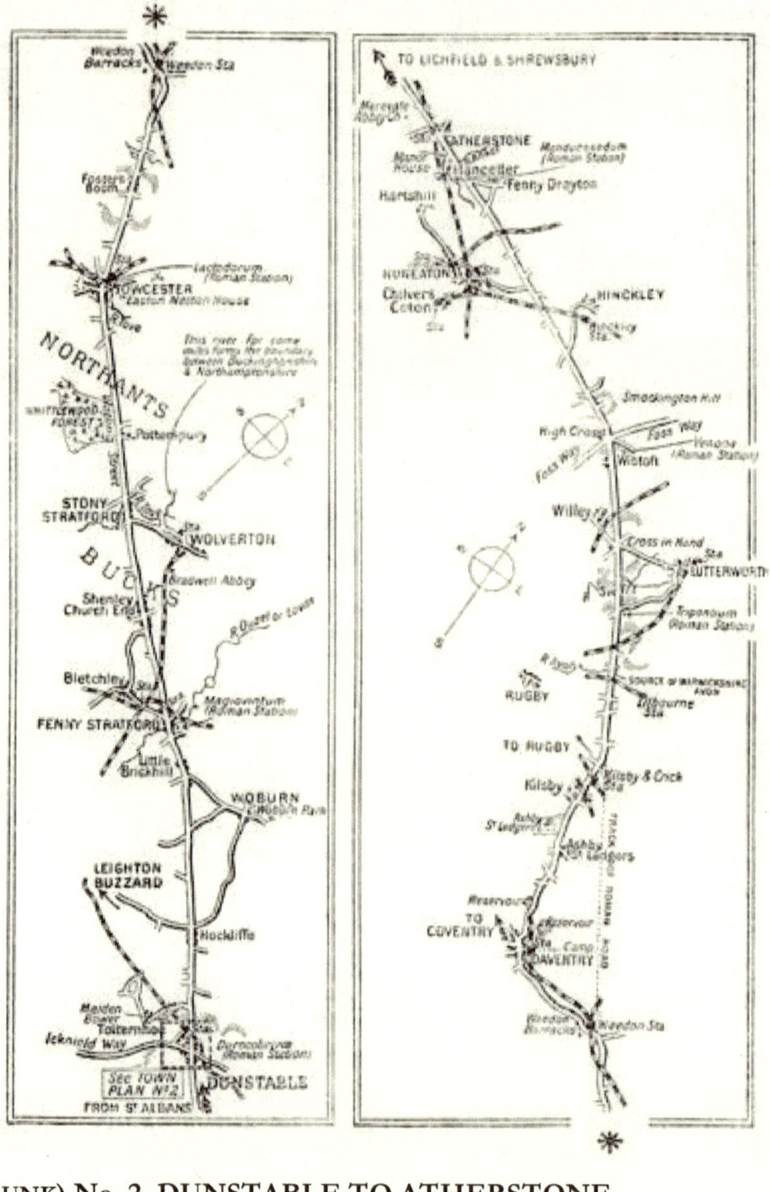

(TRUNK) No. 2. DUNSTABLE TO ATHERSTONE.

Shortly after leaving Dunstable a long, easy descent of the northern slope of the Dunstable Downs occurs, these hills being part of the Chilterns. A fine view over a large part of Bucks and Beds is seen in front, and an interesting sweep of the Downs behind. A number of sleepy little villages occur, each presenting rural features of its own in harmony with the surroundings. At Hockliffe a side-road leads to the beautiful Woburn Park and Abbey. At Fenny Stratford, a small town chiefly consisting of one street, the Roman station of *Magiovintum* was situated, and coins and other remains are frequently found; the only modern association appears to be connected with Browne Willis, the antiquary, who is buried here. The church is early Georgian, dating from 1724. Seven miles farther on, Stony Stratford, a small uninteresting town, is reached, known chiefly in history through having had an Eleanor Cross, which disappeared in Puritan days, and also from the capture of Edward V. by his uncle, the Duke of Gloucester. Bradwell Abbey, founded in 1155, now a farmhouse, lies about three miles away to the right.

From Stony Stratford to Towcester the route runs as straight as an arrow, and one can imagine the metalled track of the road the legions tramped lying but a few feet beneath the surface. Towcester is the ancient *Lactodorum*, and the later Tove Castra, or Camp on the River Tove, which flows through the town. Few, if any, Roman remains are now visible, and Easton Neston House with its picturesque park is the only feature of interest in the neighbourhood.

The road to Weedon is somewhat undulating, and rises in places to 500 feet above sea-level, an altitude which has not been reached since leaving Dunstable. At Weedon it is necessary to make a detour to the left, as the Watling Street for some considerable distance has been allowed to fall into disrepair; in fact, it is merely in some cases a trackway through grassy fields, with farmers' gates across the vanished road. The restoration of this part of the Roman way has been proposed at times, but never carried out, the considerable cost and the paucity of towns and villages probably accounting for it. This gap in continuity is to be deplored for sentimental reasons, but not for practical utility, as the track is at times more than undulating.

DAVENTRY

Daventry is a small town possessing but few attractions beyond its historic hotel, the Wheat Sheaf, built in 1610, and known in the annals of Warwickshire as the resting-place of Charles I. (after the taking of Leicester) for six consecutive days in 1645, the Royal troops, both horse and foot, in considerable numbers occupying the surrounding fields. The regal bedchamber may be seen and even occupied, while the courtyard, famous in duelling days, is visible from its window. In one encounter in 1696 a young ensign, named Gardner, gasped out his life after a duel to the death with his lieutenant. Near Daventry lies Althorp Park, the seat of Earl Spencer. In this medieval house, not greatly altered since, James I. and William III. were entertained.

On leaving Daventry the road turns sharply to the right to K i l s b y , with a poor surface most of the way. It passes through a well-wooded country, and a short distance beyond Kilsby joins the Watling Street at an acute angle. Upon looking backwards, the line of the ancient highway may be distinctly traced through the fields. From this point until Atherstone is reached, a distance of nearly twenty-three miles, Leicestershire lies upon the right-hand side of the road and Warwickshire upon the left.

D u n s m o r e   H e a t h is then crossed, and shortly afterwards two lines of railway are passed, the source of the Warwickshire Avon being near the first at Dove Bridge. At Churchover is the birthplace of Cave, of *Gentleman's Magazine* fame. The main road from Rugby to Lutterworth branches off to the right. Near this point, on the brow of the hill, just north-west of Cave's Inn and on both sides of the Watling Street, is the site of the great Roman station *Tripontium.* The remains have almost disappeared, but pieces of pottery are plentiful, and coins are now and then unearthed.

RUGBY

lies a few miles to the west of the main route, and is famous for its great school, founded in 1567, being one of the four great public schools in England. The buildings are chiefly in the Tudor style, and date from 1808, with many subsequent additions. Besides the school, there are practically no objects of interest in the town. The road to Lutterworth is slightly undulating, with a good surface.

LUTTERWORTH

is a quiet little country town of about 2,000 inhabitants, lying in a pastoral district fissured occasionally with wooded valleys. It is a typical foxhunting centre. The main street descends a hill somewhat abruptly, and crosses a small bridge over the River Swift, from which point the ashes of Wycliffe were scattered. The church is endeared to the champions of Protestantism by its associations with Wycliffe, and by the tangible relics which are preserved in it of his residence here from 1375 to 1384. The architecture of the church is chiefly of the fourteenth century. The nave is early Perpendicular, but a Decorated window occupies the end of the south aisle, where there was formerly a Lady Chapel. The chancel also is Perpendicular, with an Early English window and door. It is thus somewhat difficult to point out work which belongs to that period when Wycliffe ministered in the building. The greater part of the nave, however, may be thus assigned, and also the fresco over the north doorway, showing a queen between two kings. Over the chancel arch is another fresco. The nave roof is Perpendicular, but the pulpit, from which the reformer preached, is the great object of interest, dating as it does from a period anterior to Wycliffe's incumbency, and is thus over 500 years old. A fragment of a cope or chasuble is interesting as an undoubted relic, but the chair, table, and wooden candlesticks must be regarded with suspicion—the chair more than the others. The 'Morning Star of the Reformation' was buried in the chancel, where his remains rested for thirty years; they were then dug up, burnt, and cast into the river.

The road from Lutterworth, rejoining the Watling Street, emerges at the Cross-in-Hand, where care must be taken in the selection of the right road. From Cross-in-Hand to High Cross there is nothing of particular moment, but at the latter place, where five roads meet, was one of the most important junctions of Roman highways for the Watling Street. It is crossed here by the Foss Way coming from Gloucester, and leading through Leicester to Lincoln. The great station of *Venonæ* or *Benones* was situated here, but has entirely disappeared. Taking the road marked 'To Holyhead,' the road leads over Smockington Hill, and a few miles farther on a turning on the left to Nuneaton (two miles off the main road) is reached.

Nuneaton lies in the centre of the 'George Eliot' country, and is the Milverton of the novelist, while Chilvers Coton near it figures in 'Scenes of Clerical Life,' and 'Oldinport' may be traced in 'Newdegate,' the family name of the residents at Arbury Hall, a delightfully situated country-seat a few miles to the south-west of the town. Beyond this Nuneaton possesses no special features, except a church built in the Decorated period, and another—St. Mary's—a modern replica of the Abbey Church which formerly occupied the site.

The spire of Hinckley Church is now seen upon the right, six miles to the north of which lies the Battlefield of Bosworth. The North Warwickshire Coalfield has now been reached, and in the high ground upon the left there is an interesting geological district. The stone quarries worked there were formerly supposed to produce Millstone Grit of the Carboniferous formation, but which has recently been proved to be pre-Cambrian, and necessarily the most ancient of rocks. Hartshill is in this district; it is the birthplace of Michael Drayton, and contains a few ruins of a Norman castle dating from 1125. To the right of the Watling Street lies Fenny Drayton, where George Fox, the founder of the sect of Quakers, was born. Before entering Atherstone the small village of Witherley is passed upon the right, and the River Anker here divides the site of the great Roman station of *Manduessedum* into two parts. The name has been anglicized into Mancetter. The oblong earthwork yet remains, about 630 feet long and 440 feet broad. The church stands on the ruins of the western side of the camp. Many coins have been found here, and great masses of Roman masonry lie beneath the soil. The summer camps lie upon the adjacent hills. The first turning on the left, after passing the bridge, leads in a few minutes to Mancetter Manor House, originally built in 1135, and presenting a quaint

Edwardian appearance at the present day. In 1432 the Glovers occupied it, one of whom suffered martyrdom in the Marian persecution.

ATHERSTONE,

a singularly uninteresting looking town, whose staple manufacture is felt hats, has a long, straggling street, a portion of the Watling Street, and during sewage operations about fifty years ago the remains of the original Roman road came to light, at some depth below the present surface; some of the paving-stones, grooved by chariot wheels, were in places cemented together. Henry of Richmond slept at the Three Tuns Inn, now demolished, the night before Bosworth Battle, and heard Mass in the church, which is not of great archæological interest.

SECTION III
(TRUNK ROUTE)

ATHERSTONE TO SHREWSBURY, 59 MILES

DISTANCES ALONG THE ROUTE

	Miles.	
Atherstone to Fazeley	7	
Fazeley to Tamworth	1	½
Tamworth to Lichfield	7	
Lichfield to Muckley Corner	2	¾
Muckley Corner to Four Crosses Inn	8	¾
Four Crosses Inn to Gailey Station	2	¾
Gailey Station to Shifnal	11	¾
Shifnal to Oakengates	4	¾
Oakengates to Shrewsbury	12	¾

NOTES FOR DRIVERS

Atherstone to Lichfield.—Undulating road with fine surface.

Lichfield to Shifnal.—Almost level; surface fairly good, but the direct road (Watling Street) is rough and has some steep hills near Oakengates. The **Shifnal Loop** is, therefore, recommended. (See Route Map 3.)

PLACES OF INTEREST ON THE ROUTE

Tamworth.—An ancient town; historic castle; Perpendicular church.

Lichfield.—Cathedral; statue of, and associations with, Samuel Johnson.

Shifnal.—Pretty town, with quaint timbered houses; church Norman, Early English, and Decorated.

Wroxeter.—The Roman *Uriconium*; Roman remains.

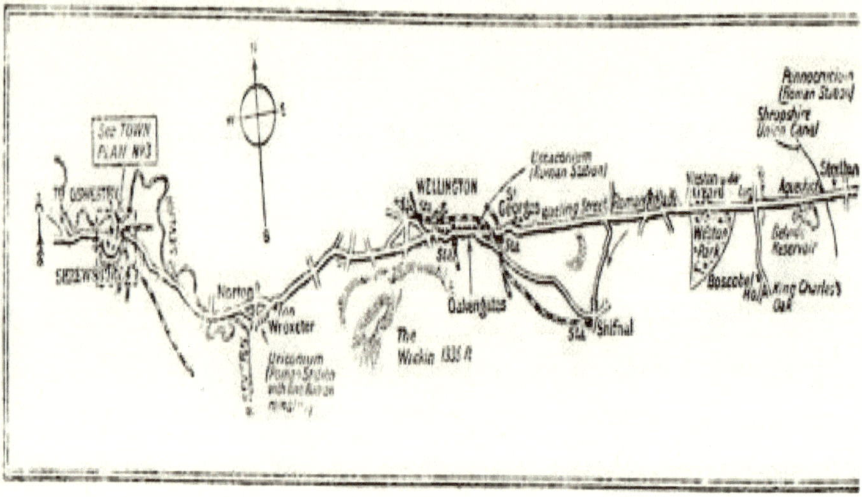

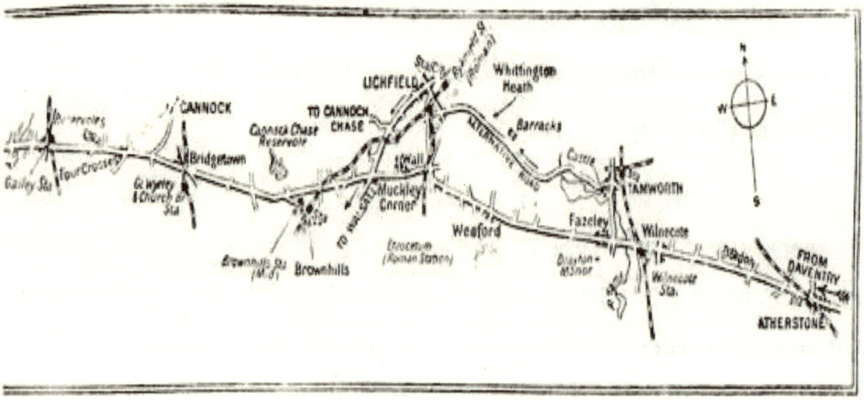

(TRUNK) No. 3. ATHERSTONE TO SHREWSBURY. (TRUNK) No. 3.

At Atherstone the railway is passed by a bridge, superseding a former level-crossing. Immediately to the left a road leads to the site of the almost demolished Merevale Abbey, the chapel of which is still used as a parish church, and contains recumbent effigies of the Ferrers family. The road to Fazeley is undulating and uninteresting. To the south of the town lies Drayton Manor, the seat of the great Sir Robert Peel. Here one is forcibly reminded by ocular evidence that this is a mining district. A turning to the right leads to

TAMWORTH,

one of the most ancient towns in Warwickshire and Staffordshire, for it stands in both counties. It was a royal residence in the time of the Heptarchy, and from that remote period to the present time the castle has been of more or less importance—in fact, it is one of the most ancient buildings in Central England. The mound upon which it stands is of British origin; Queen Ethelfleda (died 918) erected the castle which, with many alterations and additions, meets the view at the present day. It has recently been acquired by the Corporation, and is open to visitors. The ancient causeway leading to the entrance presents the finest example of Saxon 'herring-bone' masonry to be found in the kingdom. The circular keep is of picturesque red sandstone, which does much to mitigate the effect of the Perpendicular windows. The venerable building was the home of the Marmions, the Frevilles, and the Ferrers, and in 'Marmion' we find:

'They hailed him lord of Fontenaye,

Of Lutterward and Scrivelbaye,

Of Tamworth Tower and Town.'

The last of the Marmions died in 1291. The bases of the dungeon walls are four yards thick, and a visit to the castle interior gives the impression of massive solidity.

Tamworth Church, founded in the eighth century, was destroyed by the Danes in 874, and rebuilt by King Edgar. In 1345 it was burnt, but rebuilt. The crypt and two Norman transept arches remain of the early building. The late Perpendicular tower contains a curious double staircase, and is a prominent feature for many miles round.

LICHFIELD

The road to Lichfield lies by the side of the River Tame for some distance, but it passes through a colliery district; some finely wooded knolls, however, occur on either side of the road. About three miles before reaching the city the barracks are seen upon the right, with an extensive common for training purposes; at the same time the three Cathedral spires, 'The Ladies of the Vale,' form an attractive feature in the landscape. The road leads directly to the C a t h e d r a l, which is one of those exquisitely pretty ecclesiastical edifices which one wishes to put under a glass case for preservation from the elements. It has been the seat of a bishopric since the seventh century, and is connected with St. Chad. A Norman church succeeded the Saxon edifice, but has entirely disappeared. The earliest part of the present building, the west choir, dates from *c.* 1200; the south and north transepts followed, and the nave and west front date from about 1275. The eastern parts were finished in 1325. The central spire was destroyed during the Civil War, and rebuilt by Sir Christopher Wren.

The Cathedral is open to the public from 9.30 to 5 on weekdays.

LICHFIELD CATHEDRAL.
It is one of the smaller cathedrals, but its workmanship is of an exquisite richness.

Upon entering the west front, which is one of the most beautiful in England in the Decorated style, the Early English nave with dog-tooth mouldings, the clustered pillars, and the fine vaulting, impress one by their beauty and gracefulness. In the north transept one finds five lancet windows, with Perpendicular examples on either side. In the south transept the vaulted roof, with its huge bosses, and the large Perpendicular window are special features, and here the rich stained glass and the warm appearance of the red sandstone produce an effect upon which the eye delights to dwell. The choir, with its side aisles, richly vaulted roof, and huge windows springing from the triforium, at once attract the visitor's attention. The early Decorated blank arcading of the aisles is interesting, as is also the peep afforded into a building upon the south side. In the south aisle of the retro-choir a celebrated monument, the 'Sleeping Children,' touches a chord that vibrates in the nature of all who possess the tenderness of human sympathy. The Lady Chapel has rich Decorated arcading upon its walls, from above which spring nine windows with trefoil tracery. In seven of these is the stained glass that once adorned the great Cistercian nunnery of Herckenrode, in the Bishopric of Liège. It dates from 1530, and was brought to England after the suppression of the nunnery in 1802. Although one of the smallest of English cathedrals, Lichfield is singularly impressive by reason of beautiful details and graceful proportions. Although actually situated in a valley, its site is the highest in England, with the exception of St. Albans.

In the Market Square stands the statue of Samuel Johnson, opposite the house in which the great lexicographer first saw the light.

In order to rejoin the Watling Street, the road marked 'To Cannock' should be taken, and about one and a half miles from the city a turning to the right leads to that place. Continue, however, in the same straight line for another one and a half miles, and the Watling Street will be struck, leading off to the right at Muckley Corner. The Roman station of *Eteocetum* lies about one mile to the south-east at Wall, where the Rycknield Street starts for the North. This is missed by the detour to Tamworth and Lichfield.

Near Brownhills Common a large piece of water—Cannock Chase reservoir—lies to the right, and farther on another reservoir is passed. Two miles beyond Gailey railway-bridge is the site of the Roman station of *Pennocrucium*, near a roadside inn, and immediately afterwards the Shropshire Union Canal crosses the road by an aqueduct. Boscobel House and Park lie about a mile towards the south, with the famous oak in which Charles hid himself after Worcester. A straight run of seven miles passes by Weston Park, renowned for its beauty, and brings one to a turning on the left, the main road to Shifnal. It is advisable to pass through Shifnal and regain the Watling Street farther on, and thus avoid the extremely bad road between Redhill and Oakengates.

S h i f n a l is an interesting little town, possessing many quaint old timbered houses, with overhanging upper stories, often enriched by carving. A turning to the right in the middle of the town leads to the C h u r c h . It possesses many curious remains of Norman architecture, among which are the chancel arch and a portion of the south transept. The main structure is Early English and Decorated, the tower arches being of the former period. The tomb and effigy of the Prior of Wombridge, 1526, and some Elizabethan monuments are in the chancel. Over the south porch is a parvise, which projects in a novel manner into the church, and is supported there upon two pillars.

From Shifnal to Oakengates, the reputed site of *Uxaconium*, is mainly downhill, and through a colliery district, with all the usual concomitants pertaining to it. After a run of about six miles, during which the Wrekin, 1,335 feet high, lies to the left, a turning at an inn is reached leading to

WROXETER

This is the ancient *Uriconium*, destroyed by fire in the fifth century, and the imposing Roman remains form one of the chief attractions for visitors in the immediate vicinity of Shrewsbury. To the archæologist it is of supreme interest, as an immense variety of Roman remains have come to light, including many parts of the massive walls, the basilica and public baths. There are also exposed to view well-preserved examples of the hypocausts of villas. Should a detour be made to the site of this important Roman town, the largest encountered since leaving *Verulamium*, a good road will be found leading back to the main route, and thence to Shrewsbury. Continuing on the main road, one crosses the Severn, and keeps it for some time upon the right hand. Entering Shrewsbury, the centre of the town is approached by a steep hill, 1 in 10, where caution must be exercised on account of the traffic.

(*For town plan of Shrewsbury, see p. 77.*)

LOOP No. 1

FIRST PORTION: SHREWSBURY, WHITCHURCH, CHESTER—**SECOND PORTION**: CHESTER, MOLD, ST. ASAPH, RHYL—**THIRD PORTION**: RHYL, DENBIGH, RUTHIN, CORWEN, LLANGOLLEN, RUABON, WREXHAM, ELLESMERE, SHREWSBURY

SHREWSBURY TO CHESTER, 39½ MILES

DISTANCES ALONG THE ROUTE

	Miles.	
Shrewsbury to Wem Church	10	¾
Wem Church to Whitchurch	8	¾
Whitchurch to Broxton	10	
Broxton to Chester	10	

NOTES FOR DRIVERS

On leaving **Shrewsbury**, descent of 1 in 10 in the town; dangerous.

Road to **Chester** usually in good condition; surface splendid; no steep gradients.

Between **Shrewsbury** and **Wem**, undulating.

From **Whitchurch**, general fall from about 400 feet to sea-level at **Chester**.

PLACES OF INTEREST ON THE ROUTE

Battlefield of Shrewsbury, 1403.—About 3 miles from Shrewsbury; Battlefield Church, Perpendicular.

Wem.—Obelisk to Rowland Hill.

Whitchurch.—Busy country town; church dating from 1711.

Rowton Moor.—Three miles from Chester; battlefield, 1645.

Chester.—One of the most picturesque walled towns in England; Cathedral; town walls; the 'Rows' and other old houses.

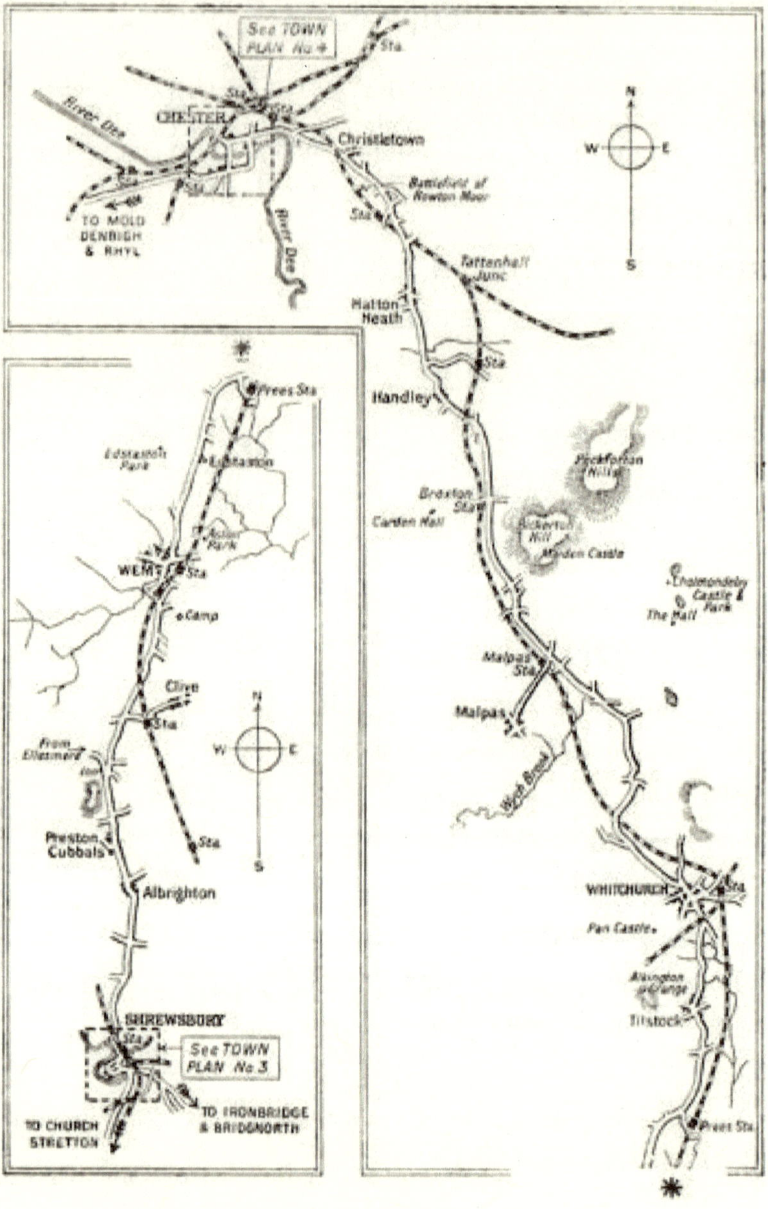

Loop 1. SHREWSBURY TO CHESTER.

Leaving Shrewsbury by the Battlefield Road, and passing through the unprepossessing parts of the old town, the church standing upon the site of the battle becomes a conspicuous object when the higher ground is reached, about a mile from the town. This remarkable memorial of the terrible slaughter which took place in 1403 is necessarily of the Perpendicular period, and at the present time is a simple parish church, to which flocks a congregation eminently agricultural. Restorations have taken place at various periods, but sufficient remains of the original to make it of great interest. The site is that upon which the fiercest part of the battle occurred, and where, after the fight, the dead were crowded by hundreds into vast pits; for the slaughter upon that fatal day was tremendous, numbering probably 8,000 men. The army of Glendower, the Mortimers, and the Percies lost 5,000 men by the most moderate estimate, and that of the victor, Henry of Bolingbroke, was but little less, chiefly owing to the deadly accuracy of the Cheshire bowmen of Percy's army, who at first almost succeeded in winning the fray. But the King's army was double the number of his opponents, and that always told in a civil war. For three hours before sunset the struggle waged round the site of the church, and when at last Percy's army broke and fled, they made for Wem to the north, or the higher, wooded ground to the east. The road to Whitchurch passes through Wem, from which Hawkstone Park may be seen towards the west upon high ground, and the obelisk to Rowland Hill. The scenery upon the route is eminently characteristic of English pastoral life, with farmsteads and cottages nestling in charming seclusion amid a wealth of foliage, or upon the summits of the small undulations which diversify the Shropshire plain. At intervals stretches of heath alternate with the cultivation, while along the whole route the Welsh mountains form a broken sky-line to the west.

Whitchurch is a busy country town with a market, and forms a centre for the trade of the district. The remains of the castle which once existed here were visible down to 1760, but now no traces can be seen.

The Church.—The old church of Whitchurch fell in 1711, and the edifice built upon the site is in heavy Romanesque architecture. There are monuments in it to the Earls of Shrewsbury, one in armour being representative of John, the first Earl, who was killed at Bordeaux in 1453, and whose remains were brought from France to be interred here.

Soon after leaving Whitchurch, Overton Scar forms a conspicuous feature in the landscape, lying to the left near the vale of the Dee.

Cholmondeley Castle, three miles to the west of Malpas Station, is the seat of the Marquis of Cholmondeley, and is situated in the Peckforton Hills. The younger son of David le Clare settled here in Norman times. The present castle is a modern building erected in the Norman style, while the old hall, of Elizabethan foundation, was, unfortunately, placed in the hands of Vanbrugh for restoration, and became so completely altered in appearance that one would hardly guess its origin. The district lying around these hills was the scene of many encounters between the Royalists and Parliamentarians. Near Broxton Station stands Carden Hall, one of the most beautiful examples of timbered mansions in the country. It was built in the time of Elizabeth, but the Cardens were here in the reign of Henry VIII. The Hall was garrisoned by the Royalists, but after being captured by the other side was plundered, like most of the mansions in this county. About a mile farther on Aldersey Hall stands to the left, about ten furlongs from the road. It is asserted that it has been occupied by the family of that name since the Norman Conquest.

In Handley Church a good brass may be seen of the Venables family, and Calveley Hall, once a manor-house and now converted into a farmhouse, has a good oak staircase and some excellent wainscotting in the rooms.

Rowton Moor is reached next, where the Royalists suffered a defeat in 1645. The road passes through the battlefield.

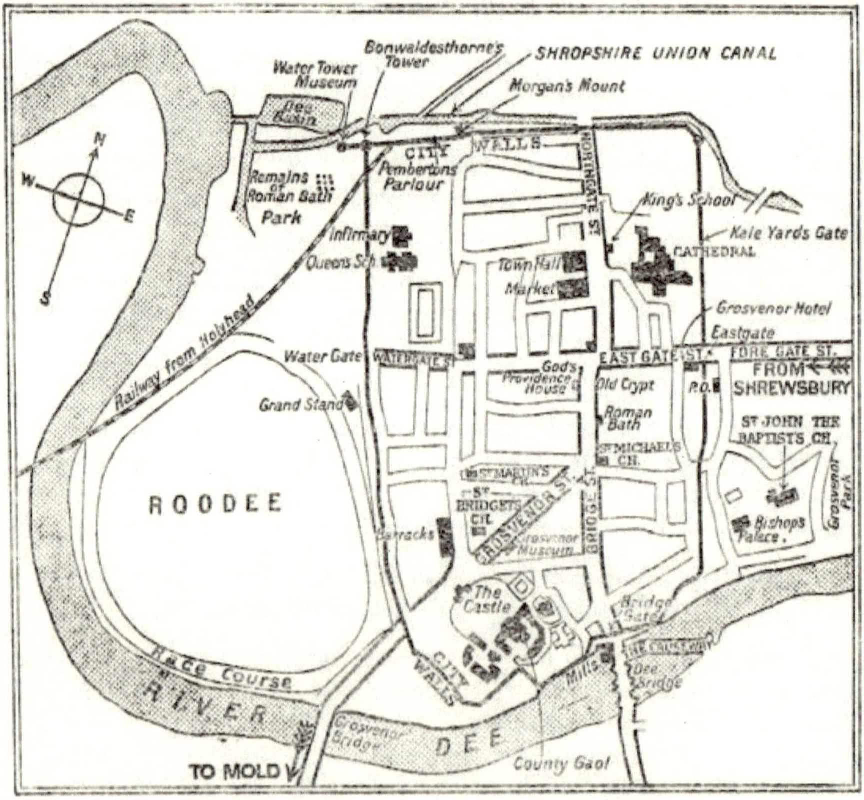

TOWN PLAN NO. 4—CHESTER.

CHESTER

From Shrewsbury the road into Chester leads into Foregate Street, and presently, after passing through a street of uninteresting suburban character, the city proper is entered by the east gate in the walls, the archway of which passes over the road. Upon the left is the Grosvenor, a comfortable and well-managed hotel, conveniently situated as a centre for seeing the many features of interest in Chester. The journey from London along the Watling Street has been upon the track of the Roman legions, and here at Chester—the ancient Deva—is found the ultimate object of their journey, for this was the headquarters of the famous Twentieth Legion, which occupied the town shortly before the Boadicean Rebellion in A.D. 61, and remained there until the evacuation of Britain in the early part of the fifth century. The old town is suggestive of Rome's imperial power, for the ichnography of the city to-day resembles in a remarkable fashion the great military castra of the conquerors of the world.

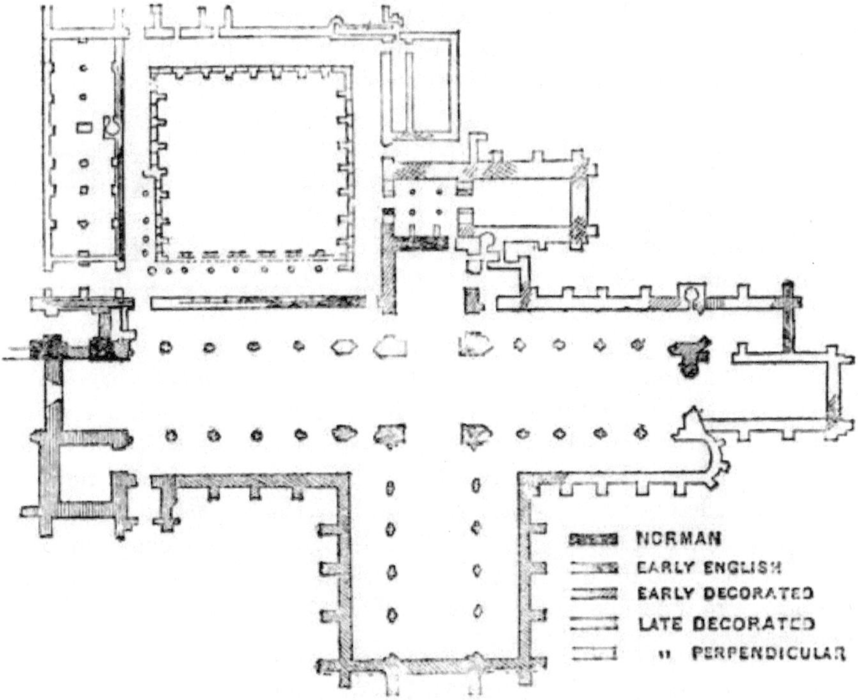

PLAN OF CHESTER CATHEDRAL.
Based on that published by the late Dean Howson.

One of the first objects of interest is the C a t h e d r a l , situated about two minutes from the hotel by passing up Werburgh Street. It is one of the red cathedrals, and owing to the sandstone of which it is composed being of a friable nature, the veneering of the edifice with new stone unfortunately deprives it of that aspect of age so characteristic of the majority of the great churches of England. The earliest building standing on the site is said to have been put up in the second century, but of that no traces exist. The present structure dates from the twelfth century, and has architecture as recent as the sixteenth. Upon entering by the west door some Norman work is apparent at the end of the nave, but its general style is Perpendicular; there is no triforium, and the fenestration springs directly above the arches, where an unornamental balustrading breaks the junction. The huge Perpendicular window at the west end is not of any particular merit. The large south transept was until recently used as a parish church, and is remarkably spacious; it is late Decorated, and possesses beautiful tracery in the window of the west aisle. Passing into the choir, which is early Decorated, and has been completely restored, one finds some exquisite work in the canopies of the stalls, which are undoubtedly the finest in the kingdom. Especially interesting are the quaint misereres; the Bishop's throne and pulpit are, however, modern. A characteristic feature of architecture occurs in the triforium, where four arches are superposed upon each of the bays below them. In the north aisle wall are preserved some magnificent mosaics, presented to the cathedral in 1886. The screen across the choir is Perpendicular, and of singular beauty, but it prevents the eye from perceiving the full length of the church, making it appear shorter than is actually the case. The north transept is small, with Norman work below and Perpendicular above. It will readily be seen that there are two periods in the Norman work. The large tomb on the floor of this transept is the resting-place of Bishop Pearson, who died in 1696. He is well known for his work on the Creed. The cloisters are entered through a Norman doorway at the east end of the north wall of the nave; the style throughout is Perpendicular, and the work on three sides of the square is picturesque; the south side, which had perished, has been rebuilt. An early Norman passage lies along the west side of the cloister. The chapter-house, which may be entered from this spot, is exceptionally worthy of a visit. It is of Early English architecture and a beautiful example of the style; the vestibule is, perhaps, more chaste than the chapter-house, and the manner in which the mouldings of the pillars run up unbroken into the vaulting is a striking feature.

Upon leaving the cathedral by the same door at the west front and turning to the right, the imposing Town Hall is seen in Northgate Street, and opposite to it is the abbey gateway, a fine example of Norman and Early English work, deserving more than a passing glance. Continuing up Northgate Street, the T o w n W a l l s are reached, and can be climbed by steps; the masonry here is probably of Roman origin. A few paces to the right lead to the Phœnix Tower (*entrance 1d.*), from the summit of which Charles I. witnessed the defeat of his troops on Rowton Moor, September 27, 1645, and not September 24, as stated on the tablet. Retracing one's steps, the Shropshire Union Canal lies below, occupying a portion of the ancient moat. The raised platform upon the right which is now encountered affords a very fine view of the surrounding country, and beyond is the Half-moon Tower, called 'Pemberton's Parlour.' From here the battlements lead to Bonwaldesthorne's Tower, now used as a museum, and upon the level sward below the visitor may perceive a number of Roman remains, including a hypocaust, or warming apparatus, altars, and other remains. The projecting isolated defence at this point is known as the Water Tower. Continuing the walk, the well-known racecourse, called the 'Roodee,' or 'Isle of the Cross,' is seen upon the right, enclosed by a loop in the river, and presently the group of buildings, consisting of the assize courts, gaol, and barracks, appear upon the left, the whole being classified under the name of 'the Castle.' The picturesque old bridge is next encountered, and here it is advisable to leave the walls, as the remainder of the route is devoid of interest.

Passing up Bridge Street, the third turning upon the right is Pepper Street, and after traversing this strangely named thoroughfare, the Church of St. John the Baptist is soon reached, one of the most interesting buildings in the city. It was originally intended to be the cathedral for the former diocese, which embraced practically the whole of Mercia, but the dignity was conferred upon Coventry. The ruins consist of very picturesque Norman work, with Norman and Early English flanking arches. By applying to the sexton, who is usually in the church, the Norman crypt may be visited. The nave of the church has Norman cylindrical pillars, dating from about 1090; the triforium arches are Early English of about a century later. A very fine lancet window is at the west end. The central tower fell in 1574, and crushed the east end of the church, which has never been rebuilt. The base of the tower shows rich Norman arches, with clustered columns supporting them. Traces of frescoes may be seen here. There are many displaced monuments now resting at the west end; one, a knight, dates from *c.* 1240, and a lady from *c.* 1400.

Retracing one's steps through Pepper Street, and passing up Bridge Street, St. Peter's Church is reached. It was built on the site of the Roman Prætorium, and in A.D. 907 the Church of SS. Peter and Paul was removed here by Ethelfleda from the site of St. Werburgh's. The edifice is mentioned in Domesday as the Church of St. Peter. The rectors' names are preserved from 1195. The church is square in plan, and consists only of four aisles; the architecture is Perpendicular, and rude Georgian galleries disfigure two of the aisles. The far-famed Rows of Chester may be visited from this point; they are found in Eastgate Street and Bridge Street in particular, but Watergate Row should on no account be missed, because two houses of the south side are striking specimens of seventeenth-century architecture. One bears the inscription 'God's Providence is mine inheritance,' which is supposed to allude to the preservation of the family occupying it from the plague. On the same side, No. 11, is a remarkable medieval crypt, now occupied by Quellyn Roberts and Co., wine merchants, who readily allow visitors to descend into the vaulted chamber.

This list of interesting sights of Chester is by no means exhaustive; an exploration of the streets in almost any direction will afford glimpses of old-time quaintnesses nestling in unsuspected byways, and the eye can dwell with pleasure upon many architectural details and rich colour schemes.

LOOP No. 1—SECOND PORTION

CHESTER TO MOLD AND RHYL, 35½ MILES

DISTANCES ALONG THE ROUTE

	Miles.	
Chester to Broughton	5	
Broughton to Mold	7	
Mold to Caerwys	9	½
Caerwys to St. Asaph	8	
St. Asaph to Rhuddlan	3	¼
Rhuddlan to Rhyl	2	¾

NOTES FOR DRIVERS

Chester to Mold.—Tramcar-lines to Saltney, flat; then splendid surface.

Broughton.—Ascent 1 in 21; then level to Mold.

Mold.—Fairly long hills to Caerwys; then level to Rhyl, except a descent near Trefnant.

PLACES OF INTEREST ON THE ROUTE

Mold.—Small county town; church of florid Henry VII. architecture; Bailey Hill, site of a British fortress; scene of the 'Alleluia Victory.'

Cilcain.—Church with magnificent oak roof.

Caerwys.—Pretty scenery; the residence of Llewelyn.

Bodfari.—Roman station.

St. Asaph.—Small town, with cathedral, smallest in England and Wales.

Rhuddlan.—Edwardian castle, ruins.

Morfa Rhuddlan.—Scene of a great battle between Offa of Mercia and Caradoc.

Rhyl.—Watering-place; splendid sands.

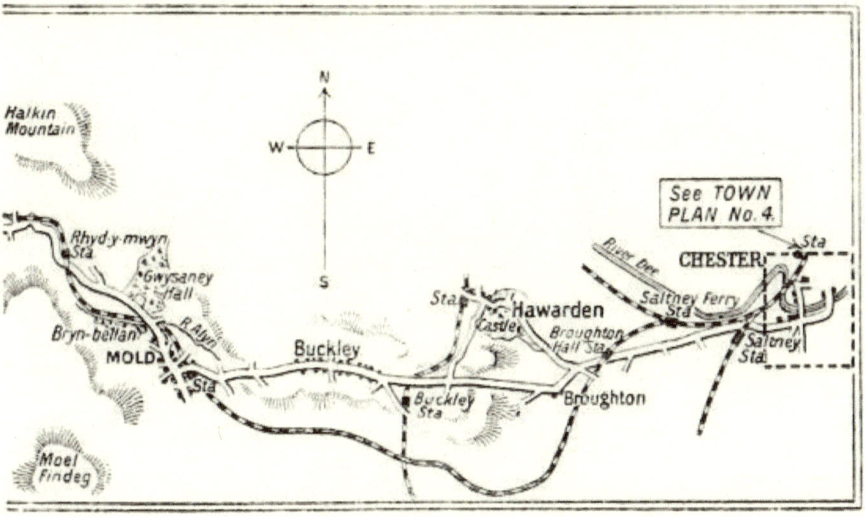

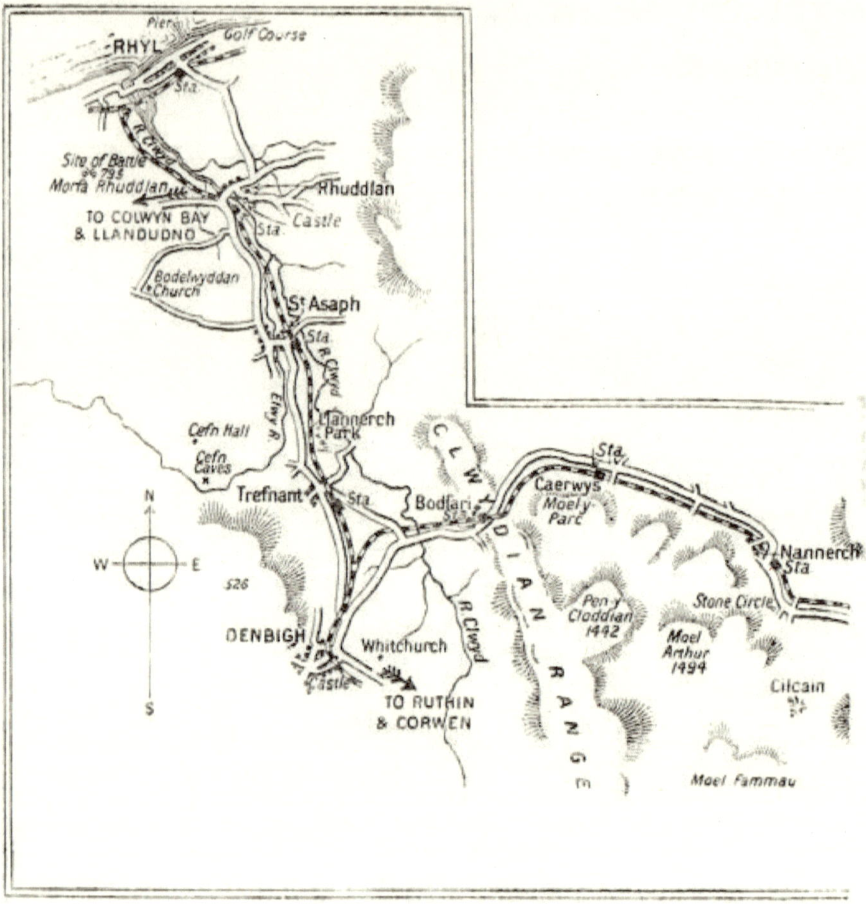

CHESTER TO MOLD AND RHYL.

LOOP 1 (SECOND PORTION).

NOTE.—Denbigh is omitted on the way from Mold to Rhyl.

On leaving Chester the Grosvenor Bridge is crossed, and as far as Saltney the road is occupied by tram-lines, while on looking backwards a fine view of the city walls is obtained. After Saltney an excellent road through the marshes enables one to see the wide estuary of the river; but at Broughton, where the left-hand road should be taken, a stiff rise of two miles leads to a plateau with an average elevation of nearly 500 feet above sea-level, upon which the road remains for the next twelve miles. The country here is well wooded, and Halkin Mountain presents a fine appearance in front. The outskirts of a small colliery district, with its centre at Buckley, are passed near Padeswood, and presently Mold, the county town of Flint, is reached.

MOLD

The town, which is rather sleepy and depressing, contains a church at the summit of a steep hill to the right, thoroughly rebuilt in the florid Tudor period early in the sixteenth century. The nave has some ornate four-centred arches, and in the chancel some reputed eighth-century work has been incorporated.

Behind the church is the commencement of the ascent to Bailey Hill, an eminence partly natural and partly artificial. It was once a British fortress, and was subsequently occupied by a medieval castle, now entirely vanished, and pleasure-grounds occupy the site. In the immediate neighbourhood of Mold there are many objects of considerable interest to the antiquary and geologist, such as the site of the 'Alleluia Victory,' won by an army of Christian converts under Germanus, and who, by shouting 'Alleluia!' struck the Picts and Scots, to whom they were opposed, with panic. In 1833 a gold breastplate of Celtic workmanship was unearthed near the town, and is now a treasured object in the British Museum. The ascent of Moel Fammau, 1,823 feet, the highest peak in the Clwydian range, from which a magnificent panorama is obtained, is easily accomplished from this town.

Mold was once a flourishing place, with mines and smelting-works in its vicinity, but they have now become unprofitable, with the inevitable result of lowering the vitality of the town. The road leading to St. Asaph passes a few coalpits near Mold, but presently winds about in a valley between the Clwydian Range and the Halkin Mountain. The village of Cilcain lies to the left of the route, at a distance of two miles, on the lower slopes of Moel Fammau, and is noted for the magnificent carved oak roof of its church, brought from Basingwerke Abbey, near Holywell. Nature is now in her pleasantest mood, and as the road winds with many a sharp turn down the long slope towards Caerwys, the mountains on both sides become softened and rounded, and clothed in many parts with trees to their summits. Upon the hills to the left lie a succession of interesting British camps, the strongest and most extensive being Moel Arthur, 1,494 feet, reached just before Nannerch appears by a road which branches off close to a stone circle. Caerwys is believed to have been a Roman station. It was at one time celebrated for its meetings of the bards, or Eisteddfodau, and also as being the residence of the last native Welsh Prince, Llewelyn ap Gruffydd. The whole of this district is rich in memories of the past, and abounds in interest. After passing Bodfari, where the railway crosses the road, a bridge over the River Clwyd is reached, and directly afterwards the turn to the right should be taken. (That to the left leads to Denbigh.)

At this point one says good-bye to the track of the Roman legions, Bodfari (*Vara*) being the last of the stations to be passed. The Roman road went straight ahead towards the west, and finished at *Segontium*, which will be seen when passing through Carnarvon. Thus, nearly all the way, from St. Albans through Shrewsbury to Chester, the Watling Street has been followed.

ST. ASAPH

This small village-city of 2,000 inhabitants is of consequence only on account of its cathedral, conspicuously placed upon high ground, and a prominent feature for many miles. To reach the time when this ancient see did not exist, one must travel back before the sixth century. The first building, of wood, was destroyed by fire in 1282, and the edifice which succeeded it was nearly razed to the ground during the wars under Owen Glendower. The present church practically dates from 1482; the choir, however, was not completed until 1770. It was restored by Sir Gilbert Scott. St. Asaph is the smallest British cathedral, being 182 feet long and 68 feet across the nave. The interior presents the aspect of a spacious parish church, and possesses only a few objects of interest. The east window is Decorated, and the tracery of the side-windows based upon traces of Early English work. The effigy of an Abbot in Episcopal robes, and probably dating from the fifteenth century, lies in the south transept. The road out of St. Asaph descends a steep hill, requiring caution, and a run of about three miles along a level road, with a sharp turning to the right over a bridge, leads to

RHUDDLAN CASTLE

The entrance to the Vale of Clwyd is one of the chief strategic points in Wales, and the elevated knob upon which the castle stands has, from the most remote antiquity, been a place of strength. The early Welsh fortress had additions early in the tenth century; it was taken by the nephew of the Earl of Chester in 1098, and enlarged about sixty years afterwards. The Welsh, however, captured it from the English in 1167, and Llewelyn subsequently held it; but Edward I. gained possession, and built the whole castle anew in 1277 upon an adjacent site. The enormous walls, impressively grand in their massive proportions, are his work. The castle appears to have remained in an efficient condition to the time of the Civil War, when it was held by the Royalists; but General Mytton captured it in 1646, and not long afterwards it was dismantled. As one stands on the site, one endeavours to visualize some of the many scenes of desperate warfare which have happened upon and around this bold sandstone bluff, and the cattle standing knee-deep in the translucent waters of the Clwyd, and lazily brushing aside the clouds of flies, seem strangely out of harmony with the memory of the wild hordes that have dashed against these frowning walls. Within its easily traced fosse, and enclosing a large area, there was formerly a priory of Dominicans, which has now disappeared, but relics of it are preserved in Rhuddlan Church. From the grassy strath within the walls the level plain reaching to Rhyl is spread out very distinctly, and if the eye is allowed to wander to Morfa Rhuddlan, which lies like a great alluvial marsh within the triangle of Rhyl, Abergele, and Rhuddlan, the most desolate stretch in Cambria, the site of that great battle in 795 is seen, when Offa, the great king of Mercia, defeated the hordes of Caradoc, the king of North Wales, with terrific slaughter. There probably exists no more pathetic wail—the death-sob of a great nation—than that of 'Morfa Rhuddlan,' which, next to the 'Men of Harlech,' is the most sung of Welsh airs.

The road to Rhyl is gained by passing through the village and taking the first road to the left. This takes one directly to the esplanade opposite the pier, where the Belvoir, a comfortable hotel, stands in a convenient position.

RHYL

Rhyl is essentially a watering-place, a watering-place pure and simple, and it does not pretend to be anything else. Its bathing facilities are magnificent, its sands are excellent for a gallop, and the *beau idéal* of parents with families, who fear that their offspring may meet disaster unless a smooth sweep of sand is available. It is healthy, bracing, peaceful, an excellent 'brain-emptier'—and that means much to the jaded man. He may be exasperated by the pier entrance, which can only be termed doubly debased Scottish architecture, but architecture by the sea is seldom free from glaring faults. As a jumping-off ground for the Vale of the Clwyd, and for the sea-gate of Wales at Abergele, it is convenient both by road and rail.

LOOP No. 1—THIRD PORTION

RHYL TO CORWEN, LLANGOLLEN, WREXHAM, AND SHREWSBURY, 86½ MILES

DISTANCES ALONG THE ROUTE

	Miles.	
Rhyl to Denbigh	15	
Denbigh to Ruthin	7	¾
Ruthin to Corwen	12	½
Corwen to Llangollen	10	
Llangollen to Wrexham	12	¼
Wrexham to Ellesmere	16	½

Ellesmere to Shrewsbury 12 ½

NOTES FOR DRIVERS

Rhyl to Trefnant.—A good road.

Trefnant.—Ascent 1 in 14, then good to Denbigh.

Denbigh to Ruthin.—Undulating; steep ascent in Ruthin, 1 in 11, then good road until 2 miles from Corwen, when there is a descent of 1 in 13.

Corwen to Llangollen.—Slightly hilly; first-class surface.

Llangollen to Wrexham.—Llangollen to Trevor excellent; Trevor to Ruabon bumpy, then fairly good to Wrexham.

Wrexham to Ellesmere.—Steep hill 1 mile from Wrexham, then exceptionally good to Ellesmere; afterwards undulating to Shrewsbury.

PLACES OF INTEREST ON THE ROUTE

Bodelwyddan Church.—Two miles from Rhuddlan, *off the road*; excellent example of modern architecture.

Cefn Caves.—Three miles from St. Asaph, or 2½ miles from Trefnant, off the road.

Denbigh.—The castle; ruins of the garrison church.

Llanrhaiadr.—Church, with fifteenth century 'Jesse' window.

Ruthin.—Castle, with beautiful surroundings; church, Perpendicular, with splendid roof.

Corwen.—Church, with eighth-century cross in churchyard.

Llangollen.—Valle Crucis Abbey; Eliseg Pillar; Dinas Bran castle; Plas Newydd, the Bridge.

Ruabon.—Church; Wynnstay Park and Monument.

Wrexham.—Church, one of the Seven Wonders of Wales, Perpendicular architecture.

Ellesmere.—Church, with hatchet-work screen; old timbered houses; picturesque lakes.

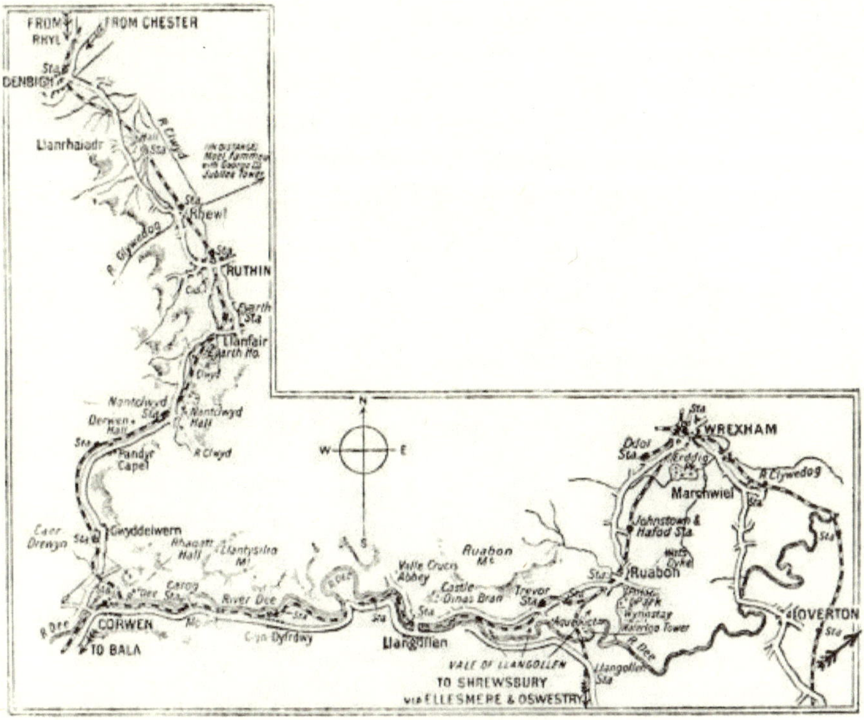

LOOP 1 (THIRD PORTION).
DENBIGH TO SHREWSBURY.

[For the route from Rhyl to Denbigh see previous map.]

For the first part of this section of the route the road is retraced through Rhuddlan, and here, if the traveller be interested in a grand example of modern ecclesiastical architecture, Bodelwyddan Church may be visited. It lies two miles from Rhuddlan, to the right of the road; was erected by Lady Willoughby de Broke; cost £60,000; and is called the 'Marble Church,' from the whiteness of the local limestone of which it is built. The spire and exterior are extremely pleasing, while the richness of the interior, with its marbles, wood-carving, stained glass, and excess of structural adornments, make it well worth a visit. A good road leads back to the trunk route.

THE CEFN CAVES,

reached by a side-road about two and a half miles from Trefnant. These lie in the grounds of Cefn Hall, and are *open on Tuesday and Friday afternoons*. They are deep cavities in the limestone rock, at one time inhabited by primeval man, whose bones and many interesting relics of his existence have been found by careful excavation of the floors. A very fine view of the Vale of the Clwyd, which has been rather overpraised, is obtained at this spot.

SHREWSBURY HOUSE, CHESTER.
One of the many picturesque frontages for which the town is famous.

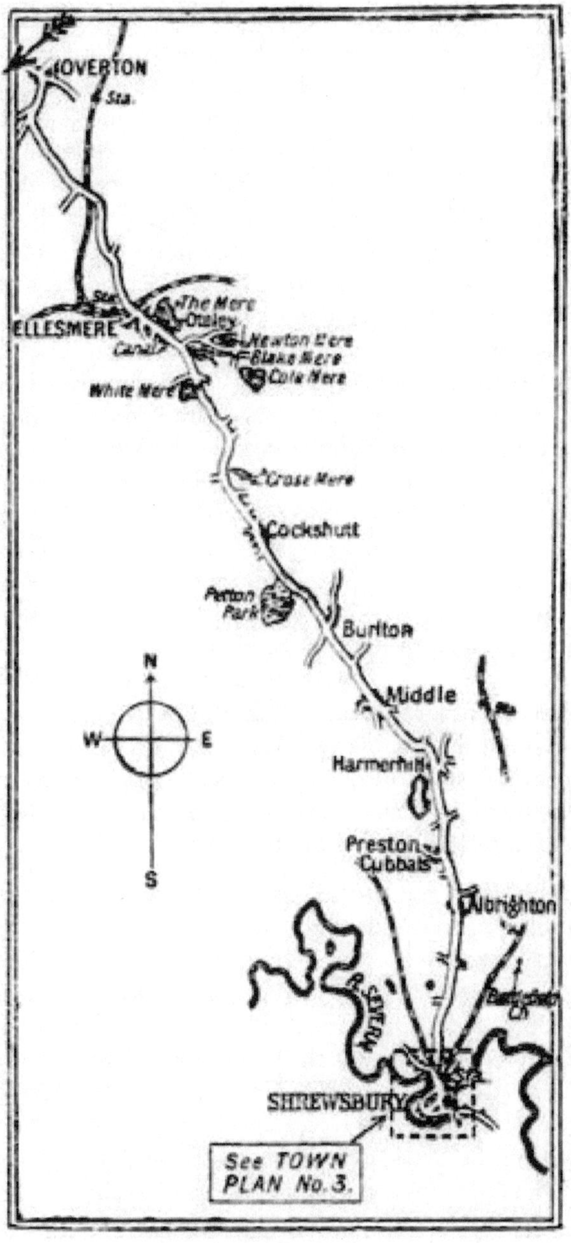

DENBIGH TO SHREWSBURY.

DENBIGH

In Denbigh a long, broad street leads up to the centre of the town, and here the chief attraction, the castle, may be visited. Passing up through a Norman gateway, which once formed part of the boundary of the ancient town, and was called Burgess's Tower, the ruins of the long-abandoned parish church, or garrison church of St. Hilary, are seen on the spacious castle green. The old parish church of the town is at W h i t c h u r c h , on the road to Ruthin. The stately ruins of the great Norman fortress, which kept watch and ward over this portion of the Vale of the Clwyd for so many centuries, crowns the summit of this conical hill, and is perched nearly 500 feet above sea-level. Long before the Norman invasion this vantage-point had been seized upon for a stronghold, but the great epoch for Denbigh happened when Edward I. sat down in Rhuddlan and gathered into his conquering hands the fair lands of Wales, consolidating his power by building a castle in each. Denbigh and Ruthin, ruled by the Laceys and the Greys respectively, formed the nuclei of two counties. Here Henry Percy, in the wars with Glendower, tried to stem the tide of insurrection; and later, in the Wars of the Roses, it was a centre of that desolation and destruction which overwhelmed the valley under Jasper Tudor and the Earl of Pembroke, and reduced it to a land of smouldering embers. But one of the most stirring episodes in the history of the castle was the grand defence made by Colonel William Salusbury, the stout old Royalist, who, in the summer of 1646, valiantly held the walls against the Parliamentarians. From April until November it was assaulted in vain, for Salusbury had sworn that he would not surrender it except at the bidding of his King. This was eventually obtained, and the garrison marched out with, if possible, more than the honours of war. Soon afterwards the castle was completely dismantled, and now chiefly serves as a place of assembly for the townspeople, a recreation-ground, and a coign of vantage, under favourable circumstances, for a splendid view over the Vale.

The road to Ruthin leads out of the busy market-place, and a mile beyond the town one reaches the fine old church of W h i t c h u r c h , now only used for burial services. It belongs to the Perpendicular period, and in it parts of the rood-screen may be seen, converted into a reredos, and a screen at the west end of the north aisle. An interesting brass to Richard Myddelton, who died 1575, is preserved here; he was the Governor of Denbigh Castle, and is represented with his wife and a small family of sixteen. The Myddeltons, like the Salusburys, have left indelible traces upon this part of Wales, and of the sons represented on the brass, one became a Lord Mayor of London, and another, the sixth, is perhaps the best known to Englishmen, as he was the celebrated Sir Hugh Myddelton who brought the New River to the metropolis. The ancestral home of this family, Chirk Castle, will be visited *en route.*

After another one and a half miles, L l a n r h a i a d r C h u r c h is seen, whose interior is interesting on account of the 'Jesse' window, of fine fifteenth-century glass, purchased with the offerings of pilgrims to the holy well in the wooded glen above the church. It is in a remarkably good state of preservation, with the colours rich and brilliant. Outside the east window are the graves of five soldiers who fell in the famous siege of Denbigh; under one lies Captain Wynne, of the great house of Gwydir, near Llanrwst. He died from wounds in the castle, and by mutual arrangement the cortège was permitted to pass through the lines of the beleaguers, the Parliamentarians firing the last salute over the grave of the hero.

Between Llanrhaiadr and Ruthin the highest points of the Clwydian Range come prominently into view, the huge ruin on Moel Fammau, to which reference has been made in connection with Mold, being plainly visible.

RUTHIN (*RED CASTLE*)

The road leads into the central square of the town, from the south side of which issues Castle Street. The modern Ruthin Castle is occupied by Colonel W. Cornwallis West, Lord-Lieutenant of Denbighshire, and the ruins stand in the Park. (*Permission to enter may be obtained at the lodge.*) The remains consist of a dungeon, a 'Beheading Tower,' an armoury, and some curious passages. A whipping-post is also preserved. The ruins, deep red in hue, and mantled by the rich green of the clinging foliage, with a setting beyond of the upper part of the Vale of the Clwyd, form a picture rich in colour. Reginald de Grey owned the castle shortly after its erection in 1280, and it remained in the possession of his family until about 1480. Owen Glendower attempted its capture in 1400, but the Parliamentarians were more successful, for it fell in 1646, after a siege of three months, from which time it has been a ruin. Sir Thomas Myddelton of Chirk became owner, and the present possessor has inherited it from him in the female line. The castle was partially rebuilt in 1826, and brought to its present condition in 1852.

The Church of St. Peter is an imposing edifice, chiefly Perpendicular, and contains a finely decorated roof of Henry VII.'s period, beautifully carved in black oak and divided into 500 small panels. The old building adjacent and the church are the remains of a Priory of White Friars, and form a very picturesque addition; near them are the former buildings of the Grammar School, founded in 1574. The foundation is now accommodated in better surroundings.

The natural environs of Ruthin are of great beauty, and this part of the Clwyd Valley is a favourite place of residence. Upon Moel Feulli are the remains of a fortified British camp, enlarged by the Romans, and from it and Moel Fammau magnificent views may be obtained.

Leaving Ruthin, the upper part of the Vale of the Clwyd is traversed, and the watershed between the latter river and the Dee crossed at a height of 600 feet. After passing through the narrow Vale of Nantclwyd, with its towering limestone rocks, the small church of Derwen, lying off the road to the right of Derwen Station, is seen. It contains a handsome fifteenth-century screen and rood-loft, with a time-honoured thirteenth-century cross in the churchyard.

CORWEN

is a centre for the railway system of Wales, but possesses no special attractions, unless the mark of Owen Glendower's dagger upon the lintel of the south door of the church, inflicted, so it is said, when in a pet, be deemed one, though probably the tradition had its origin in the dagger carved on the shaft of an eighth-century cross in the same churchyard. The summit of the rock behind the town, whereon stands a cairn, was the point whence Glendower reviewed his troops previous to the Battle of Shrewsbury. The short climb is rewarded by a pleasing view.

LLANGOLLEN

is reached by a part of the Telford-Holyhead road, which is generally in magnificent condition. Pretty views of the Dee, the Berwyn Mountains on the right, the Llantysilio Mountains on the left, and the Eglwyseg rocks in front, are obtained, and the most beautiful part of the hill country of Wales, as contrasted with the mountain scenery, is presented to the eye. The loveliest views are those lying round the town, rivalling in beauty, and perhaps surpassing, any found elsewhere in Britain. The Bridge is one of the "Wonders of Wales," dating from 1345, and Plas Newydd, lying about half a mile from the bridge, the residence of the famed ladies of Llangollen, should on no account be missed. The romance of their lives is too lengthy for inclusion here, but may be readily learnt on the spot. The house is an aggregation of carved oak within and without. No one should visit Llangollen without ascending Castell Dinas Brân, which towers to a height of 1,000 feet above the village. The origin of the quaint ruins upon the summit is lost in antiquity, but is attributed to one of the early Princes of Powis. The tide of war has raged scores of times round the hoary fragments upon the crest, which look like the eyrie of a robber baron or the fantastic imaginings of a Doré. When the castle emerges into the light of history we find that Griffith, the son of Madoc, occupied it in the thirteenth century, and that about a hundred years afterwards it fell into ruin.

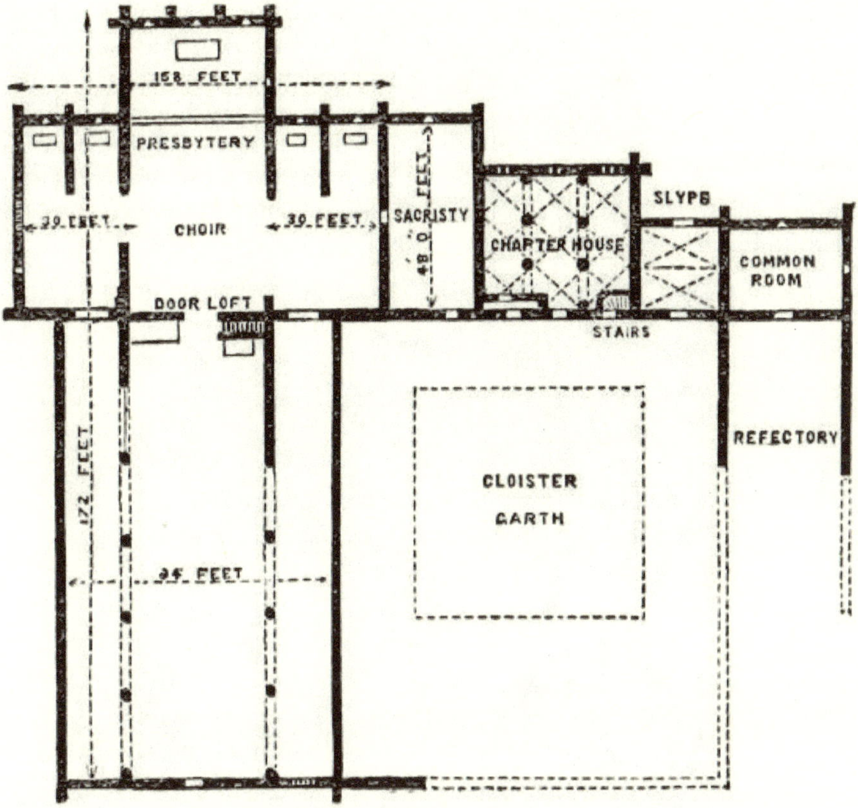

VALLE CRUCIS ABBEY: GROUND PLAN.

VALLE CRUCIS ABBEY

(*admission 6d.*) lies two miles by road from Llangollen. Founded by the above-named Griffith in A.D. 1200, it is necessarily in the Early English style, and dog-tooth ornamentation may be discovered in the west end. The beautiful ruin appeals to artist and antiquary alike, and is considered the most picturesque in Wales. A little way off to the north is Eliseg's Pillar, a most astonishing early monument put up by Concenn ap Cadell ap Brochmail to the memory of his great-grandfather, Eliseg, who lived as far back as the beginning of the seventh century. It is no longer possible to read the Latin inscription giving these facts, and the remarkable monument itself has suffered much mutilation. Llangollen is a town in which a week can be spent with profit and pleasure, so numerous are the places of interest in the immediate neighbourhood. The fine escarpment of the limestone rocks, the Eglwyseg, lying above the village, are conspicuous on the left for some distance on leaving for Ruabon through the Vale of Llangollen, where the famed Wynnstay Park is situated, the residence of Sir H. Watkin Williams-

Wynn, Bart. The house is not on view, but admission to the park is freely given by application at the lodge gates, close to the town. The associations of the park are, however, the chief point in connection with it, for the Wynns go back into remote antiquity, and the history of North Wales and the members of this family are inseparable. The pillar standing above the swiftly rushing Dee is a cenotaph perpetuating the names of those who fell in the Irish rebellion of '98, when a Wynn took his company of yeomanry over the water to help in the suppression.

THE SWALLOW FALLS, BETTWS-Y-COED.
The finest waterfall in Wales.

WREXHAM

From Ruabon to Wrexham tram-lines run by the side of the road, but they do not cause much inconvenience, and the road is good. The chief object for visiting the town is to view the church, which is one of the finest, if not *the* finest, in the Principality, and enumerated among the "Seven Wonders of

Wales." It was erected in 1472 to replace a former structure destroyed by fire. It is a splendid example of Perpendicular architecture, the tower of six stages and 135 feet in height being probably unsurpassed, and the rich peal of ten bells it contains are celebrated far and wide—they were made in 1726. The church contains monuments to the Myddelton and other families, and in the churchyard the Elihu Yale tomb is of exceptional interest to Americans.

ELLESMERE

At Wrexham one turns towards the south to Shrewsbury, and Ellesmere is the first town calling for comment. There are many old carved timber houses to be seen, a beautiful contrast to the modern box-of-bricks erections which now so frequently serve for dwellings. No trace of the castle now remains; its site is occupied by a bowling-green, whence a view into nine counties is obtained. The church is chiefly of Perpendicular architecture, and is worth visiting. The chancel screen is of hatchet-work, and over the door may be seen the groove in which the rood formerly stood. The Oteley Chapel has a quaint figure, *temp.* Edward IV., on the north-west pier, and also an altar-tomb with recumbent figures. The mere from which the town gained its name lies close at hand; four other meres are in the vicinity, and these, with other pleasant concomitants, help to make very pretty and charming scenery for some distance on the road to Shrewsbury. Shortly after leaving the town the Ellesmere Canal—one of Telford's great works—is crossed.

SECTION IV
(TRUNK ROUTE)

SHREWSBURY TO LLANDUDNO, 81½ MILES

DISTANCES ALONG THE ROUTE

Miles.		
Shrewsbury to Oswestry	17	
Oswestry to Chirk	5	¾
Chirk to Llangollen	6	¾
Llangollen to Corwen	10	
Corwen to Cerrig-y-Druidon	9	¾
Cerrig-y-Druidon to Pentre Voelas	5	½
Pentre Voelas to Bettws-y-Coed	6	¾
Bettws-y-Coed to Llanrwst	4	½
Llanrwst to Tal-y-Cafn	6	¾
Tal-y-Cafn to Glan Conway	3	¾
Glan Conway to Llandudno	5	

NOTES FOR DRIVERS

The Holyhead Road.—Splendid surface; perfect condition generally.

Dangerous hill in **Shrewsbury**.

A fairly stiff ascent at **Chirk**, 1 in 18.

Road ascends from **Corwen to Cerrig-y-Druidon**.

Last 9 miles into **Bettws-y-Coed** downhill.

Bettws-y-Coed to Tal-y-Cafn.—Level, then a hill, up and down, 1 in 12.

Near Llandudno Junction.—Steep ascent, 1 in 10.

PLACES OF INTEREST ON THE ROUTE

Shrewsbury.—Castle; free library and museum; market-house; churches; public gardens; town walls.

Montford Bridge.—Pretty road.

Oswestry.—Castle mound; church, with a fine tower.

Chirk.—Castle of great interest; viaduct; aqueduct.

Llangollen.—Valle Crucis Abbey; Eliseg's Pillar; bridge. The really fine scenery lies beyond Llangollen.

Corwen.—Church, with eighth-century cross in churchyard.

Conway Falls.—Pandy Mill and Falls, Swallow Falls, all about 2 miles short of Bettws-y-Coed, upon the left, where the Conway Falls Inn will be seen.

Bettws-y-Coed.—Waterloo Bridge (Dolwyddelan Castle).

Llanrwst.—Bridge; Gwydir Castle and Chapel.

Conway.—Castle; bridge; walls of the town; church.

Llandudno.—Watering-place; Great Orme's Head; St. Tudno's Church.

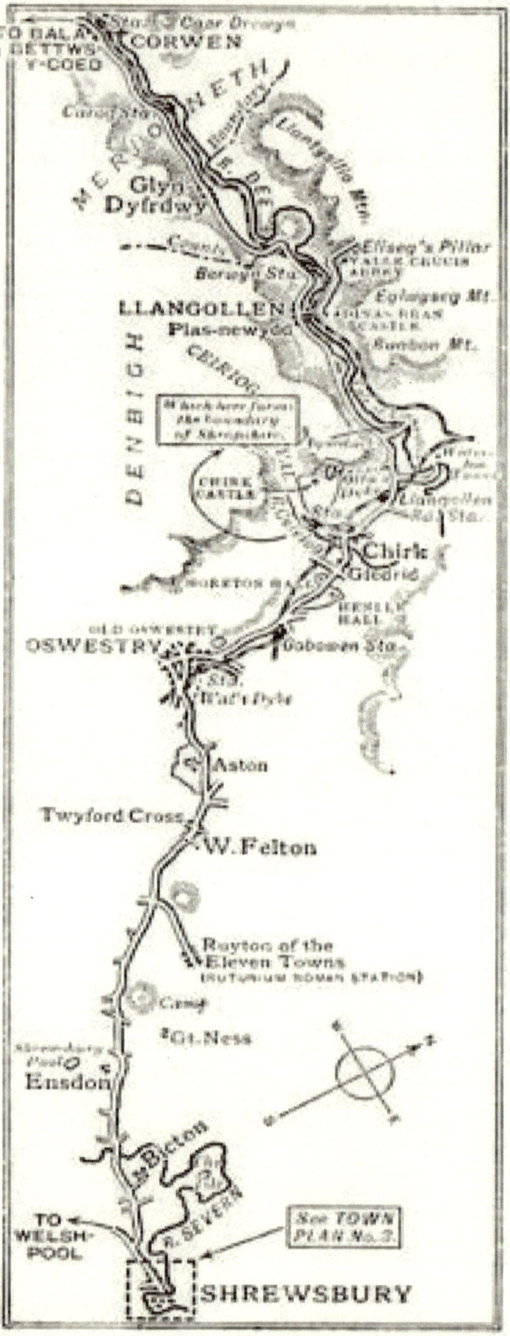

(TRUNK) No. 4. SHREWSBURY TO CORWEN.

S h r e w s b u r y . —To pass through Shropshire without seeing Shrewsbury would be tantamount to journeying through Italy without visiting Rome. Its physical features are strikingly picturesque, and it has almost as many antiquities as Chester. Fortunately, too, the objects of interest are grouped together.

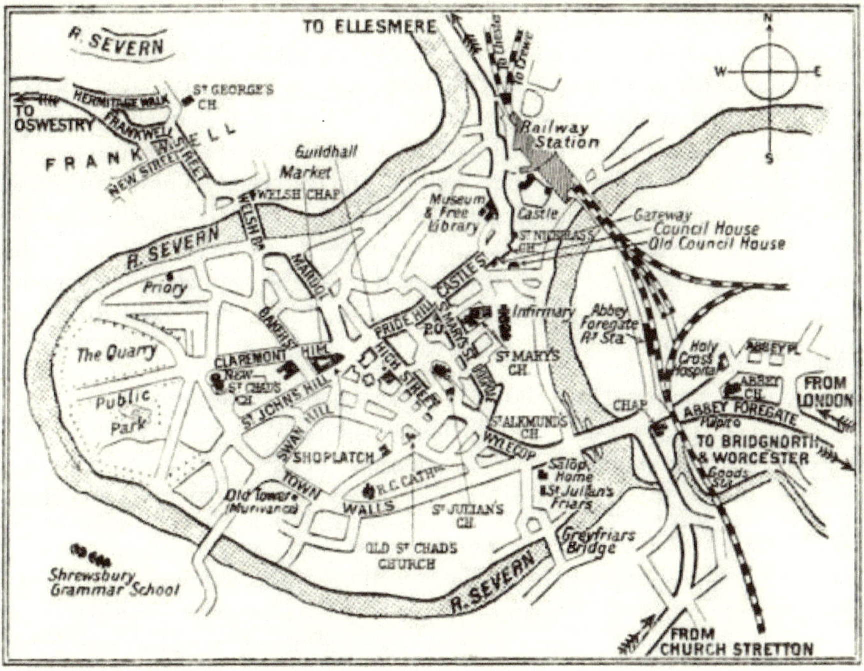

TOWN PLAN NO. 3—SHREWSBURY.

The town lies in a loop of the Severn, with the castle protecting the opening. It is of red sandstone, and dates in part from the time of Edward I. The grounds are open, but the building is private. The free library and museum, opposite the castle, occupy the old buildings of Shrewsbury School, founded in the reign of Edward VI. The museum contains many 'finds' from *Uriconium.* The school now occupies magnificent buildings south of the town. Passing up Castle Street, the old Council House gateway is upon the left, and soon after a turn to the left at the post office brings one to S t . M a r y ' s C h u r c h , a noble building, of which the base of the tower and the nave are Norman, the transept Early English, and the aisles Perpendicular, and other portions late Perpendicular. The tower, with its spire 222 feet high, is the third loftiest in the kingdom. The general appearance of the interior is very beautiful, and the Jesse window of fourteenth-century glass should be especially noticed; it was originally in the Grey Friars' monastery. The glass as a whole excels that of any other English parish church; the St. Bernard window, for example, on the north side of the altar, attributed to Albert Dürer, came from a church at Cologne. St. Alkmund's Church can be seen from St. Mary's, and passing that, and also St. Julian's Church, the old Wyle Cop may be reached. Among the ancient timbered houses there is one in which Henry VII. stayed prior to Bosworth in 1485. Passing over the English Bridge, the Abbey Church is reached, with its imposing west front and great Perpendicular window, and the tower, the base of which is Norman, rising from the west end of the nave. Internally the latter possesses three massive Norman bays, and two of the Early English period, a fine arch in the latter style dividing it from the tower. The chancel and clerestory have been rebuilt recently in good taste. There are some interesting monumental effigies; one in the south aisle is supposed to represent the founder, Roger, Earl of Shrewsbury, died 1094. In this church, then the Chapel of the Monastery of the Holy Cross, Richard II. held the 'great Parliament' in 1377.

Returning to the town, the road by Beeches Lane will lead by way of the old walls to Murivance Tower, the only one remaining of the twenty which once guarded the town. A short distance farther on, the 'Quarry,' with its beautiful avenues of lime-trees by the river, is reached, one of the spots of which Shrewsbury is justly proud.

Having safely negotiated the dangerous hill in Shrewsbury, the road to Oswestry is easily found, and, as nothing of supreme importance is encountered before that town appears, the beauties of the Holyhead Road may be appreciated.

OSWESTRY

The Church possesses a remarkably fine tower, which presents a venerable appearance by reason of the growth of vegetation upon it. A portion was pulled down during the Civil War, and rebuilt some time after the Restoration. The interior should be visited, although there are no special features upon which to dilate. About a mile to the north of the town lies Old Oswestry, a very fine and well-preserved earthwork, consisting of three concentric circles of defences. A portion of Wat's Dyke lies adjacent. This was the first ditch made by Offa, King of Mercia, in the eighth century to prevent Welsh incursions; the second, called Offa's Dyke, was dug a few miles nearer the Welsh border, and generally parallel to the first.

A stiff rise in the road announces that Chirk is at hand, and the celebrated castle is the first point of interest.

CHIRK CASTLE,

anciently, Castel-y-Waen, is the only example of the thirty great fortalices in Shropshire erected to control the Welsh border which remains in complete repair and is occupied at the present time. It is indelibly associated with the Myddeltons, an ancient Denbigh family who have been identified with every popular movement in that part of the country for centuries past. The present owner is Mr. Richard Myddelton.

(*The Castle is open Mondays and Tuesdays 2 to 5 p.m., 1s. each person; other days special orders, Estate Office, Chirk, 5s. for three persons.*)

The builder of the existing fortress was Roger Mortimer, Lord of Chirk, who in 1310 commenced work upon the site of Castell Crogen, which dated from 1011. In 1595 it came into the possession of Sir Thomas Myddelton, subsequently Lord Mayor of London. Sir Hugh Myddelton, of New River fame, was his brother. The Royalists seized the castle in the absence of the second Sir Thomas Myddelton, a Parliamentarian, who had the pleasant experience of battering his own property in the endeavour to retake it. Becoming disgusted with Parliamentarian excesses, he became Royalist again, and was besieged. So much damage was done by the artillery of Cromwell that £30,000 were spent subsequently on repairs.

It is a quadrangular structure, with embattled walls, four towers of great strength at the angles, and another defending the gateway. A court of considerable area occupies the centre. Some very interesting pictures form part of the treasures of the house, and among them is the exquisite cabinet given to Sir Thomas by Charles II. The exterior aspect is extremely pleasing, with ivy-covered walls and red-grey stonework forming a background to the old-world gardens. Traces of Offa's Dyke occur near the farmhouse at the foot of the castle. The beautiful Ceriog Valley is an attractive feature of this neighbourhood.

The road to Llangollen from Chirk commands a fine view of the vale, and a sight of one of the most striking features of the Dee Valley, the great aqueduct conveying the canal across it at a height of 120 feet above the river. An iron trough in the stonework contains the water. There are nineteen arches, and the length is over 1,000 feet. It is one of Telford's masterpieces.

(*For a description of the route from Llangollen to Corwen, see pp. 69-71.*)

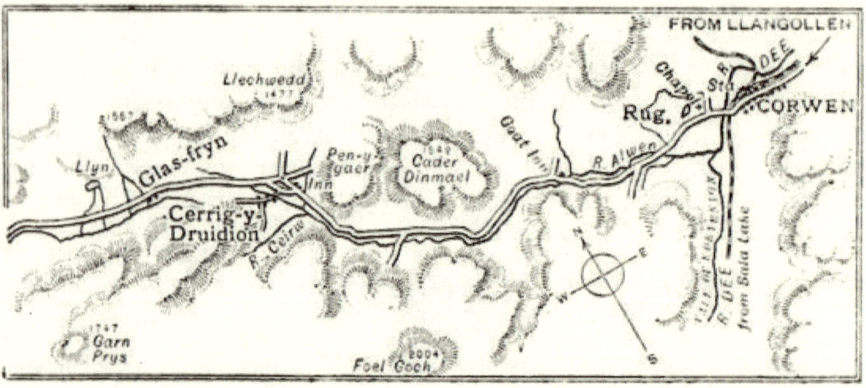

(Trunk) No. 4. CORWEN TO LLANDUDNO.

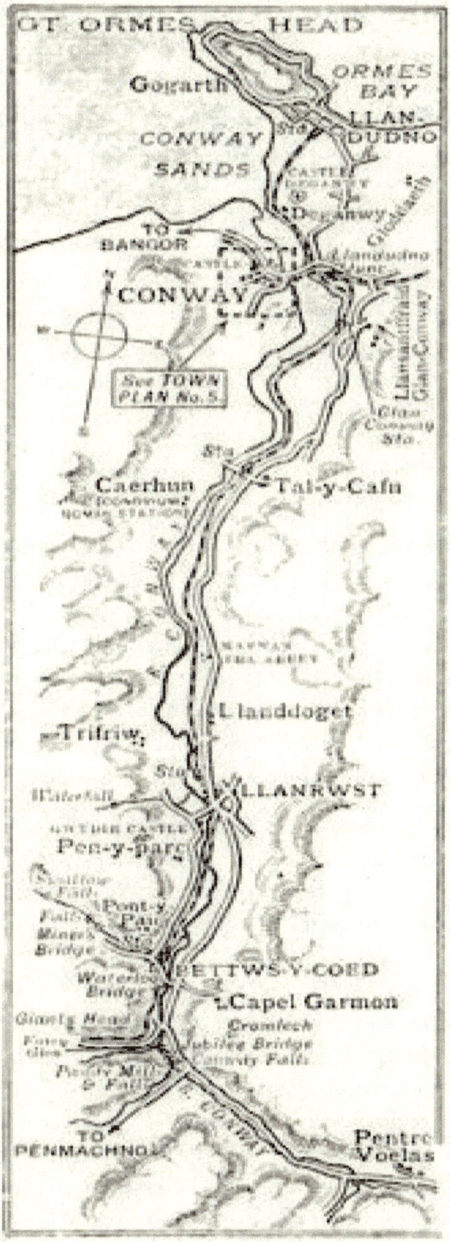

Leaving Corwen, the river is passed by a bridge, and a glimpse afforded up the Vale of Edeyrnion to the left, at the end of which lies Bala Lake and the source of the Dee. There are many glimpses of charming scenery and nestling homesteads to be seen between Corwen and Cerrig-y-Druidon, although the latter lies upon a somewhat bare tableland perched nearly 1,000 feet above sea-level. The British camp of Pen-y-Gaer lies to the right of it. Pentre Voelas is situated at the beginning of the long descent into Bettws, and this part of the road commands as beautiful scenery as one could wish to see. A little more than four miles beyond Pentre Voelas is a turning on the left to Penmachno, and a few yards farther on the Conway Falls are seen at the bottom of a deep ravine. The celebrated Fairy Glen may be reached by means of a broad green path, which leaves the main road at the same place as that leading to the Conway Falls. The wicket-gate, beyond which the glen is reached, is nearly three-quarters of a mile down this track. The beauty of the glen is so conspicuously appealing that it has won for itself an almost world-wide renown. The road from this point descends rapidly, crosses the Waterloo Bridge, and enters Bettws-y-Coed.

BETTWS Y COED.

The charm of this delightful locality is felt by everyone who comes within its influence. From the village itself not a mountain is visible, but all around are beautiful glades and the profuse richness of vegetation flourishing in subtle, harmonious accord with rocks and dashing waters. The Miner's Bridge lies about a mile along the Capel Curig Road, with the Swallow Falls a mile farther. To Capel Garmon a footpath ascends, and also a zigzag road. It affords a magnificent panoramic view of the chief heights of the Snowdonian Range, with the exception of Snowdon itself, which is hidden by the grand mass of Moel Siabod. An interesting cromlech lies near Capel Garmon.

Resuming the journey, the road to Llanrwst passes over the Waterloo Bridge and turns sharply to the left. Llyn-y-Parc is seen across the Conway, lying at the base of spurs projecting from the mountains beyond, and Gwydir Castle appears at the farther end of it.

LLANRWST

This ancient market town contains a church dating from the fifteenth century, when it replaced a much older one. It contains several interesting monuments and an elaborate screen. The beautiful Gwydir Chapel was designed by Inigo Jones; it dates from 1633, and contains five brasses of members of the Wynne family. The large stone coffin of Llewellyn the Great, son-in-law of King John, is preserved here, having been removed from Conway Abbey. The effigy in armour represents Howel Coetmore, who led a hundred Denbighshire men at Poitiers.

Gwydir Castle was built in 1555, and partly rebuilt in 1816. In the absence of the family (Lord Carrington is the owner) it is possible that the interesting interior may be seen. The park contains much natural beauty, one conspicuous feature being the lofty Falcon Rock behind the house. Llanrwst

Bridge, built by Inigo Jones in 1636, is said to tremble if sudden pressure be placed on one of the parapets.

Two miles out of Llanrwst the village of T r e f r i e w is seen across the river, a summer resort and inland watering-place. Presently the site of Maenan Abbey, which disappeared at the Reformation, is passed, before reaching Maenan House. The mountains lying between the Conway Valley and Nant Ffrancon now present a fine spectacle. Shortly after Tal-y-Cafn a dangerous hill is encountered, and from its summit the Roman station of *Canovium*, situated near Caerhun on the Carnarvonshire side, may be discerned. As the fishing at this part of the estuary is noted, some coracles may perhaps be seen. The road between Glan Conway and Llandudno reveals grand views of Conway Castle and Mountain, and all the varied scenery which makes the estuary so famous.

LLANDUDNO

The 'Biarritz of Britain' is not an inappropriate name for this favoured town, which possesses every advantage of splendid climate, beautiful scenery, and perfect bathing.

Great Orme's Head is generally the object of the first excursion. In the early morning it looks very imposing, with the exquisite effect of moving mist lying upon the placid waters of the bay at its base, and the summit of the great limestone mass reddened by the hues of the rising sun. It may be seen from the carriage-road which circles it, and affords splendid views of mountain and sea, probably unsurpassed in the kingdom; but the best way is to ascend to the summit by a well-marked road north of the town leading from Church Street, and to visit St. Tudno's Church, with its quaint entrance, 4½ feet in height, of rugged stones, and its general aspect of antiquity. The church is seen from Telegraph Point, which dominates the peninsula. A cromlech lies to the left of the road leading to it, and the remains of a stone circle are above the church. There is plenty of rough scrambling to be obtained.

The carriage-drive is best entered near the pier (*motors one shilling toll; pedestrians one penny*). The way rises and falls like the Corniche Road; red rocks alternate with white or grey limestone; at times the track is at a giddy height, and presently near the surface of the water. The view up the Menai Straits, with the coasts of Anglesey and Carnarvon nearing each other at the bridges, is very fine, but when the farthest point of the headland is reached, that which leads back to the town is no less beautiful, affording as it does one of the finest prospects of the noble outline of the Carnarvonshire Mountains.

The visitor should not fail to visit the Little Orme, where the sheer cliffs and grassy summit often offer a seclusion much appreciated after the boisterous exuberances of an August crowd. There are many coigns of vantage around

Llandudno from which the appreciative traveller can gaze over mountain, sea, and strath, and also a number of interesting edifices that may be visited if sufficient time is allowed.

Unlike Aberystwyth, there is a considerable choice of hotels at Llandudno. The Queen's is recommended for its fine position on the front and for its general excellence.

CONWAY FROM BENARTH.
On the left is the famous Edwardian castle and leading to it is Telford's tubular bridge. Great Orme's Head appears in the distance.

SECTION V
(TRUNK ROUTE)

LLANDUDNO TO BANGOR, 18¾ MILES

DISTANCES ALONG THE ROUTE

	Miles.	
Llandudno to Conway	3	¾
Conway to Penmaenmawr	4	½
Penmaenmawr to Llanfairfechan	2	¾
Llanfairfechan to Bangor	7	¾

NOTES FOR DRIVERS

At **Penmaenmawr** a gradient of 1 in 14.

Before reaching **Llanfairfechan** 1 in 12. Surface good.

PLACES OF INTEREST ON THE ROUTE

Conway.—The suspension bridge by Telford; castle; church; the medieval town walls and bastions; Plas Mawr, a sixteenth-century house.

Penmaenmawr.—Fine cliff scenery; large British fort above quarries.

Llanfairfechan.—A typical Welsh watering-place.

Aber.—Falls.

Bangor.—Model village of Llandegai; Penrhyn Castle; cathedral; University buildings.

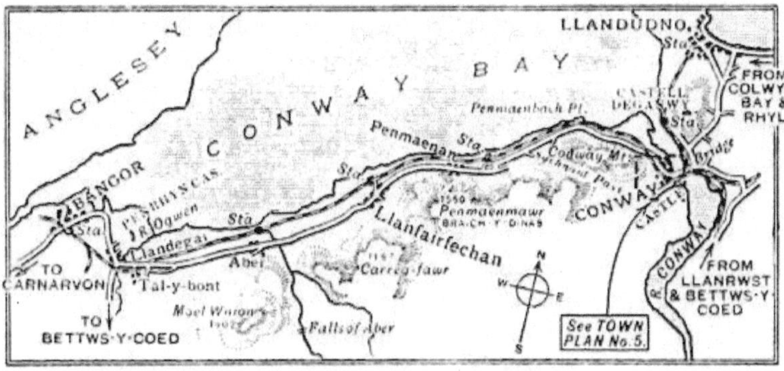

(TRUNK) No. 5. LLANDUDNO TO BANGOR.

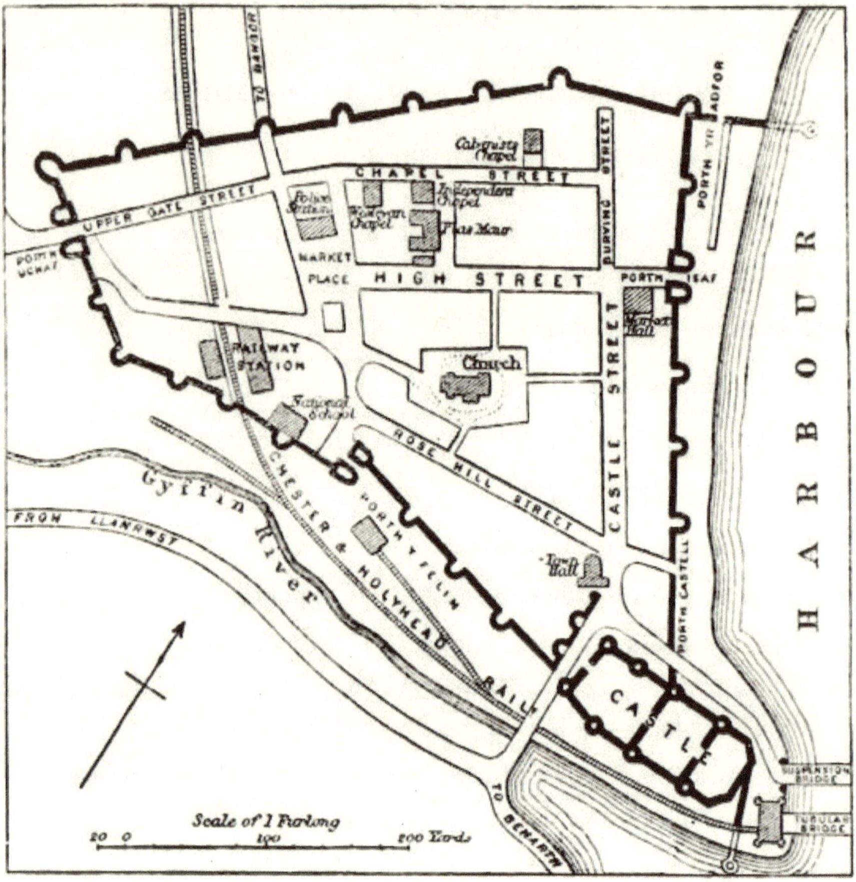

TOWN PLAN NO. 5—CONWAY.

The road into Conway leads over the suspension bridge built by Telford, the harmony of the towers with the adjacent castle being a subject of general congratulation. The entrance to t h e C a s t l e (*admission 3d.*) is close to the end of the bridge. The structure possesses the characteristics of Edwardian castles, with more ornamentation than usual, and was undoubtedly, when perfect, one of the most magnificent fortresses in the kingdom. It commands, as usual, one of the roads through the passes leading from Wales—that from the Snowdon district and Anglesey. The chief points of interest are the Queen's Tower, with its oratory, the Great Hall, the King's Tower, and the Broken Tower. It is a matter for surprise that so much remains of interest in the castle to the present day, which, like nearly all the castles in Wales, was dismantled by the Parliamentarians. The soft grey colour of the stone, and the warm, rich greens and browns of the foliage which creeps over them, is exceptionally pleasing; the delightful views of the surrounding country, and the wonderful position occupied by the massive walls, all conduce to render Conway Castle a conspicuous landmark in the recollection of the traveller.

In passing down Castle Street, a late Perpendicular carved stone on the front of a house on the south side is of interest, and so also is a quaint building, now a temperance hall, dating from the year 1400.

One of the entrances to the Church lies in this street. The building is of the Decorated period, and is of great interest, as it contains a Perpendicular rood-loft, richly carved, with priests' entrance in perfect preservation, and a fine screen; a lace humeral and corporal 400 years old, preserved behind glass in the vestry; and a curious post-Reformation arched tomb on the south side of the chancel.

The Walls of Conway are unique, and form the best example in Europe of thirteenth-century scientific fortification. The Saracenic influence engendered by the Crusades is strongly exemplified in their construction; they are one mile in circuit, about 12 feet thick, with four gates and many semicircular towers. The feature of piercing the merlons of the battlements for the discharge of arrows is exemplified here, as in the castle. This undulating, encircling wall, clothed with creepers in parts, and presenting picturesque features at every turn, is a dream of medievalism not often encountered. Upon the quay stands the reputed smallest house in Great Britain, squeezed into a corner of the fortifications; one can stand in the road and shake hands with a person in the upper story.

Plas Mawr, or Queen Elizabeth's Palace (*admission 6d.*), dates from 1585, and has its chief frontage in Crown Lane. It is a perfectly preserved example of the architecture of that period, and abounds in archæological objects of interest. The 365 windows and 52 doors are not merely a coincidence.

Leaving Conway, the Sychnant Pass may be traversed if desired; it is a steep road leading over the mountains to Penmaenmawr, revealing fine views over the whole district.

The main road leads round the coast via Penmaenbach Point, near Conway Mountain (upon which are traces of an ancient fort). At Penmaenmawr one finds a cluster of modern villas, of every size and design, nestling at the foot of an enormous mass of stone towering up to a height of 1,550 feet—the well-known Penmaenmawr Mountain. Upon the summit, which affords a magnificent view for many miles round, are the ruins of one of the strongest of the early British forts, said to have accommodated 20,000 men. It is a matter for infinite regret that this important link with primitive Wales should be doomed to disappear through the steady advance of the huge quarries now eating into the hill. These quarries, and the steep tramway-lines up to them, also very seriously detract from the beauty of the spot. After leaving the village, the great round hump upon the summit of the mountain can be plainly seen from the road.

At Llanfairfechan, a small seaside resort, one reaches a typical Welsh resort—bathing-machines and sands combined with incipient mountain-climbing.

The Falls at Aber are two miles from the road, and can only be reached by footpath. The effect of the falls varies greatly with the season; but the climb up the valley towards Foel Fras is very fine. The road now passes inland somewhat, and the views of the Straits, of Beaumaris, and of Puffin Island, hitherto enjoyed, become obscured by trees. Near Bangor one of the entrances to the park surrounding Penrhyn Castle is seen upon the right, and here is the Model Village of Llandegai, interesting to those engaged in the social problems of the day. Workmen on the Penrhyn estate are housed in pretty cottages grouped in twos or threes, and placed in gardens. Avenues of trees shade the village roads, in the middle of which is Llandegai Church (*the key generally hangs up in the porch*). A tomb with two recumbent effigies of interest lies within: it came from Llanfaes Priory, but whom it represents is not known; the armour of the knight and the costume of the lady point to *c.* 1470. The church is charmingly clean and well kept. In the village no public-house is allowed, a state of things which has been productive of the very best results.

The road runs some distance by the park, and at times affords a view of Penrhyn Castle, the entrance to which is seen upon taking a sharp turn to the right, when Penrhyn Port is perceived; the bridge leads up to the gateway. (*Open Tuesday and Thursday afternoons, 10 to 5; 2s. for one person; 1s. extra for each additional one. Half the proceeds goes to local hospitals.*) The castle is an impressive modern reproduction of a Norman fortress; the keep reminds one of Rochester, and is really fine. The interior is worth a visit, if only to see how Lord Penrhyn has adapted modern luxury to the rough Norman architecture.

BANGOR

Upon leaving the castle, University College is passed upon the right, and a drive through the street leads to an open triangular space, where the cathedral comes into sight. Although the cathedral site has a rich history, having been occupied by the first church about 525, yet the present edifice is singularly uninteresting and unimpressive. This is undoubtedly due to the fact that the Saxon church was destroyed in 1071, the Norman successor in 1211, and the

Early English building in 1407, when it was reduced to ruins, and remained so for nearly a century. Consequently, the main part of the present edifice only dates from Henry VII.'s reign, and the tower from 1532. There is nothing of interest in the cathedral and but little outside. The clock, however, upon the occasion of the writer's recent visit, was worth noting, as the hands, the striking parts, and Greenwich time, were all at variance. Thus, when the hands pointed to 9.54, Greenwich time was 9.49, and the clock struck 10.

CONWAY VALLEY.
A peep of the River Conway between Bettws-y-Coed and Conway.

From the road leading downwards by the cathedral there is a view of the new University buildings, placed upon a commanding site overlooking the town. Lower Bangor lies in an amphitheatre of hills, upon which Upper Bangor is being built, the latter embracing the fashionable part of the town, and also the goal of pleasure-seekers, who patronize the sands and the pier.

LOOP No. 2

BANGOR TO BETTWS-Y-COED, 20¼ MILES

(The scenery of these twenty miles is so remarkably impressive that this short run is strongly recommended. The return journey can be made via Conway (as described in Section V.), a distance of thirty miles, or a return by the same road need not be shirked, for the scenery unfolds fresh glories when travelling in the opposite direction.)

DISTANCES ALONG THE ROUTE

	Miles.	
Bangor to Bethesda	5	¼
Bethesda to Llyn Ogwen	4	½
Llyn Ogwen to Capel Curig	5	
Capel Curig to Bettws-y-Coed	5	½

NOTES FOR DRIVERS

A steady rise from **Bethesda to Llyn Ogwen**, then level for 2 miles.

A long descent to **Bettws-y-Coed**, steep at times. Surface good.

PLACES OF INTEREST ON THE ROUTE

Penrhyn Castle.—Modern Norman structure (open to public).

Llandegai Model Village.—Church, with interesting tomb.

Bethesda Slate Quarries.

Nant Ffrancon.—Scenery wild and grand.

Llyn Idwal and the Devil's Kitchen.—Stern rock and lake scenery.

Llyn Ogwen.—A wild lake among the mountains.

Capel Curig.—The Cyfyng Falls; grand view of Snowdon.

Bettws-y-Coed (see p. 84).—A charming village in a steep leafy valley.

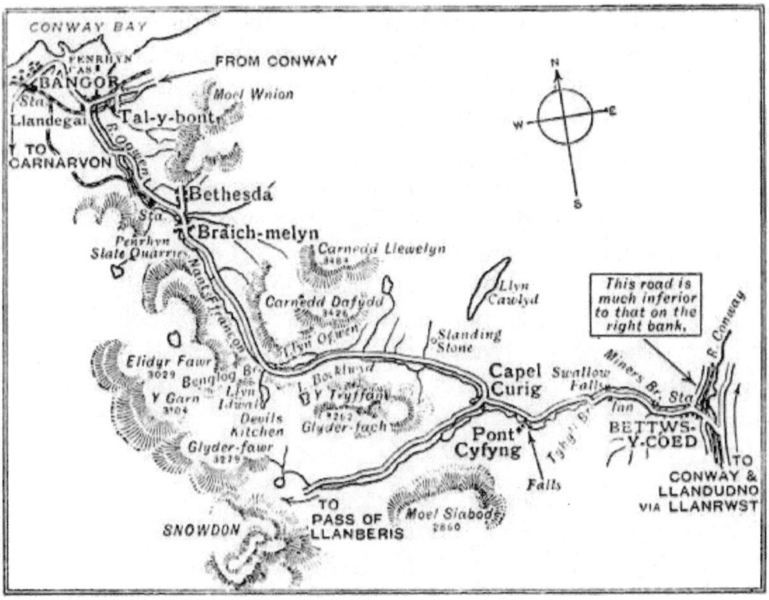

LOOP 2. BANGOR TO BETTWS-Y-COED.

Those who wish to see Wales in all its aspects should on no account miss the twenty-mile run from Bangor to Bettws. It has been termed the most impressive pass in North Wales, and poetically referred to as 'Beauty sleeping in the lap of Horror.' To fully grasp the feeling of the place a walk through it on a mild winter's day is desirable, and on January 1 of last year one of the writers experienced that sensation, when flying scud and wild lashing torrents of occasional rain from whirling masses of black clouds upon the sombre peaks added a realistic force to the wildness of the scene.

The road leading to Penrhyn Castle and Llandegai is that which should be taken. At Bethesda a typical slate-quarrying town is reached, with great 'tips' of refuse encircling it; the continual roar and rattle of engines, dragging tramloads of slate, high above the roadway, is punctuated with the occasional boom of the blastings. The quarries may be visited if desired, when a memorable sight will be witnessed.

There is nothing in this centre of Welsh Nonconformity of antiquarian interest, and soon a steady ascent leads from it into the Nant Ffrancon Pass, presumably the Valley of Beavers. Upon the right lies a range of mountains, each over 3,000 feet in height, and well known to climbers—Elidyr Fawr, Y Garn, and Glyder Fawr, with Glyder Fach straight in front, and the giant mass of Moel Siabod behind it. On the left, Carnedd Llewelyn, 3,484 feet, and Carnedd Dafydd, 3,426 feet, send down great shoulders into the pass, where the winding road, ever ascending, climbs above the grassy valley lying between the encircling giants. At Benglog Bridge, where the foaming Afon Ogwen leaps down the boulders in a torrent, one is nearly 1,000 feet above sea-level. Here the lonely Llyn Ogwen comes into view, but before passing it the short clamber over rocks to Llyn Idwal should on no account be omitted. The path begins behind the little inn, and winds by the side of the stream draining from the lake which abruptly comes into view. This lonely tarn, with its waters reflecting the black scarp of Glyder Fawr, seldom or never lit up by the sun's rays, and often lashed into foam by the fierce eddies sweeping down from the mountains, is the very embodiment of awe-inspiring impressiveness. Even if the day be beautiful there is a wild loneliness, which is accentuated by the legend of Prince Idwal being brutally murdered here by Dunawt at the instigation of his father, to whom the youth had been entrusted by his parents.

The terrific black chasm seen in the rocks overshadowing the pool is named Twll Du, or the Black Cleft, but popularly 'The Devil's Kitchen.' It is 450 feet high and 100 feet deep, narrowing in places to 6 feet wide. A foaming cataract of troubled waters pours down, forming in its fall the hollows at the base termed 'The Devil's Pots.' Many fatal accidents to climbers have occurred here in ascending to Llyn Bochlwyd, lying nearly 700 feet higher, on Glyder Fach, last year (1910) being by no means immune.

South of Lake Ogwen, Tryfaen, the three-headed mountain, is remarkably impressive. Soon after the lake is passed a descent commences to Capel Curig, where a magnificent view of the eastern slopes of Snowdon is obtained between Moel Siabod and Glyder Fawr. The combined waters of the Llugwy and Nant-y-Gwryd accompany the road as it leads downwards to Bettws-y-Coed, with the Swallow Falls and Miners' Bridge, as previously noticed (see p. 84).

SECTION VI
(TRUNK ROUTE)

BANGOR TO DOLGELLEY, 65¾ MILES

DISTANCES ALONG THE ROUTE

Miles.		
Bangor to Carnarvon	9	
Carnarvon to Llanberis	7	½
Llanberis to Pen-y-Gwryd	6	½
Pen-y-Gwryd to Beddgelert	7	¾
Beddgelert to Penrhyn Deudraeth	7	½
Penrhyn Deudraeth to Harlech	6	½
Harlech to Barmouth	11	
Barmouth to Dolgelley	10	

NOTES FOR DRIVERS

Bangor to Carnarvon.—Nearly level and splendid surface.

Carnarvon to Llanberis.—Steep hills for 4 miles, then easy gradients and good surface.

Steady rise through **Pass of Llanberis**.

Remainder of the route splendid surface, with occasional moderate hills.

PLACES OF INTEREST ON THE ROUTE

Carnarvon.—The Roman town of *Segontium*; magnificent thirteenth-century castle; town walls; St. Mary's Church.

Splendid views of the **Snowdon precipices**.

Llanberis.—A popular resort consisting of old and new villages; Dolbadarn Castle; waterfall; slate quarries; mountain railway.

Pass of Llanberis.—Cromlech, so called; impressive scenery.

Beddgelert.—A picturesque village; Gelert's grave; church; prettiest part of route.

Aberglaslyn.—Pass and bridge; delightful scenery.

Penrhyn.—Ffestiniog Toy Railway; Deudraeth Castle, of modern construction.

Harlech.—County town (small) of Merioneth; castle in commanding position.

Llanbedr.—A village; Llyn Cwm Bychan, a wild lake; Roman steps.

Llanddwywe.—Church; Cors-y-Gedol cromlechs.

Llanaber.—Church, Early English architecture; interesting stone relic.

Barmouth.—Modern watering-place; bridge; panorama walk; magnificent views of the estuary of the Mawddach.

Bontddu.—Water-fall.

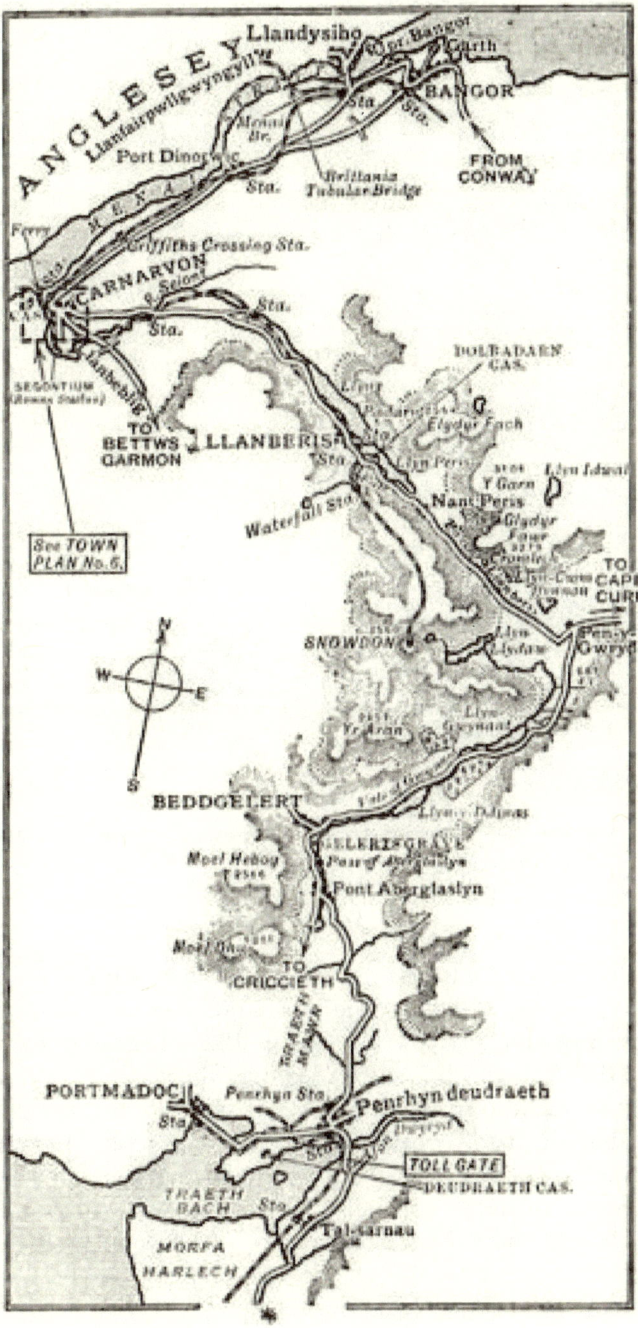

(TRUNK) No. 6. BANGOR TO DOLGELLEY.

No. 6. BANGOR TO DOLGELLEY.

The road from Bangor leads past the Menai Suspension Bridge over the Straits, once a wonder of the world, but now overshadowed by the Forth Bridge and others. It was opened in 1826. The total length of the roadway is 1,000 feet, which is suspended over the water at a height of 100 feet above the highest spring-tide. The view from the bridge is most picturesque, but it is hardly worth while to take a car over. (*Motor-car 2s. toll; foot passengers 1d. each.*) The bridge has a very distinct swing in a high wind. Farther on one sees the Britannia Tubular Bridge, opened in 1850, and carrying the railway across in two hollow tubes of enormous strength. No one can accuse this engineering feat of being beautiful, but it has thoroughly proved its efficiency. The Anglesey Column forms a prominent landmark at the farther end of the bridge; it was erected as a memorial of the Marquis of Anglesey who distinguished himself at Waterloo. The well-known Plas Newydd, the residence of the present peer, lies adjacent, and there also is the village of L l a n f a i r , sometimes Llanfair Pwll Gwyngyll, and a full name of fifty-four letters if one is still more respectful. At Port Dinorwic vessels load up with slates from Bethesda. The view of the Anglesey coast is fine at first, but the shores gradually deteriorate as one reaches Carnarvon, eventually spreading out in mud flats.

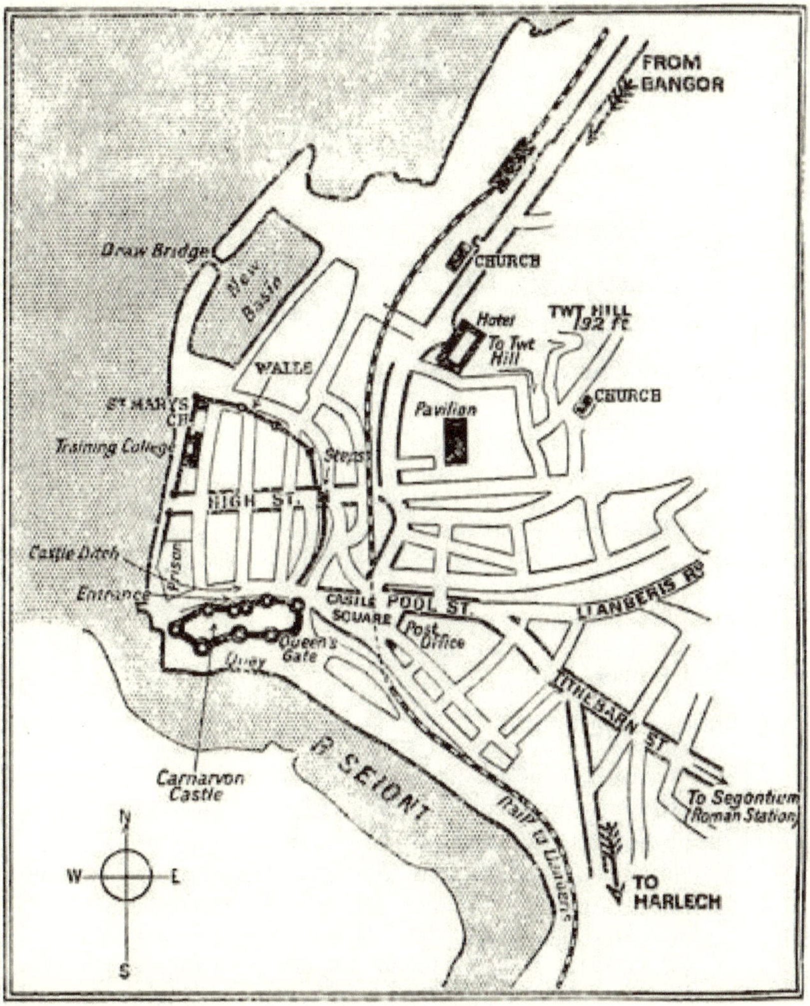

TOWN PLAN NO. 6—CARNARVON.

CARNARVON

As the great Roman town and fortress of *Segontium*, the reputed birthplace of Constantine the Great, the site of a famous feudal fortress, and the birthplace of the first Prince of Wales, Carnarvon undoubtedly occupies a unique position in British history, and, as it still possesses tangible evidences of most of its past record, the traveller is unwise who passes by without a stay of at least a few hours' duration, though a few days would be more appropriate.

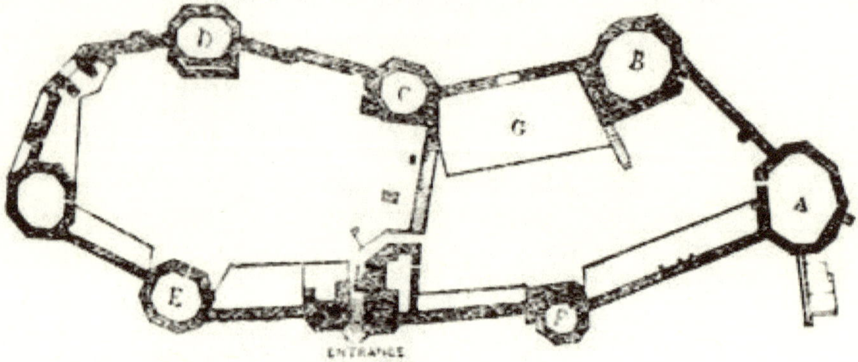

GROUND PLAN OF CARNARVON CASTLE.

- **A. Eagle Tower.**
- **B. Queen's Tower.**
- **C. Chamberlain's Tower.**
- **D. Black Tower.**
- **E. Granary Tower.**
- **F. Well Tower.**
- **G. Banqueting Hall.**

Behind the Royal Hotel, which is passed on entering the town, is a small rocky knob, easily climbed, called Twt Hill, a coign of vantage for viewing the Carnarvon mountains, the Straits, Anglesey, and Carnarvon itself. On a clear day the mountains of Wicklow can be seen, and as a practical exponent of the ichnography of the town the hill is of great use. The approach to the castle by a narrow road suddenly reveals a view of Carnarvon Castle, the vast dimensions of which may probably be best gleaned by walking down to the slate wharf on the River Seoint, laving the walls. Here the great height of the walls, the quality of the excellent stonework, and the general effect of impregnability, are realized. Returning to the main entrance, the great arch known as the Queen's Doorway is passed high up in the wall; it is the traditional spot whence the infant Edward was shown to the Welsh chieftains by his father. The drawbridge at one time crossed the street at this point; an inn now occupies the sight of the barbican. Within the castle (*admission 4d.*) the visitor is at once struck with the idea that a medieval fortress in its entirety is presented to the view; there are no crumbling ruins or ivy-clad masses of fallen masonry, as in the majority of structures of this nature. This is accounted for by the fact that it belongs to the Crown, and every stone as it becomes weathered is carefully replaced. The castle is, in fact, a most interesting study for the archæologist, as illustrating medieval methods of defence. The Eagle Tower, the reputed apartment where Edward II. was born, the Queen's Gateway, and other interesting parts, are pointed out by the keeper. It should be remembered that the castle is the finest in Europe except one; that it was built by Edward I. in 1283, heightened by Edward II., garrisoned by the Royalists in the Civil War under Lord Byron, and after an able defence surrendered to the Parliamentarians, who ordered its demolition in 1660, which was fortunately not carried out. The Town Walls of Carnarvon are interesting objects to the visitor, as is also St. Mary's Church, built into the walls, a tower forming the vestry and the walls two sides of the church.

Of *Segontium*, the great Roman station, but little remains. A portion of the wall, in bad condition, lies in a narrow lane at the top of the hill, gained by ascending Pool Street and Tithebarn Street and passing round to the right, at the back of the Rectory, before reaching Llanbeblig Church. There are other and better sections to be seen by making inquiries. In one instance, in the front-garden of a house, it is some 20 feet in height, formed of beautifully squared stones, and can be seen from the roadway; by the courtesy of the occupiers it is quite possible for a nearer view to be obtained. This wall undoubtedly extended to the river.

The road to Llanberis leads from Castle Square up Pool Street for a short distance, when Llanberis Road is entered. The route is to a certain extent spoilt at first by intrusive chimneys and other industrial manifestations. Llyn Padarn has also been ruined by quarries, and probably was never celebrated for scenery. The peak of Snowdon is seen intermittently upon the right, but the chief mountain features are Elidyr Fawr (the other side of which has been seen from Nant Ffrancon) and Carnedd Dafydd, 3,426 feet.

Llanberis is a favourite tourists' resort for fishing and mountain-climbing, and a headquarters for excursions to neighbouring points.

Dolbadarn Castle is of remote antiquity, and probably existed in the sixth century, its position making it a fortress of importance. It has probably seen as much wild work as any castle in Wales, especially during the Glendower period, being the master-key to the Snowdon region.

O l d L l a n b e r i s , beyond Llyn Peris, is more picturesque than the new, and contains a church, which is chiefly interesting on account of the graves in the churchyard of those who have lost their lives on Snowdon. The entrance to the famous P a s s o f L l a n b e r i s , between Glyder Fawr and Snowdon, is very impressive, and the narrowness of the valley gives it a distinct character compared with Nant Ffrancon. It is probably the finest mountain defile traversed by a carriage-road in the Principality. A huge mass of rock, which in falling has produced a natural cromlech, is to be seen on the left. The summit of Glyder Fawr appears before the end of the pass is reached, but that of Snowdon is still hidden. The highest point of the pass is 1,179 feet above sea-level. The views obtained upon reaching Pen-y-Gwryd are a relief after the wildness of the route traversed. Moel Siabod to the left front, with the sugar-loaf height of Cynicht, are prominent features, while the view down the Gwynant Valley is one of the sweetest prospects in Wales. At the hotel occurs an abrupt turning to the right, and a sharp descent leads to Llyn Gwynant, a picturesque lake, from which a grand view of the rugged slopes of Snowdon is obtained. Llyn-y-Ddinas, farther on, is scarcely less pleasing. Soon afterwards

BEDDGELERT

is entered, the most romantically situated village in Wales, standing at the junction of three valleys, leading respectively to Carnarvon, Portmadoc, and Capel Curig, and surrounded by a grand array of mountain peaks. It derives its name from the story of Llewellyn's hound, and means 'the grave of Gelert.' The rude monument said to have been erected by the Prince in his repentance for the hasty act may be reached in a few hundred yards from the village. Moel Habog, 2,566 feet, is an easy climb from here. The road to Penrhyn Deudraeth leads through the romantic Pass of Aberglaslyn, and emerges upon the far-famed bridge, where the rich colouring of the rocks, full of exquisite contrasts with the foliage, delights the eye at every glance. There are many parts of Switzerland that afford similar visions of beauty and grandeur, but what Pont Aberglaslyn loses in size it gains in the beauty of its colour. The junction of two roads occurs here—one to Tremadoc, the other to Penrhyn. The latter drops to an extensive and dreary plain, Traeth Mawr, across which the road winds with many a sharp turn. The views of the distant mountains are very effective, while straight in front the Castle of Harlech becomes a prominent feature, with the waters of Cardigan Bay to right and left.

DISTANT VIEW OF PENMAENMAWR.
Between Conway and Bangor.

Penrhyn Deudraeth is a mining village of no interest, except as the starting-point of the Ffestiniog narrow-gauge railway. Here the river draining the Vale of Ffestiniog enters a large sheet of water called Traeth Bach, and, crossing it by a bridge, the Morfa Harlech, an uninteresting flat, is entered, with the modern Castle of Deudraeth to the right. Here the road runs between the Morfa and the high country to the left, until it reaches the little town of

HARLECH

Unless the visitor should happen to be a golfer and a frequenter of the famous St. David's Club Links, there is practically nothing of interest in the neighbourhood except the castle, famous in history and song, which occupies a precipitous elevation in the front of the town. The entry is opposite the Castle Hotel. (*Admission 4d.*) A fortress of some sort existed as early as the third century, when Bronwen, or White-Bosomed, the daughter of Bran the Blessed, lived here. About 550 a more substantial pile was raised, but this in turn was replaced by the present castle, built by Edward I. in 1280, who, however, incorporated much of the older building in his new fortress. In 1404 it was seized by Glendower, but retaken by the King's troops in 1408. Margaret of Anjou took refuge in it after Northampton in 1460. Edward IV., after a long siege, captured it in 1468, and the 'March of the Men of Harlech' dates from that period. During the Civil War the castle was alternately in possession of both parties. It is now Crown property. The magnificent view from the battlements should be seen. Across the bay, seven miles, is the sister castle of Criccieth, while the long promontory of Carnarvon, termed Lleyn, forms a bold feature on the north-western horizon. The two highest elevations on the promontory are The Rivals, and Bardsey Island is the detached fragment. To the right there is a line of mountain peaks to Moel Hebod and the Snowdon heights. Two and a half miles to the south of Harlech the Island of Mochras lies off the shore, joined at low tide by an isthmus. It is chiefly visited for its beautiful shells. Near it is the commencement of the Sarn Badrig, a curious ledge of rocks, bare at low tide, which runs far out into the waters of the bay. A similar formation, though of less extent, lies off Aberystwyth. To the antiquary the country to the east of Harlech is of the greatest interest; it teems with relics, chiefly prehistoric, such as cromlechs, stone circles, and dolmens. The far-famed Roman Steps, the Lake of Cwm Bychan, with its abnormally savage surroundings, the Drws Ardudwy, all lie in this interesting hinterland, mostly far away from the main road. Near Llanbedr, however, between the road and the river, and just short of the village, are two long stones, and another bearing an Ogham inscription. L l a n d d w y w e C h u r c h is not of any particular interest, but two cromlechs stand nearly opposite the King's Head Inn, about eighty yards from the road. The large cromlech known as Arthur's Quoit is at some distance, near Cors-y-Gedol, the old seat of the Vaughans, or Vychans, of Cors-y-Gedol. The church at L l a n a b e r is of Early English architecture, and should be visited. An inscribed stone of much interest and with various decipherings stands near the north-west door; it was found below low-water mark on the beach near the church.

BARMOUTH

This rather overbuilt watering-place is situated in a romantic position at the mouth of the Mawddach, and is remarkable for its genial winter climate, the town being protected by the high hills surrounding it. Apart from the visitors who crowd into the town during the summer season, there are a great number who utilize it as a centre for mountaineering, antiquarian, geological, and fishing excursions. The houses are built up the face of the cliff, so that the chimney-pots of one house are opposite the front-door of the house behind, and it is possible to diagnose a neighbour's dinner by the odours thus conveyed. The church is new, but some interesting geological contortions occur near it. The view from the railway bridge is one of the most remarkable in Wales. (*The toll is 2d., and one of the best times for seeing the estuary and its mountainous setting is at sunset.*) High tide helps the scene enormously. A rich and sombre purple, partly clothing the mountains, melts into exquisite gradations of green and velvety browns. Cader Idris, upon the right, fills all that side of the picture; the Arrans furnish the centre distance; while the outliers of Llawr Lech and Y Garn occupy the left. A well-known projection on the flanks of Cader is the Giant's Nose.

The Panorama Walk is a favourite stroll from Barmouth; it is commenced at a terrace bearing the curious name of Porkington, and direction-boards indicate the route. The path truly deserves the name it has been given, although the labelling of scenery in this way is exceedingly distasteful.

THE ESTUARY OF THE MAWDDACH

The road to Dolgelley lies upon the northern shore of this famous estuary, and for beauty and impressiveness cannot easily be overpraised. The many windings in the road accentuate its charm, glimpses, sometimes of entrancing beauty, being frequently presented to the traveller. Besides the scenery there are no special objects to be indicated upon the road; just beyond Brintirion, however, a stream descends which has passed through the gold-field of St. David's, lying upon the slopes of the mountain above. The ruins of Cymmer Abbey, near Llanelltyd, remind one forcibly of Valle Crucis Abbey, so charming and reposeful are the surroundings. It was founded *c.* 1200 by the Cistercians, and dissolved at the Reformation. The adjoining farmhouse contains parts of the refectory and abbot's lodging. The eastern portion of the church is in the best preservation, and upon the south are a few Early English arches and pillars. The road here turns sharply to the right to Dolgelley, and, entering this quaintly-situated little town, the Golden Lion Hotel is found in the market-place near the church.

LOOP No. 3

DOLGELLEY TO CEMMAES VIA TAL-Y-LLYN, 40 MILES

DISTANCES ALONG THE ROUTE

	Miles.	
Dolgelley to Penmaenpool	2	½
Penmaenpool to Arthog	4	½
Arthog to Llwyngwril	5	
Llwyngwril to Llanegryn	4	
Llanegryn to Abergynolwyn	6	
Abergynolwyn to Tal-y-llyn	3	
Tal-y-llyn to Corris	4	
Corris to Machynlleth	5	
Machynlleth to Cemmaes	6	

NOTES FOR DRIVERS

Surface to **Llwyngwril** excellent.

Near **Arthog** gradient of 1 in 10.

Near **Friog** gradient of 1 in 14.

Ascent of 1 in 9 near **Abergynolwyn**, and descent of 1 in 6 into the village.

After **Tal-y-llyn** ascent of 1 in 7, and descent to **Corris** 1 in 16.

Surface generally good to **Machynlleth**.

Then excellent road, but hilly, to **Cemmaes**.

PLACES OF INTEREST ON THE ROUTE

Arthog.—Waterfalls.

Llwyngwril.—A village; remains of Castell-y-Gaer.

Llanegryn.—Church with magnificent rood-loft; Bird Rock in distance.

Tal-y-llyn.—A lake near Cader Idris.

Corris.—Toy railway; slate district.

Machynlleth.—Market town; remains of old Senate-house.

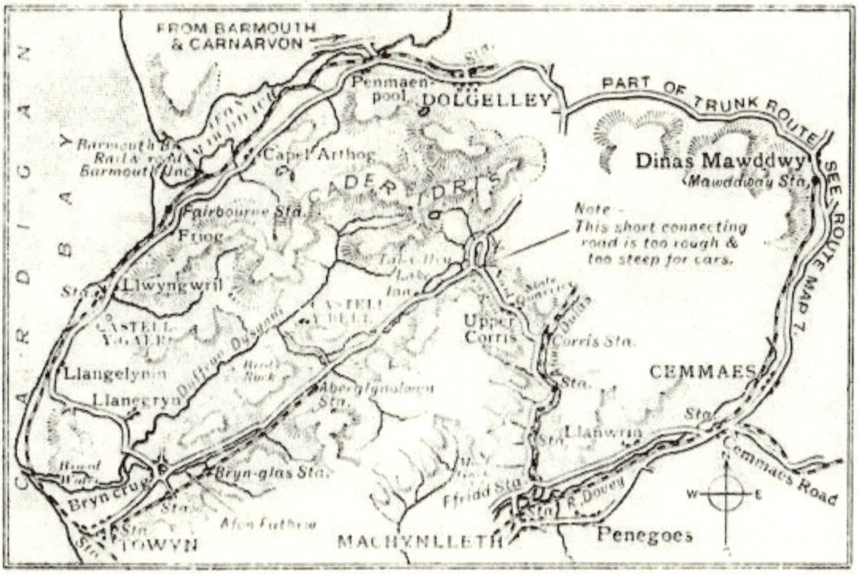

LOOP 3. DOLGELLEY TO CEMMAES VIA TAL-Y-LLYN.

The road from Dolgelley passes, with many windings, from the town to the estuary at Penmaenpool, to which place excursion steamers run during the summer from Barmouth. Although the scenery upon the south bank of the Mawddach is not so fine as that upon the north, yet the mountains of Ardudwy, as the hinterland of Barmouth was anciently called, present an imposing aspect, and sometimes compose a pretty picture when seen through the umbrageous foliage which lines the road on both sides. If the tide be high, the view is accentuated by the reflections in the broad expanse of water, and singularly beautiful glimpses are at times displayed. The undulating road, flanked at times by the universal whitewashed cottages, reaches A r t h o g , a small village situated at the base of a finely wooded, diversified ground, about a mile from which are the Arthog Lakes, and at a short distance from the hotel a waterfall, of considerable beauty after a heavy fall of rain, but much attenuated in dry weather. At Friog the slate quarries are apparent on the left of the road, and a steady rise begins, leading to an excellent retrospective view of Barmouth, Harlech Castle, and the Lleyn Peninsula to Bardsey.

SNOWDON FROM TRAETH MAWR.

LLWYNGWRIL

is a small village, with the Dyffryn River passing through it under a bridge. Castell-y-Gaer lies upon its banks at a short distance up the stream, consisting of small masses of broken ivy-clad masonry, of an unknown fortress so far as history is concerned. Upon the bridge before mentioned on Sunday evenings after church or chapel the youths and maidens of the village congregate to sing the sweet Welsh refrains handed down through long generations, and harmonized with a beauty of feeling which only a music-loving nation can express. Among the men singularly rich basses prevail; north of Barmouth, strange to say, tenors predominate. The route turns abruptly inland beyond Llangelynin, and the village of

LLANEGRYN,

lying off the main road, but approached by a lane, appears on the left. It contains a church well worth visiting, inasmuch as the superb rood-screen is among the finest in the British Isles. It is of early Perpendicular work, and the loft above is quite perfect except for the actual rood and the figures of saints. A good roof and an interesting Norman font should also be noticed.

THE BIRD ROCK

may be seen from this point, an isolated crag of peculiar shape standing up black and dour against the mountains beyond. The weird beauty of the landscape can hardly be overpraised. The road leading straight onwards passes almost underneath the rock, but the main route to the right descends to the bridge over the river, draining the Dysynni Valley, and Tal-y-llyn. Here are some sharp turns, but presently the very narrow road is reached, leading directly to the lake. Passing another vehicle is not an easy matter. The scenery increases in beauty as one progresses, the little railway to the right having scarcely the smallest deteriorating effect upon the valley. The ruins of Castell-y-Bere, formerly one of the largest in Wales, and once visited by Edward I., lie in the adjacent valley to the left, to which the narrow road leads, coming into Abergynolwyn on the left.

TAL-Y-LLYN

Tal-y-llyn is a quarter of a mile in width, and a little over a mile in length. It lies under Cader Idris, although the summit is not visible from it; two great craters, however, carved in its rocky flanks, form a fitting background on the left. In front lies a valley, by ascending which the Cross Foxes Inn is reached, and subsequently Dolgelley. Extravagant praise has been lavished upon the lake by many travellers, but one misses some essentials to claims of exceptional beauty. No quality of mystery appeals to the imagination; the lake does not lie in an appalling neighbourhood of black riven rocks or in a glen of surpassing beauty. All is open, and the whole is seen at one vision. Anglers, however, find Tal-y-llyn an ideal spot. At the farther end of the lake the road, after a branch track to the right by a cottage has been passed, turns to the right up a steep ascent, from whose summit a retrospective view of the lake is perhaps the best obtainable. The road to Corris through Nant Gwgan is pretty, with occasional waterfalls and stone slides from the shoulders of mountains towering hundreds of feet above the pass. The rich browns and greens and subtler shades of grey form charming contrasts of colour. Unfortunately, the lower end of the pass is disfigured by many slate quarries. Upper Corris is strongly reminiscent of Bethesda. A monument is erected here on the left side of the road to Alfred W. Hughes, F.R.C.S., who died in 1900 of fever during the war in South Africa. A quarry railway, with a miniature station and a gauge of 2 feet 3 inches, runs by the side of the road. At Corris, which is a slate-mining town pure and simple, the road trends to the right, and the view becomes less circumscribed as the vale of Afon Dulas widens out. When the Dovey Valley is reached a wide expanse of alluvial land comes into view, through which the river meanders westwards towards its estuary.

MACHYNLLETH

Machynlleth is a spacious and well-built market town and borough with two main streets, wide and pleasant, with well-kept shops, thus forming a marked contrast in that respect to the majority of Welsh towns. It forms one of the centres of the woollen industry of the county, and indulges somewhat in the tanning business as well. The clock-tower is a prominent object; the church has no features of interest worth recording; the Market-house dates only from 1783, and of antiquarian curiosities there are but few. An old black-and-white cottage at the end of Maengwyn Street, which branches off to the left at the chief main street, has 'OWEN PUGH O VXOR 1628' for 'Owen Pugh and wife.' The 'O,' however, is baffling as a conjunction. Opposite are portions of the old Senate-house, the reputed building in which Owen Glendower succeeded in persuading the nobles and commons to acknowledge him Prince of Wales in 1402. Upon the hills surrounding Machynlleth remains occur which appear to indicate that the town was a Roman station, and coins have occasionally been found to confirm this. A good road up the Valley of the Dovey leads to Cemmaes, where the trunk route is again reached.

(*For a description of the road from Cemmaes to Dolgelley, see Section VII.*)

LOOP No. 4

CEMMAES TO ABERYSTWYTH AND LLANGURIG, 49¾ MILES

DISTANCES ALONG THE ROUTE

	Miles.	
Cemmaes to Machynlleth	5	½
Machynlleth to Talybont	10	¾
Talybont to Aberystwyth	9	¼
Aberystwyth to Goginan	7	½
Goginan to Ponterwyd	4	¼
Ponterwyd to Dyffryn Castell Hotel	2	
Dyffryn Castell Hotel to Llangurig	10	½

NOTES FOR DRIVERS

Cemmaes to Aberystwyth.—Good surface all the way, but hilly; worst gradients before and after Talybont, 1 in 13 and 1 in 11.

First 12 miles after **Aberystwyth** splendid surface, then becomes a little rough and bumpy to **Llangurig**.

There are some steep hills in the neighbourhood of the **Devil's Bridge**.

PLACES OF INTEREST ON THE ROUTE

Glandovey (or **Glan Dyfi**).—Entrance for the beautiful Lyfnant Valley; view over the estuary.

Aberystwyth.—A considerable town, with ruins of an Edwardian castle and the University buildings.

The Devil's Bridge.—Grand scenery; the Parson's Bridge; the Punch Bowl.

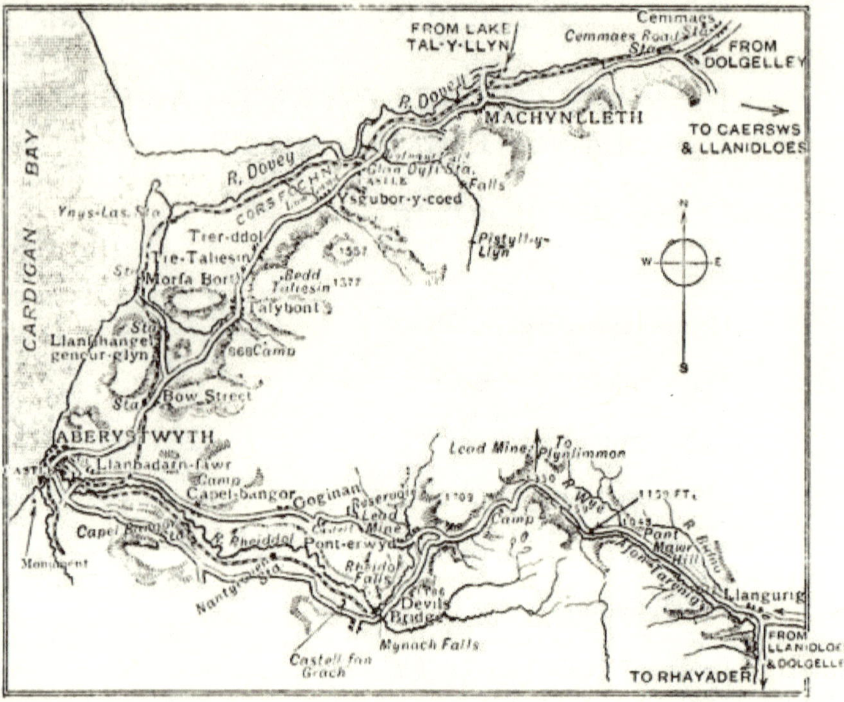

Loop 4. CEMMAES TO ABERYSTWYTH AND LLANGURIG.

The road down the Valley of the Dovey presents a pretty panorama, but possesses no particular feature to arrest attention—it is merely a pleasant drive.

GLANDOVEY

This small place stands at the entrance to the Lyfnant Valley, one of the most distractingly beautiful little glens in the whole of Wales, with waterfalls, torrents, and utter wildness of vegetation, and stern, bleak splendour at the farther end, where Pistyll-y-Llyn showers its two foaming torrents headlong into the black caldron beneath. The first cataract met, the Glaspwll Cascade, is a fine one, but it cannot vie with the more remote example. There is a prettily situated small castle on the left of the road. The estuary of the Dovey now appears, and if the tide be at the flood, presents a very fine prospect. Aberdovey generally has a brig or two lying off the quay. An extensive salt marsh now comes into view, between which and the high land the road runs. B o r t h lies on the coast of this plain; its hydro, links, and beautiful sands attract visitors during the summer. At Tre-Taliesin we are reminded of the grave of Taliesin, the 'King of the Bards' during the sixth century; the pilgrimage to his grave, which lies about a mile to the left of the road, is a favourite one from Aberystwyth. Two miles farther on the remains of a British camp or fort crown the summit of Moel-y-Gaer, close to the road upon the right; they are remarkably well preserved, and in the neighbourhood are some Druidical circles. In this district the open country around is quite park-like in many places; at times, however, it reminds one of parts of Devonshire. About two miles from Aberystwyth there is a beautiful vista of Cardigan Bay and the coast laved by its waters, with the town lying below at the termination of a long and rather trying hill.

ABERYSTWYTH

Aberystwyth not only boasts of a high antiquity, but also of having been the commercial centre for the Mid-Welsh counties. The trade has now dwindled, but as a watering-place it easily holds its own as one of the most frequented in Wales. The chief points of interest are:

The Castle, the ruins of which occupy a position of prominence in the centre of the town, was built by Gilbert de Strongbow in the reign of Henry I. It was destroyed by Owen Gwynedd, and rebuilt by Edward I.; in the Civil War it was dismantled by the Parliamentarians. The grounds are now laid out in pleasant walks, affording fine views of the coast.

The University Buildings adjoin the castle, and may be termed one of the finest examples of recent architecture in the Principality. The general effect of the modern buildings in the town is depressing, probably owing to the use of the dark Silurian stone, covered with the universal slate roof.

The town is happy in having an immediate neighbourhood of great interest to the antiquary and to the ordinary tourist, inasmuch as many pleasant excursions may be indulged in, such, for example, as the visits to Strata Florida Abbey, the Monk's Cave, Lyfnant Valley, and the Devil's Bridge.

The route to Llangurig commences in Aberystwyth, in Northgate Street, and runs through Llanbadarn. At Pont Erwydd a road leads south to the Devil's Bridge, fifteen miles, a feature which should not on any account be missed.

An alternative route, eleven and three-quarter miles to the bridge, is a part of the direct road to Rhayader.

(*a*) First Route, the Pont Erwydd.—Road level for first six miles, then rise to 1,027 feet; hilly.

Llanbadarn.—Church much restored.

Bangor to Goginan.—Lead-mines have destroyed scenery. A wild country around Pont Erwydd, where the route turns to the right.

(*b*) Alternative Route.—The direct road to Devil's Bridge commences in Bridge Street, crosses the harbour, and passes under the railway.

About five miles out Cader Idris appears, twenty miles away to the left. The view afterwards into the Rheidol Valley is very fine. The highest point of the road, 989 feet above sea-level, commands a fine view of the two peaks of Plynlimmon. Castell-fan-Crach is a prehistoric earthwork.

The Devil's Bridge is situated in what is probably the finest and most picturesque glen in the British Isles; the approach to it by either of the roads described gives only a slight idea of its merits. The monks of Strata Florida Abbey are supposed to have built the arch in the time of Rufus; the second bridge dates from 1814. The Devil's Punch Bowl, the Robbers' Cave, and the Falls of the Rheidol, should be seen.

The road to Llangurig from Pont Erwydd leads through a bare valley containing a large number of abandoned lead-mines—the dead hopes of thousands of sanguine speculators. The highest point of the road, 1,368 feet, is only two and a half miles from the summit of Plynlimmon (2,469 feet high), about two miles from the source of the Wye, and four miles from that of the Severn. The mountain is dull and uninteresting, being more of a flat spreading lump than a peak, and has extensive tracts of bog-land and marsh. Descending towards Llangurig, the Wye is crossed near an inn, and accompanies the road down the valley, which is cultivated to a certain extent in its lower portion. At Llangurig the main route is reached between Llanidloes and Rhayader.

(*For a description of the 30½ miles between Llangurig and Cemmaes, see Section VII.*)

SECTION VII
(TRUNK ROUTE)

DOLGELLEY TO LLANGURIG, 48¼ MILES

DISTANCES ALONG THE ROUTE

	Miles.	
Dolgelley to Cross Foxes	3	½
Cross Foxes to Dinas Mawddwy	7	
Dinas Mawddwy to Cemmaes	7	¼
Cemmaes to Llanbrynmair	5	¾
Llanbrynmair to Carno	6	
Carno to Caersws	5	¼
Caersws to Llandinam	2	½
Llandinam to Llanidloes	6	
Llanidloes to Llangurig	5	

NOTES FOR DRIVERS

Steady rise to **Cross Foxes**, then very steep ascent to top of **Cold Door Pass** (1 in 8), 988 feet high.

Easy descent to **Dinas Mawddwy**.

Dinas Mawddwy to Carno.—Undulating, but a rise just before Carno, 1 in 12.

Carno to Caersws.—Steady descent, occasionally sharp.

After **Caersws** undulating, with a few stiff hills to **Llangurig**.

PLACES OF INTEREST ON THE ROUTE

Dolgelley.—Small town possessing little interest in itself. Surroundings include Torrent Walk, Precipice Walk, Cader Idris, and innumerable spots to which excursions on foot may be taken.

Cross Foxes.—Splendid view from near this inn.

Dinas Mawddwy.—A little town, prettily situated; grand view of Aran Mawddwy, 2,970 feet.

Talerddig.—A natural rock arch.

Caersws.—Small village on site of Roman station, with visible earthworks.

Llanidloes.—A typical Welsh market town; the church; Van Mines.

Llangurig.—The highest village in Wales.

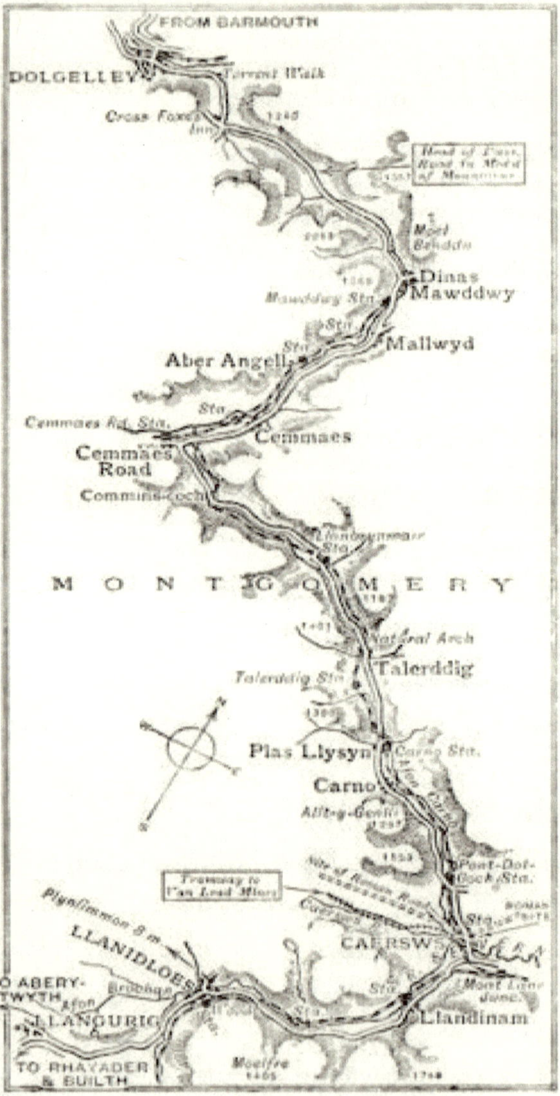

(TRUNK) No. 7. DOLGELLEY TO LLANGURIG.

DOLGELLEY,

the capital town of Merionethshire, is situated in a wide and fertile valley of singular beauty at the foot of Cader Idris. The streets are exceptionally short and irregular. The parish church of St. Mary has no particular merits; in it is preserved a fourteenth-century effigy of one of the Vaughans, or Vychans, of Nannau. From Dolgelley various excursions may be made to such places of rare beauty as the Precipice Walk, cut high up on the face of Moel Cynwch, with views over the Gaullwyd Valley. The Torrent Walk is beautified by the rich greens and browns lavished by Nature on the rocks by the foaming torrent of the Clywedog. Three fine waterfalls are also to be found in the neighbourhood, one the well-known Pistyll-y-Cain, while the ascent of Cader from this town is a very desirable one.

The road from Dolgelley to Dinas Mawddwy is an interesting one, both by reason of the stiff climbs and also the fine views that accompany it. The surface is generally inclined to be rough, and upon the occasion of the writer's recent visit the portion leading down into Dolgelley was appallingly bad. No doubt this state of things does not exist now. At the Cross Foxes Inn the road turns sharply to the left and mounts to Cold Door Pass, situated upon a bleak moor, with a splendid view of Cader Idris standing in grand isolation and beauty. Many mountains suffer by the proximity of other heights, but Cader is an exception. From the pass the road gradually descends through a valley, increasing in beauty of verdure and foliage, to Dinas Mawddwy.

DINAS MAWDDWY

This sequestered little town lies in a deep hollow formed by the junction of two valleys, which discharge the streams they respectively contain into the Dovey, occupying the main valley. The town consists of one long street, with the grounds and house of Plas at the termination. The church is chiefly known for its enormous yews, one in particular being of really vast dimensions. Dinas Mawddwy is a centre for anglers, sportsmen, and artists, and, during the season, for excursionists. From the road a waterfall is a prominent feature.

The road from Dinas Mawddwy follows the course of the Dovey, and lies in a valley of singular beauty; although the mountains on either side seldom approach 1,500 feet, yet they possess a beauty of form which seems characteristic of the district, and are, as a rule, well wooded.

CEMMAES

is a fairly large village lying off the main road, and nestling for shelter under an outlying crag of the mountains to the west. Shortly after, at Cemmaes Road, the route turns sharply to the left (by going straight on one approaches

Machynlleth), and looking backwards a fine array of familiar peaks are seen up the broad valley just traversed. The road to Caersws is at first very winding, with occasional sharp dips; pleasant glimpses are obtained into well-wooded glens, where tributaries of the river flow over their troubled course to join the Afon Garno, or Carno, and before reaching Carno an extraordinary stratification of the rocks is revealed, chiefly in the railway cutting. A natural arch of anticlinal stratification occurs at Talerddig, with every appearance of being built of masonry. At Carno the valley becomes open and pastoral.

CAERSWS

stands at the confluence of the River Carno and the Severn, and was a place of considerable importance in the Roman period. Their influence is still seen in the straight piece of road just traversed, and in other sections still to be passed. In the centre of the village the winter camp is seen, a rampart about 150 yards square, with the road cutting across the centre. The vallum and accompanying fosse are at some points well preserved. Several summer camps occupy the surrounding heights, and many traces of the great Roman road going east and west are to be discovered. At Moat Lane Junction, which lies at a short distance to the left of the route, is a rectangular earthen fort, with a moat adjacent surrounding a high mound, now covered with firs. At L l a n d i n a m a statue to a certain David Davies stands prominently by the roadside. The Severn Valley here is wide and open, with many plantations of firs; the railway runs close beside the river for miles. In the distance upon the right may be seen the rounded summits of Plynlimmon, often dark and sombre against the sky.

LLANIDLOES

This is a typical Welsh market town, extremely uninteresting and remarkably dull, with the depressing style of architecture so characteristic of the majority of houses in the Principality. Externally dreary, too, are the places of worship, and one longs for a board of architects and artists who will supervise new building plans and save the land from further ugliness, so conspicuous where Nature is so full of artistry. The town is devoted to the Welsh flannel industry, and is well known to climbers as the jumping-off point for the ascent of Plynlimmon, about ten miles to the west as the crow flies. In the deeply furrowed shoulders of this mountain are the birthplaces of two famous rivers, the Wye and the Severn. About two miles north of the town are the Van Lead Mines, once so important; and upon Van Hill, close to them, occurs a large hill-fort, of which so many are scattered about this district.

The Market-house is of wood, and decidedly quaint; the church possesses a ceiling of carved oak, reputed to have been transported from the suppressed

Abbey of Cwm Hir, in Radnorshire; it stands near the bridge, and is dedicated to St. Idloes. From this point a rather pretty view is obtained of the Severn uniting with a tributary, the Clywedog.

The five miles between Llanidloes and Llangurig present occasionally landscapes reminding one forcibly of English pastorals, if the mountains can possibly be kept out of sight. The village of L l a n g u r i g possesses a small church of no very great interest; perhaps the chief fact connected with the place is that the village is the highest in Wales, for it stands at an elevation of nearly 1,000 feet above the level of the sea.

(*For the road between Llangurig and Talgarth, see pp. 180-185.*)

LOOP No. 5

FIRST PORTION: TALGARTH TO ST. DAVID'S—**SECOND PORTION**: ST. DAVID'S TO HEREFORD

TALGARTH TO CARDIGAN AND ST. DAVID'S, 117¼ MILES

DISTANCES ALONG THE ROUTE

	Miles.	
Talgarth (Bronllys) to Brecon	8	¼
Brecon to Llandovery	20	¾
Llandovery to Llanwrda	4	¼
Llanwrda to Pumpsaint	8	
Pumpsaint to Lampeter	8	¼
Lampeter to Newcastle	23	
Newcastle to Cardigan	10	½
Cardigan to Newport	12	
Newport to Fishguard	6	¾
Fishguard to St. David's	15	½

NOTES FOR DRIVERS

To **Brecon** good road, and thence to **Llandovery** splendid.

Llandovery to Lampeter.—Very good; to **Cardigan**, steep hills at times.

Cardigan to Fishguard.—A succession of steep hills, mostly 1 in 11 or 12; at **Fishguard** descent and ascent of 1 in 7, dangerous turns; dangerous hairpin turn on the hill into **Nevern**.

Fishguard to St. David's.—Undulating, but good.

PLACES OF INTEREST ON THE ROUTE

Brecon.—Very pleasant town; the Priory Church, a massive structure, chiefly Early English and Decorated; fragments of town walls.

Llandovery.—A small and not unpicturesque town; ruins of the castle.

Llanwrda.—A pretty village in fine mountain scenery.

Lampeter.—A small town famous as a fishing centre. The college is the chief building.

Newcastle Emlyn.—Small town with beautiful ruins of the castle.

Cardigan.—A considerable town; the bridge over the Teifi; the remains of the castle; church not interesting. Within three miles are—(1) St. Dogmael's Priory ruins; (2) the beautifully-situated Kilgerran Castle.

Nevern.—Castle ruins; a very interesting church with early inscribed crosses.

Newport.—A small fishing town; the castle.

Fishguard.—Goodwick Sands; the harbour; the Pen Caer Peninsula; fine coast scenery.

St. David's.—A small scattered place, scarcely more than a village; beautiful cathedral; picturesque ruins of the palace. Grand coast-line, deeply indented.

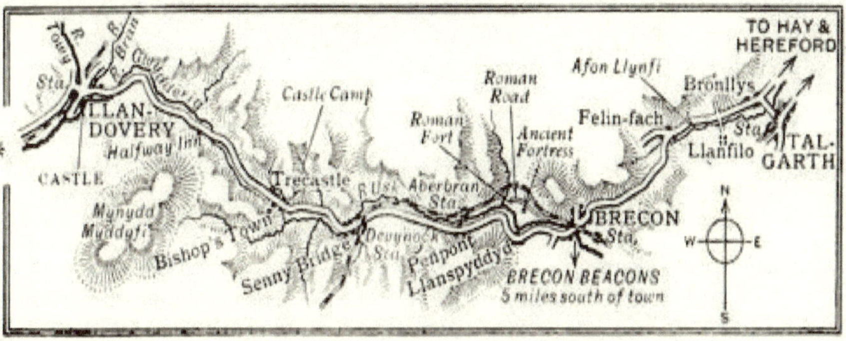

LOOP 5 (FIRST PORTION). TALGARTH TO LLANDILO.

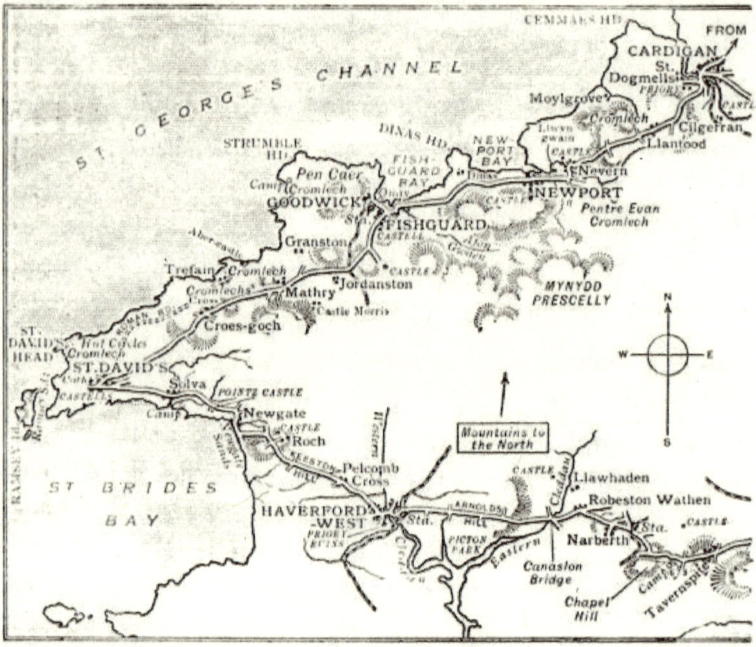

LOOP 5. TALGARTH TO ST. DAVID'S AND HAVERFORDWEST.

The road from Talgarth to Brecon presents no special features except those of picturesque hill and dale, with various streams crossing the road at intervals.

BRECON

Brecon, the county town of Brecknockshire, lies upon the River Usk, and was formerly defended by walls and gates. Of the castle, destroyed as usual during the Civil War, only a few fragments near the Castle Hotel have survived, and one restored section facing the river.

St. Mary's Church has suffered so much from bad restoration that practically nothing of archæological interest remains in it.

The Priory Church.—This building is only excelled in Wales by the Cathedrals of St. David's and Llandaff. It is a massive cruciform structure, with a central tower, high roof and gables, and an external aspect almost devoid of ornamentation. The eastern portions are of Early English work, and the nave was gradually transformed during the fourteenth century into a Decorated building, with great octagonal piers, broad arches, and a lofty clerestory. The carved Norman font should be noticed, and also a number of effigies, one dating from 1359. An interesting feature are the chapels on either side of the presbytery, called respectively the Chapel of the Normans and the Chapel of the Men of Battle, the priory being a cell of Battle Abbey. The guilds of the town had chapels in the nave, those of the tailors, weavers, tuckers, and courvisors, or shoemakers, being at the west end. The domestic buildings still remain, and are attached to the southern side of the west end of the nave; the building has been restored by Sir Gilbert Scott. The town is a pleasant one by reason of the many public walks in and about it, and fine views may be obtained of the well-known Beacons, some of them approaching 3,000 feet in height.

The district round Brecon abounds in prehistoric camps and various remains of the British, Roman, and Saxon occupations. On the road to Llandovery, for instance, near Llanspyddyd, there is a Roman fort, and another of unknown origin adjoining, with a Roman road passing round them. Senny Bridge merely consists of a long street of uninteresting houses. At Trecastle there is an important mound, at one time crowned with a fortalice. From the centre of this village there is a steep ascent. The River Usk accompanies the road, and appears under various surroundings—now as a placid stream winding through meadowlands, and again as a foaming torrent in a deep, tree-shaded glen. This road through the outliers of the Beacons abounds in picturesque views of a well-wooded country, backed by the great swarthy slopes of the hills, called the Black Mountains, although the dark brown sandstone of which they are composed is the same colour as the brown heath upon them.

LLANDOVERY

Llandovery consists chiefly of two streets, which converge at the market-place, and a welcome change is the red wash with which many of the houses are covered, as a relief from the ubiquitous whitewash of the rest of Wales.

The Castle.—This has nearly disappeared, and only two dismantled circular towers, with a curtain wall between, remain. They may be found standing on a grassy knoll near the Castle Hotel. The River Bran is fairly wide at this point, and passes under a fine bridge.

Upon leaving Llandovery a level crossing has to be negotiated; the road crosses the River Towy, and then turns sharply to the left.

Llanwrda is a pretty village situated amid lovely pastoral scenery, and with a fine prospect over the valley. The road here turns at right angles towards the north, and between this point and the Hafod Bridge Inn, nearly four miles, the scenery is distinctly and strikingly beautiful. The small stream, the Dulais, accompanies the route, passing and repassing under the road. Near Pumpsaint lies a gold-mine, the Ogofan, and here the River Cothi, beloved of piscators, comes down from the mountains on its way to the Towy. Between Pumpsaint and Lampeter high ground is crossed, and a portion of the Sarn Helen Roman road appears near an inn beyond Pont-ar-Twch. Near Lampeter a village occurs bearing the ominous name of Rain.

LAMPETER

is one of the best-known fishing centres in Wales, the River Teifi affording exceedingly good sport. It is a well-built town, situated in a fertile valley. The bridge over the stream is said to have been erected in the time of King Stephen, from which the town claims the name of Lampeter Pont Stephen. The chief building is St. David's College, theological, designed for those who cannot afford Oxford or Cambridge. To gain the road for Newcastle Emlyn and Cardigan the river at Lampeter must be recrossed, and the turning taken to the right at 'Gwar Gate' Inn. The route gives a striking view over the valley of the Teifi, whose extraordinary meanderings and loopings appear as a huge serpent of silver lying in the broad landscape. The road for a considerable distance is of Roman construction—the Sarn Helen, but even those conquerors of the world could not conquer Nature in Wales and make their roads straight.

Llanbyther is a small and prettily-situated village, with one of the numerous 'Pen-y-Gaer' camps lying close to the road. The New Quay Road Station of Llanfihangel-ar-Arth turns off to the right soon after the Aber-Iar Inn; it is of a second-class character, but saves a considerable distance and some hills on the way to Llandyssil.

Llandyssil is a romantically-situated village upon the banks of the Teifi, which here assume a rocky character. Its church is dedicated to St. Tyssul, who lived in the early part of the sixth century. From Llandyssil the road south of the river should be taken to Newcastle Emlyn; it has many awkward turns.

NEWCASTLE EMLYN

is a well-situated town with a long street running at right angles to the coach-road.

The Castle is a beautifully-placed ruin, with grand views over the surrounding country. The position of the fortress for natural defence is most remarkable, for the Teifi here forms a reversed S, and in one of the loops so made the ruins are situated, the moat thus naturally formed being one of the most remarkable in existence. The most ancient building upon the site is reputed to have had a Roman origin; the second was erected by Sir Rhys ap Thomas (who built Dynevor Castle) in the time of Henry VII., who frequently resided here, and from it the town was termed 'New-castle.' The Royalists held it throughout the Civil War, but after that period it appears to have lapsed into ruin. Two octagonal towers supporting an arch give entrance to the ruins.

Three miles out from Newcastle Emlyn is Cenarth, a most picturesque and pleasantly-situated little village upon the border between Carmarthenshire and Pembrokeshire. There is a fine salmon-leap close to the hamlet which is worth seeing. The road thence to Cardigan traverses a plain, becoming more and more open as the town is approached, presenting a broad sweep of smiling woods and pasture.

CARDIGAN

The chief centre of interest in Cardigan is undoubtedly the bridge over the Teifi. It probably dates from the Early English Period, and has been widened. From this point there is a good view up and down the river, with the castle and church as prominent features.

The Castle.—The small portion hidden away in the ivy at the present time affords no clue to the former size and importance of this stronghold. It was founded in the time of Henry II. by the Prince of South Wales, and after a chequered career was dismantled at the Commonwealth. The keep is now occupied by private houses.

The Church (*key obtained at one of the cottages in the road*).—The tower is a fine one, but so far as the whole interior is concerned it must be confessed that all ecclesiological features of interest have been obliterated by paint, plaster, and incongruous additions. The chancel arch, of the Perpendicular period, has a fearful and wonderful 'skew,' which may or may not have been acquired by age.

The town contains a number of old houses, nooks, and byways, but they are only moderately interesting to the artist, who finds his best subjects by the bridge and along the river, where sailing-boats and small steamers reveal the picturesque qualities generally to be found in small ports. One feature of the town soon attracts attention—namely, the strong reluctance of the majority of chimneys in Cardigan to keep to the perpendicular.

St. Dogmael's Priory, less than two miles from Cardigan, lies upon the left of the estuary. The remains are of the Early English period, and are still considerable. Martin de Tours, who came over with the Conqueror (not St. Martin), was the founder.

Kilgerran Castle, three miles south of the town, and easily reached by road, stands upon a vast bare rock uplifted above the foaming, eddying stream rushing round its base, through a narrow channel in the rocks. Many eulogistic statements have been made concerning this beauty-spot, but none have overpraised it. The ruins consist of two towers, with part of a gateway and curtain wall, together with fragments of massive bastions. It was erected about 1223, when Marshall, Earl of Chepstow, subdued the Welsh in these districts.

On leaving for Newport, the long rise of the road affords, in about two miles, a remarkably fine view towards the left. With Mynydd Prescelly for a background, the composition of the foreground and middle distance by a beautiful vale is singularly impressive, and this view, with panoramic changes, accompanies the road to Nevern.

The hills seen in the front have massive rocky crags penetrating their otherwise smooth outline.

Nevern.—A very dangerous turn in the road ushers the traveller into this beautiful little village, embowered in the midst of rich meadows, orchards, and gardens in a situation which is eminently picturesque and pleasing. The River Nevern flows through the village, and an amphitheatre of well-wooded hills encloses it.

The Castle consists of some slight remains of a Norman building, apparently of a square plan, with bastions at the angles.

The Church is one of the largest in the county, and of very great interest. It is of Early English architecture, with a Perpendicular recess forming a chapel upon the south side. In the window-sill of the south window of this chapel is inserted a long granite stone, with an Ogham inscription upon it, together with a slab bearing an excellent example of an early interlaced cross. The church stands in a quite ideal sloping churchyard, containing a stone cross about 13 feet in height, with Celtic ornamentation and two inscriptions, not yet satisfactorily deciphered, as far as the writer is aware. Near the south porch is a menhir with an inscription.

The Pentre Evan cromlech, one of the finest known, lies about three miles from Nevern by road, but less than two as the crow flies. A car may be taken by a third-class road for the greater part of the distance, but a local guide is necessary.

NEWPORT

Newport is a small fishing town, and also a seaport, upon the estuary of the Nevern. It is a quiet watering-place, the sea-bathing being very good, while the surrounding country is of enticing interest.

The Castle was built in 1215, and used by the lords of Cemmaes for their courts. It was destroyed by Llewelyn, but restored recently by a descendant of the first baron, but in such strong contrast to the original Norman architecture that it is very disappointing externally.

The Church has been built near the castle, and partakes somewhat of its character, being stern and massive in its proportions. The interior contains nothing of particular interest.

A small cromlech lies within a few hundred yards of the centre of the town, to which any inhabitant will direct one. Occasional glimpses of the estuary, with its sands gleaming in the sun, are obtained from the main streets of the town.

The road between Newport and Fishguard reveals a wide view of the Prescelly Mountains, the highest in Pembrokeshire, and a favourite climb for visitors. A most attractive view of Goodwick Harbour, now generally known as Fishguard, is obtained from the road, or, better still, from one of the steep meadows on either hand. The great importance of this harbour in connection with the Atlantic mail and passenger service has suddenly brought a remote district into prominence. It is now a familiar sight for the natives to see a huge liner in this natural harbour take on passengers and cargo, while a few years ago the waters of the deep inlet had never been churned by propellers.

The descent into Fishguard of 1 in 7 must be taken with extreme caution; at the foot of the curving descent a bridge crosses the Afon Gwaen, and from this the road climbs with equal suddenness and at an equally trying angle. It is a hill calculated to test to the last fraction of its horsepower the capacity a car possesses in hill-climbing. At the top of the ascent the whole bay is spread out in panoramic fashion, and one can see the new breakwater, still incomplete, protecting the anchorage.

The road from Fishguard to St. David's passes first across the isthmus of the Pen Caer Peninsula, whose northern part terminates in Strumble Head. This district is the happy hunting-ground for the archæologist, as it literally teems with prehistoric remains—castles, camps, stone circles, cromlechs, and menhirs, are encountered almost at every step. Two miles out of Fishguard the turning to the right should be taken at a puzzling junction of roads. At Mathry some cromlechs occur near the road, and two miles farther on a wayside cross may be seen. The hills in this neighbourhood generally have the formation noticed previously at Cardigan—namely the projection of high tors from their summits, breaking through otherwise smooth elevations. Nearing St. David's Head it is obvious that the face of the landscape is gradually changing: the hedgerows become less in height, and are often mere mounds of turf or stone; the few trees met with are dwarfed and attenuated, and invariably lean away from the south-west. As St. David's comes nearer these characteristics become accentuated, and a barren, wind-swept moorland appears, almost unrelieved by a single tree.

PLAN OF ST. DAVID'S CATHEDRAL.

ST. DAVID'S

The modern town of St. David's has a sad and desolate air, arising from the number of abandoned houses to be seen on every hand.

The Cathedral (*nave open free on weekdays, 9 to 1 and 2 to 6; a charge of 6d. is made for admission to the eastern chapels*) is in a remarkable situation at the farther end of the town, and practically bursts upon the view when the edge of the deep hollow it occupies is reached. In such an exposed corner of Britain it is not surprising that everything should take what shelter it can find, but to walk through a rather dreary and wind-swept Welsh village, and to *discover* a magnificent cathedral cowering almost out of sight at one's very feet, is not an everyday occurrence even with the touring motorist. A score of abbeys planted in sequestered valleys will come to the mind of anyone who has explored this island, but a well-preserved cathedral built in a deep and narrow hollow in a rocky promontory almost takes away what little breath the blustering wind has left to the exploring stranger. To the left is the old tower gateway, a weather-worn remnant of the embattled fortifications which once encircled the monastery. Down below, and approached by a long and steep flight of stone steps, stands the church, with the square tower of rather unsatisfactory outline dominating the nave, transept, and eastern portions of the buildings. Beyond appears one of the most beautiful ruins that ever gladdened the eye—the remains of one of the finest episcopal palaces to be seen in the British Isles. Near the church are also grouped ruins of the conventual buildings, and the whole forms a scene that indelibly impresses itself upon the memory. Descending the thirty-nine steps, one reaches the south porch of the nave. Whatever preconceived ideas one may hold of the beauty of this part of the church, the sight of the original far surpasses them. The beautiful Norman pillars and graceful arches, ornamented with the most elaborate chevron and zigzag mouldings of the Transitional period; the clerestory springing directly from the dwarfed triforium with which it is incorporated; and the whole surmounted by a finely-wrought timber roof, make a picture of the rarest perfection. The colouring is full of subtle richness, the stonework being of a soft dove-grey combined with a bluish tinge. The building dates from 1180, the previous church having been burnt down by pirates. The tower fell in 1220, and was rebuilt at different periods. The choir and transepts are Early English, but were added to in the Decorated period. The eastern chapels are Decorated, as is also the beautiful rood-screen. The ceiling in the nave dates from *c.* 1500. Many objects of interest are contained in the building; the shrines of St. David and St. Caradoc, the tomb of Edmund Tudor, father of Henry VII., the monument of Bishop Gower, the chapel of St. Thomas à Becket, and the fan tracery of the roof in Bishop Vaughan's Chapel, are all worthy of careful inspection. Outside the north wall of the nave gigantic and ill-proportioned buttresses are seen, built in 1248 to strengthen the nave, which had suffered from an earthquake; on the opposite side are the remains of the cloisters of St. Mary's College, begun in 1362.

The exploration of the ruins of the Bishop's Palace should on no account be omitted, as the lower chambers, the row of clerestory arches, the beautiful doorways, and the general composition of the whole ruin, are worthy of the closest attention.

Upon the return to the main street the ancient cross is seen, no less than 28 feet in height; the steps were restored by Bishop Thirlwall in 1873.

The coast scenery at St. David's is remarkably wild, and the subjects for the painter in oils or water-colours, or for the less ambitious who carry a sketch-book and a good soft pencil, are full of particular attractiveness. To those who are without the desire or capacity to carry away any permanent impressions of the scenery it will be enough to lie in a sheltered spot and watch the white waves burst into columns of spray on the northern end of Ramsey Island.

LOOP No. 5—SECOND PORTION

ST. DAVIDS TO HEREFORD, 132¼ MILES

DISTANCES ALONG THE ROUTE

	Miles.	
St. David's to Haverfordwest	15	¾
Haverfordwest to Narberth	10	¼
Narberth to Red Roses	7	
Red Roses to Carmarthen	14	¾
Carmarthen to Pontacothi	6	¼
Pontacothi to Llandilo	8	¾
Llandilo to Llangadock	6	¾
Llangadock to Llandovery	5	½
Llandovery to Trecastle	9	
Trecastle to Devynock	3	¼
Devynock to Brecon	8	¾
Brecon to Talgarth (Bronllys)	8	¼
Bronllys to Three Cocks Inn	2	½
Three Cocks Inn to Hay	4	¾
Hay to Clifford	2	½
Clifford to Hereford	18	¼

NOTES FOR DRIVERS

St. David's to Haverfordwest.—This road has a fine surface, but hills are frequent and all dangerous. They range from 1 in 8 to 1 in 12.

Haverfordwest to Carmarthen.—This also has a good surface, but the hills are numerous. Near Narberth is a hill 1 in 9.

Carmarthen to Brecon.—Splendid surface and easy gradients.

Brecon to Hereford.—An excellent road without dangerous hills.

Hay.—A toll of 9d. must be paid for crossing the river.

PLACES OF INTEREST ON THE ROUTE

Solva.—A village in pretty scenery.

Pointz Castle.—An earthwork.

Roche Castle.—Very conspicuous.

Haverfordwest.—A pleasant town; the castle, now a gaol; St. Mary's Church, with ancient wooden carving; the Priory Ruins.

Narberth.—A little town with ruins of its castle.

St. Clears.—A small port.

Carmarthen.—A busy county town; the castle, now the gaol; the Guildhall; the church; Picton Monument; interesting market.

Llandilo.—Small town on high ground; Dynevor Castle; Careg Cennen Castle.

Llandilo to Talgarth.—See Loop 6, Part I.

Hay.—A little town on English border; the castle, an interesting structure (not open).

Clifford Castle, birthplace of Fair Rosamond.

Whitney.—Beautiful scenery on the Wye; old timbered houses.

Hereford.—The cathedral, Norman to Perpendicular; the Shire Hall; the castle green; interesting old houses.

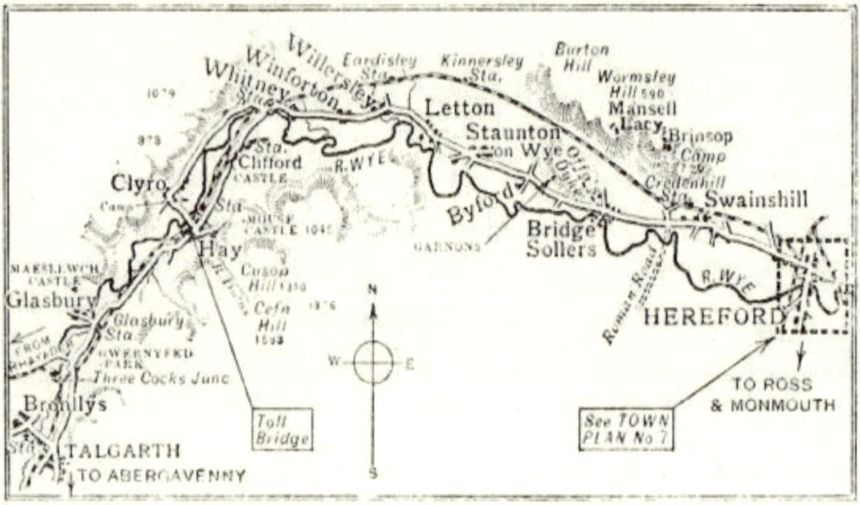

LOOP 5 (EASTERN END). TALGARTH TO HEREFORD.

The distance from St. David's to Haverfordwest is sixteen miles, or, as the natives naïvely express it, 'sixteen miles and seventeen hills.' For the switchback contour, however, one is compensated by the wide views generally obtained when the tops of the hills are reached, before plunging downwards into the next sudden hollow. The same characteristics of wild moorland and storm-swept down prevail as noticed upon the road to St. David's, and it is very interesting to note how gradually the vegetation develops as the route progresses. About two miles out the little village of Solva is passed, lying upon a romantic inlet in this iron-bound coast, and recalling, to some extent, the fishing village of Staithes, in Yorkshire. The view over St. Bride's Bay, with Skomer Island as the farthest point, is exceedingly fine on a crisp, sunny morning, and shortly after leaving Solva, Pointz Castle, an earthwork, appears upon the right hand, at a short distance from the road. The sharp descent to Newgate brings one almost within reach of the salt spray at high tide, and the road runs for a few hundred yards by the sands of that name, giving a glimpse of some fine coast scenery. There is an example here of a 'rolling beach,' an accumulation of pebbles being washed over and over upon the flat land beyond. The road now climbs to the uplands, upon which stands Roche Castle, a conspicuous landmark for many miles. It was built in the reign of Henry III., but has later windows inserted. Garrisoned for the King during the time of the Civil War, it was captured by the Parliamentarians, but subsequently retaken. Lord St. Davids, the present owner, has adapted it for modern habitation. Its position upon a rocky scar, in the midst of a treeless plain, is peculiarly imposing.

As the road approaches Haverfordwest trees of respectable proportions begin to appear, no longer leaning towards the north-east.

HAVERFORDWEST

The town of Haverfordwest occupies an important position among those of South Wales, and is the centre of commerce for a large district. The streets are narrow and steep, with sharp turnings, probably caused by the confinement of the ancient fortifications which once protected the town. Of these practically nothing remains but the shell of a strong castle, now converted into the county gaol, standing upon a rocky eminence overlooking the town. Although very impressive when viewed from a distance or from the River Cleddau in the town, it hardly repays minute inspection. Gilbert de Clare, Earl of Pembroke, is said to have built it about 1120, and it became, with that of Pembroke, one of the most important fortresses in 'Little England,' as the southern part of Pembroke was termed. It was demolished by order of Oliver Cromwell.

St. Mary's Church is of great interest, the exterior showing some fantastic gargoyles, and the nave some fine clustered columns of Early English work, with a Perpendicular clerestory above. The ceilings should be noticed, and also the early lancets at the west end. It is a beautiful church, full of light, with no gloomy corners. There is an ancient wooden carving of St. Michael the Archangel and the Dragon, dating from the fifteenth century.

The Priory Ruins are situated a short distance from the southern part of the town, and are quite picturesque. They are the remains of a priory of Austin Canons erected in the twelfth century. The very liberal grants of Robert de Hwlffordd, lord of this town, were confirmed by Edward III. The remains of the minster are of Early English work.

The road from Haverfordwest takes a sharp turn to the right upon leaving the town, and passes over the railway-lines. An isolated church stands upon a hill to the right, and soon afterwards the woods surrounding Picton Castle, two miles away, come into view. It is one of the most ancient residences in the kingdom, having been built by a De Picton in the reign of Rufus. From that time it has been inhabited by an unbroken line of proprietors, never deserted, never vacant. The alterations have not very much affected the baronial style of the building, and until quite recently it presented the appearance of a medieval fortress.

At Canaston Bridge the road crosses the eastern Cleddau, which discharges into Milford Haven, and here, upon the left, at about a mile, lies the picturesque ruin of Llawhaden Castle, once a residence of the Bishops of St. David's. The gateway, flanked by two demi-bastions, forms a very effective picture.

Approaching Narberth, the right-hand road should be taken at Robeston Wathen. Fir-trees near this point begin to make their appearance, having been conspicuously absent from St. David's to this point.

NARBERTH

There is a very steep hill in this town, leading to the ruins of a Norman castle crowning the summit. They are picturesquely covered with ivy, but the remains now apparent are small when compared with those visible in the eighteenth century. The roads in the neighbourhood of Narberth are rather misleading, as so many by-roads enter. Care should be taken to decipher the sign-boards in many cases before proceeding. Between Narberth and St. Clears, for instance, there are three roads at Tavernspite near an inn, and the centre one should be taken.

St. Clears is a long and straggling village at the head of an estuary of the Taff, and vessels of small tonnage can reach it at high tide. It formerly possessed a castle and a priory, but both have disappeared. The town itself is uninteresting. Between St. Clears and Carmarthen the small hamlet of Banc-y-Felin is particularly pleasing, with a tributary of the Taff flowing through it.

CARMARTHEN

Carmarthen, the capital of the shire, stands upon the site of the Roman *Maridunum*, and is the point of convergence of two roads, Via Maritima and Via Montana. Some parts of the town stand at a considerable elevation, and present an imposing picture from a distance. It is an excellent example of an old Welsh town, retaining a great deal of its primeval quaintness. Upon market-days, when it swarms with people from the surrounding districts, one seldom hears a word of English spoken, and the busy scenes witnessed in the bustling market are mainly transacted in the mother-tongue. Upon entering the town the Picton Monument is seen, raised in honour of the Peninsula hero, who fell at Waterloo.

The Church of St. Peter is a large building chiefly in the Perpendicular style, with a lofty square tower. The interior has been very carefully plastered so as to hide everything of interest. A Roman altar, however, may be seen below the tower.

Sir Richard Steele, who died in 1729, the friend of Addison, and the well-known man of letters, lies buried in this church. In his old age he came to reside at Llangunnor, near Carmarthen.

The Castle, which at one time made Carmarthen a place of strength, was demolished by the Parliamentarians, and the small portion remaining has been converted into the county gaol. On leaving Carmarthen the route towards Llandilo lies upon the Roman road, the Via Montana. It includes some of the finest scenery in South Wales. There are two roads running in the valley, with the railway separating them; the north one is the more picturesque.

At a loop in the road about ten miles out, Middleton Hall, lying due south, and erected by Sir William Paxton, may be recognized by the tall tower which forms such a conspicuous landmark. It is known as Paxton's Tower, but was raised by him in memory of Nelson. Almost directly afterwards, Dryslwyn Castle comes in sight, a most picturesque ruin, consisting of one tower and many fragments of walls. It was besieged in the time of Edward I., when Lord Stafford and other leaders lost their lives, in undermining the fortress, by the sudden collapse of the walls beneath which they were operating.

On Grongar Hill, a few hundred yards away to the right, the poet Dyer composed his poem 'Grongar Hill.' The view from the summit is charming. On the farther side of the valley can be seen Golden Grove, the residence of Viscount Emlyn. Dynevor Park and Castle come into view upon the right front on reaching the neighbourhood of Llandilo. The ruins stand upon a lofty mound a short distance from the road, in the most attractive portion of the park. The first castle was built in 877, and almost rebuilt in the time of William the Conqueror. For some centuries it was the residence of the Princes of South Wales. Henry VII. granted it to Sir Rhys ap Thomas, a descendant of the Princes, and ancestor of the present owner, Lord Dynevor. It was occupied until 1760. The remains consist of a round keep and a square tower, commanding a magnificent prospect. (*The ruins are open for inspection to the bona-fide visitor upon application.*)

LLANDILO

Llandilo is a small town perched upon two or three steep hills to the north of the River Towy, crossed here by a stone bridge of one span. The streets are narrow, with the public buildings grouped together in the centre of the town. The church was thoroughly rebuilt in 1848, and everything of interest then disappeared. If a stay can be arranged at Llandilo, one of the most remarkable edifices in the kingdom, Careg Cennen, should be seen. It is a castle almost without a history, standing upon a rocky height with inaccessible precipices on three sides, the foremost one over 300 feet in height. Two square towers guard the sloping ground upon the fourth side, and the main portion of the castle occupies the summits of the precipices. The situation is superb and the scenery delightful. The spirit of romance is free from any of the handicaps usually suffered by the historian, for in this castle among the clouds, in connection with which history is silent (except a reputed origin in the thirteenth century at the hands of Rhys of Wales), the wings of imagination may soar to any height. This is a site awaiting the novelist in search of a romantic setting for a story of the Middle Ages. It stands about five miles to the south-east of Llandilo, overlooking the Vale of the Towy.

Between Llandilo and Llanwrda a large Roman camp can be seen lying upon Carn Goch, and at the inn where the road turns to Llangadock a large tributary joins the Towy. In a few miles Llanwrda is reached, and the loop for St. David's is thus completed. For the road between Llanwrda and Talgarth, see pp. 143-148.

The route from Talgarth to Hay is winding, and care should be taken to avoid the numerous roads leading away from the main road, which lies on the south side of the River Wye, and for a considerable distance is parallel to the railway.

Glasbury, beyond the Three Cocks, is a small village much frequented by the fishing fraternity; a fine prospect of the Black Mountains is obtained, and the views generally are among the best to be found in the district.

The entry into Hay is very pretty, with shady hedgerows and many of the attributes of English scenery.

HAY

This little town lies upon the borders of England and Wales, at the junction of the shires of Radnor, Hereford, and Brecon. The word 'Hay' is allied to 'hedge,' meaning a boundary. It was at one time the main entry into Wales from England, and naturally, from its position, it has seen stirring times in the past.

The Castle dominates the town, and is easily reached from the main street; the entrance is at the back. The architecture now appears to be a mixture of all kinds, including Tudor, for numerous additions have been made. A residence constructed out of the old materials occupies part of the site. Sir Philip Walwyn is supposed to have built the first castle in 1090, and at the end of the twelfth century extensive additions were made. Henry III. almost rebuilt it, and in 1233 Llewelyn ap Jorweth stormed it. Thirty years later it was taken twice, and in the time of Glendower it was burnt. Many other minor happenings have occurred to lend variety to its existence. James I. made large additions to the building. The fortifying walls once enclosing the town have nearly disappeared. The road upon the town side traverses the former moat. A view across the river gives a glimpse of a Roman camp near the stream, while to the north-west stands Clyro, reached by a main road, and enclosed by beautiful woods. A mound of earth and a moat are now the sole remains of the proud and lordly Clyro Castle mentioned by Leland.

The ruins of Cusop Castle and Mouse Castle lie at a short distance from the town, and a favourite excursion is that to the far-famed Llanthony Abbey, lying amid romantic wilds some ten miles to the south.

The route to Whitney crosses the river at Hay, passes through Clyro, and in two miles affords a view of Clifford Castle, standing upon a bold eminence by the side of the river; it was the birthplace of Jane de Clifford, the Fair Rosamond of Henry II., and the former residence of the Lords de Clifford. The scenery in the environment of these beautiful ruins is most charming. The route from Hay may be taken in this direction if desired. (*A toll of 9d. has to be paid to cross the river.*)

WHITNEY

The village of Whitney is surrounded by a rich belt of pasture-land interspersed with clumps of trees, and exceedingly beautiful scenery is to be found upon the river-banks. There is no ancient church, for it was washed away in a flood in the early part of the eighteenth century. The beautiful views seen at Whitney unfold themselves more and more as one reaches Letton, Merbach Hill upon the right, rising high out of the ground like a hog's back, giving a characteristic touch to the scenery. At Letton a particularly beautiful group of black-and-white timbered cottages stand by the side of the road, and remind one that English soil has been reached, and that the never-ending monotony of the Welsh whitewashed cottages has at last been left behind. At Staunton, on the Wye, a little Early English church is perched above the village. On the right there formerly stood a castle, and near it is Moccas Park, the residence of Royalty in Saxon times. The present owners are descended from Richard, the second son of King John. After passing Byford a portion of Offa's Dyke occurs upon the left, crossing over Mansell Hill. Some quaintly-cut yew-trees may be seen near the Kite's Nest Inn, and just before entering Hereford, at White Cross, an interesting cross is noticeable. It was put up in 1347 by Bishop Charlton to commemorate the disappearance of the Black Plague, and was restored by Archdeacon Lord Saye and Sele.

HEREFORD CATHEDRAL FROM THE BANKS OF THE WYE.
It belongs mainly to the Early English period, and is built of a reddish stone.

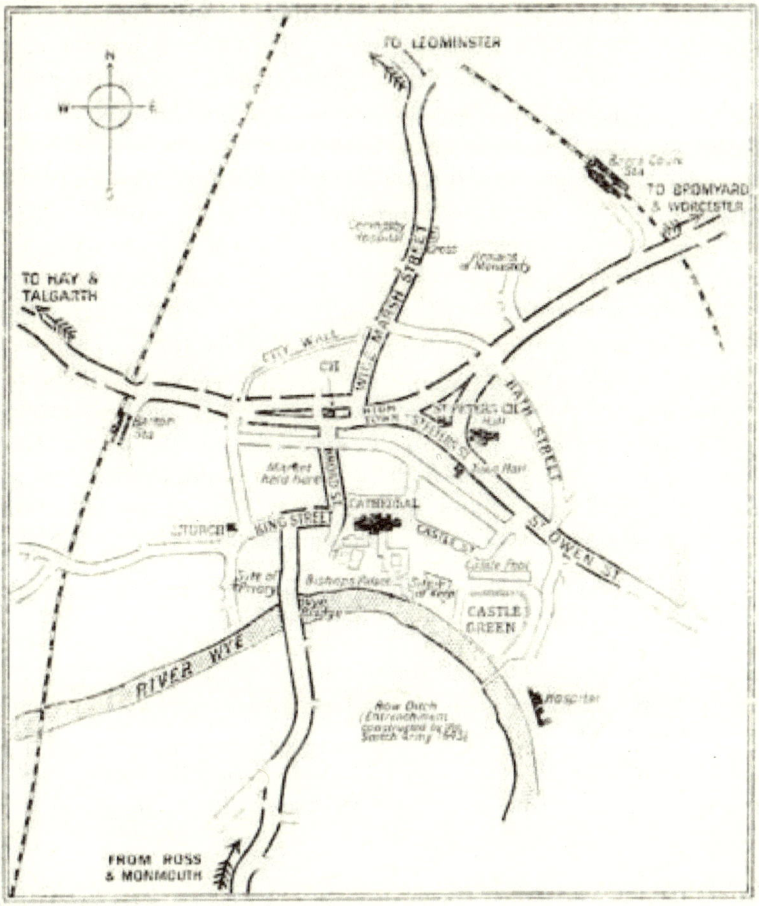

TOWN PLAN NO. 7—HEREFORD.

HEREFORD

is a pleasantly-situated town, but if it were not for the possession of a cathedral the place would not offer any particular attractions for visitors beyond the charming river scenery common to the Wye Valley.

Hereford became a separate see in 673, and Putta was the first Bishop. The first church was rebuilt in a better fashion when the remains of the murdered Ethelbert were brought to Hereford, but this pre-Norman structure was burnt by the Welsh in 1055. In 1079 Robert of Lorraine, the first Norman Bishop, began the cathedral of which much exists at the present day, using dark red sandstone. The choir up to the clerestory, the arcades of the nave, and the south transept, are Norman work of this early date.

The beautiful Lady Chapel, and the clerestory of the choir are Early English. The north and both the eastern transepts, part of tower, and the chapter-house, are Decorated. The chantries, sacristy, and a few other parts, are Perpendicular. The western tower fell in 1786, and brought down with it the west front and the first bay of the nave. This disaster accounts for the modern west front. Upon entering the nave the Norman bays are singularly impressive, especially the carved capitals. The choir is entered through a metal chancel screen; the stalls are richly carved, and 'the chair of King Stephen' is preserved in it. Scattered about in the great building there are probably more monumental tombs and effigies than in any other cathedral, and this is especially true with regard to ecclesiastics. Two notable monuments are those of Bishop Aquablanca (1245-1268), and the shrine of St. Thomas of Cantilupe in the north transept. A famous archæological treasure, the *Mappa Mundi*, a map of the world, drawn on one large sheet of parchment in the thirteenth century by Richard de Haldingham, is preserved in this building, and may be seen upon application. The Bishop's Palace is close to the Wye, on the south side of the cathedral.

The Shire Hall, a Grecian Doric building, standing in St. Peter's Square, was erected in the early part of the last century.

The Castle Green is the site of the vanished Castle of Hereford; it is one of the prettiest parts of the town. Hereford contains some interesting houses, and three of them, now used as a bank, may be seen in the High Town. It was at one time the Butchers' Guildhall, and the carving upon the outside, as well as the inside, is extremely ornate.

SECTION VIII
(TRUNK ROUTE)

LLANGURIG TO ABERGAVENNY, 68 MILES

DISTANCES ALONG THE ROUTE

Miles.		
Llangurig to Rhayader	9	¼
Rhayader to Newbridge-on-Wye	8	
Newbridge-on-Wye to Builth	5	½
Builth to Hay	19	
Hay to Bronllys	7	¼
Bronllys to Talgarth	1	
Talgarth to Castle Inn	3	½
Castle Inn to Crickhowell	8	¼
Crickhowell to Abergavenny	6	¼

NOTES FOR DRIVERS

The road is splendidly engineered, and as a rule has an excellent surface. There are no really stiff gradients.

PLACES OF INTEREST ON THE ROUTE

Rhayader.—A small and uninteresting town; Birmingham reservoirs.

Builth.—Another small town, possessing no interest besides the site of the castle and the wells.

Talgarth (1 mile distant).—Remains of Bronllys Castle; Llangorse Pool.

Crickhowell.—The church; the castle ruins.

Abergavenny.—A market town; castle, now a recreation-ground; church, with fine carved oak; earliest wooden effigy; the Blorenge.

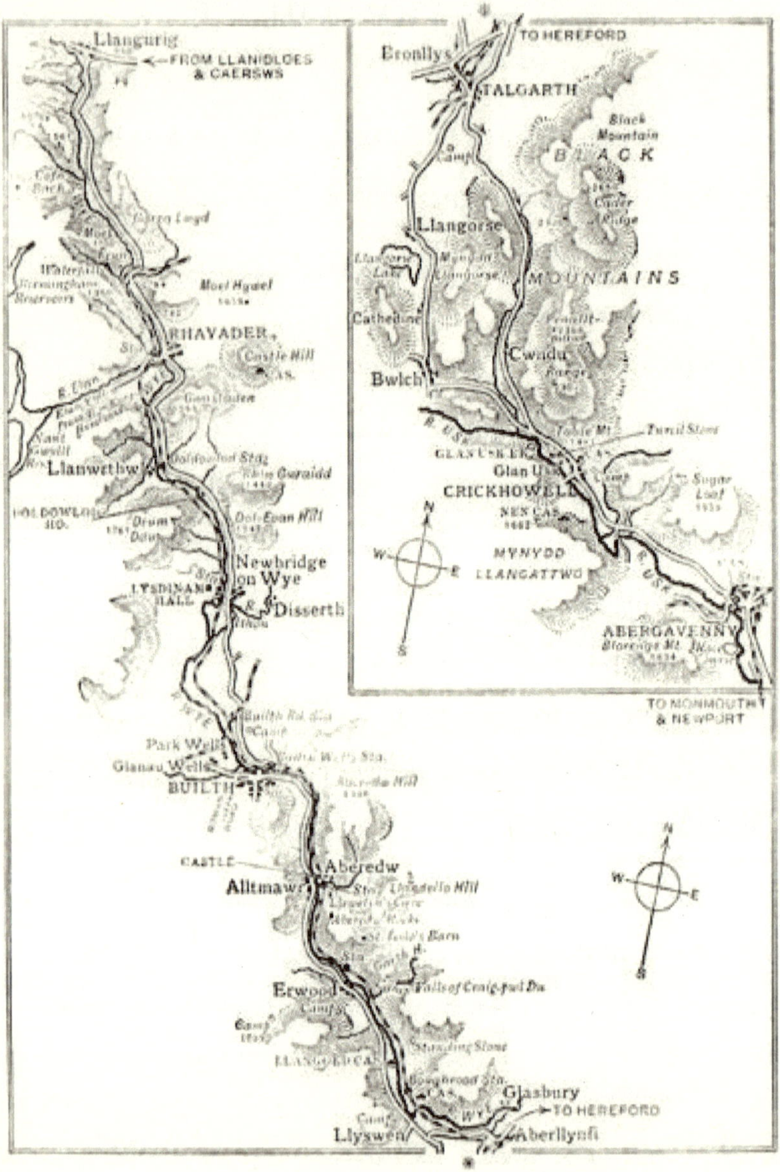

(TRUNK) No. 8. LLANGURIG TO ABERGAVENNY.

The road to Rhayader traverses part of the Upper Wye Valley, and gives frequent glimpses of troubled, foam-flecked water, alternating with long reaches where the river slides smoothly along its rocky bed. The setting is one of pastoral scenery, bounded by the rounded uplands, which help to form the catchment basin for the great lakes which now supply Birmingham with water. This gigantic undertaking, to be extended altogether over fifty years, will eventually be the means of constructing a chain of lakes in the vale of the Elan, effectually providing for the future needs of the great manufacturing metropolis so far as water is concerned.

RHAYADER

The chief attraction at Rhayader is the scenery, as nothing of particular importance meets the eye in the town. It is a good sketching-ground for artists, many excellent subjects being discoverable in the surrounding country. To the angler it is a paradise. Although it possesses two churches, they are not worthy of the time required for inspecting them. The W y e here is an impetuous mountain stream, plunging amid the rocks strewn along its course; to this point the salmon reach the upper waters at the spawning season. Between Rhayader and Builth there are several very sharp turnings in the road, requiring considerable care if risks are to be avoided. The W y e is close to the road at many parts of its course, and forms the boundary between the counties of Brecon and Radnor. Farther on the stream begins to lose its torrential character, and, traversing this well-wooded valley, assumes more of the calm and placid character with which one generally associates it. It receives the superfluous water from the great lakes of the Birmingham Corporation Reservoirs by the Afon Elan soon after passing Rhayader. To the west of Newbridge-on-Wye, Lysdinam Hall, the ancestral home of the Venables, is seen upon an eminence.

BUILTH WELLS

This ancient town, the *Bullæum* of the Romans, is the centre of trade for the neighbouring districts, and derives much importance from its wells—saline, sulphurous, and chalybeate. The population is less than 2,000, but probably a regiment might be raised locally all bearing the surname of Price or Powell.

T h e C a s t l e , or rather the site of it, is near the town, close to the Wye Bridge. It possesses a double fosse, a rampart of earth, and a keep, which, judging from the foundation, must have been of great size. It was besieged and captured by Llewelyn in 1260.

The scene of Llewelyn's death in 1282 lies near the Radnor road at Cefn-y-Bedd, a few miles from the town. The Prince was refused a refuge in Builth (hence 'The Traitors of Builth'), and, reversing his horse's shoes, fled in the deep snow for safety, but was overtaken and slain.

The church of Builth is a modern erection, and the town is uninteresting.

The road from Builth to Talgarth passes through Erwood, at some five miles' distance, and Garth Hill, crowned by an earthwork, lies to the left; it is also the place where the English troops in quest of Llewelyn forded the river in 1282. Two miles away to the left are the celebrated Falls of Craig-pwl-du, a fall of 40 feet into a weird ravine. The neighbourhood is full of interest to the antiquary and the geologist. About three miles beyond Erwood the castle and woods of Llangoed are passed, and Boughrood Castle appears on the left. Lyswen is reputed to have been an early residence of the Welsh Princes. The general character of the road between Builth and Talgarth may be stated as not wildly grand, but an exquisite combination of river scenery with eminently beautiful surroundings, where the ruggedness of the rocks is softened by a covering of verdure, and foliage in subtle gradations of beauty appears on every hand. It is probably one of the most splendid roads for scenery of this character in the Principality.

THE WYE, SYMOND'S YAT, NEAR MONMOUTH, HEREFORDSHIRE.
At this point the view embraces some of the finest river scenery in Britain.

TALGARTH

This quiet little town, nestling under the shadow of the Black Mountain, is chiefly noted for the proximity of Bronllys Castle, one mile distant, of Early English and reputed Norman architecture. It is a round tower, 70 feet high, standing upon a mound, and its history appears to have been lost. The Black Forest now lies upon the left hand, and upon the right, at a few miles' distance, is Llangorse Lake, a large but shallow sheet of water 500 feet above sea-level, and much referred to as a probable source for the future supply of water to London. The scheme is considered a feasible one, and the water would flow to the metropolis by gravitation. According to tradition, the lake covers the site of a large city which perished in some terrible catastrophe—a similar type of legend to that of Semmerwater in Wensleydale. As the road nears Crickhowell the great Sugar Loaf (1,955 feet) becomes prominent, with a number of small villages, farmsteads, and cottages dotting the slopes of the lower hills. The River Usk now appears descending a valley from Brecon, together with the main road from that place.

CRICKHOWELL

The Church is a building of some dignity, with nave, chancel, aisles, and spire standing near the bridge.

The Castle remains consist of a square tower in fair preservation, flanked by a round one, together with tumbled mounds of masonry and earth. Several beautifully-situated seats are near the village. From Crickhowell to Abergavenny two roads run, one on either side of the valley, that upon the right being slightly longer, but it is more picturesque. The Sugar Loaf Mountain lies to the left across the valley, while an opening in the hills to the right reveals a glimpse into the Black Country of the South Wales Coalfield. Near Llangrwyne there is a most romantic stretch of country, with many beautiful features.

ABERGAVENNY

This flourishing market town claims a high antiquity in history as being the direct descendant of the Roman *Gobannium.* Its quaint narrow streets contain some houses of interest, while the splendid country lying around tempts the tourist to stay.

The Castle, standing upon an eminence overlooking the Usk, was an important Norman stronghold. William de Braose, in the twelfth century, invited many Welsh chieftains to a Christmas feast in the castle, and then foully murdered them; in retaliation their relatives burnt the castle. It, however, rose again, and came after a time into the Warwick family, passing eventually to the Nevilles, represented now by the Marquis of Abergavenny, who lives at Neville Court, up the river. As a ruin, now laid out as something between a tea-garden and a recreation-ground, the castle is exceedingly disappointing. The steeps of the Blorenge are well seen from the terrace.

The Church is near the post office and market hall. The Herbert and Lewes Chapels are the chief points of interest in it, but attention should be drawn to the ancient carved-oak seats in the choir, and also to the font. A colossal recumbent figure of what must at one time have been a 'Jesse tree' is preserved here; it is 10 feet long, and the stump of the tree remains, springing from the side of Jesse. When complete it must have formed a splendid screen, standing behind the high-altar. The wooden effigy of George de Cantelupe in the Herbert Chapel (1273) is the finest example of early wood-carving extant in these islands.

Near the church stands Priory Mansion, with a good garden, and splendid oak panelling in the interior.

Abergavenny is an ideal place for the budding mountain-climber, who can have excellent practice upon the Blorenge, the great Skyrrid, and the Sugar Loaf.

SECTION IX
(TRUNK ROUTE)

ABERGAVENNY TO GLOUCESTER VIA NEWPORT AND MONMOUTH, 84¼ MILES

DISTANCES ALONG THE ROUTE

	Miles.	
Abergavenny to Raglan Castle	9	
Raglan Castle to Usk	5	¼
Usk to Caerleon	7	¾
Caerleon to Newport	3	¼
Newport to Caerwent	11	
Caerwent to Chepstow	5	
Chepstow to Tintern	5	¼
Tintern to Monmouth	11	
Monmouth to Whitchurch	4	½
Whitchurch to Ross	6	
Ross to Lea	4	½
Lea to Dursley Cross	3	
Dursley Cross to Gloucester	8	¾

NOTES FOR DRIVERS

Abergavenny to Newport.—No steep hills, fine surface.

Newport to Ross.—A splendid road; at Chepstow a hill 1 in 12.

At **Whitchurch** a dangerous hill, 1 in 10, with poor surface.

After passing **Goodrich** the Wye is crossed by Kerne Bridge, where a toll is charged for motor-cars.

Ross to Gloucester.—Very good; no stiff gradients.

PLACES OF INTEREST ON THE ROUTE

Raglan.—Village and church; beautiful ruins of the castle; picturesque scenery.

Usk.—A village, with ruins of castle and a Norman church.

Caerleon.—A village, with museum of Roman antiquities; the amphitheatre.

Newport.—A busy port; ruins of the castle; interesting church of St. Woollos; the docks.

Caerwent.—Small village with Roman remains; Caldicott Castle is a little to south of route.

Chepstow.—A market town; the castle, a fine example of a Norman fortress; the church, chiefly of Norman architecture.

Tintern Abbey.—One of the most beautiful ruins in England.

Tintern Parva.—Hamlet, with small Early English church.

Monmouth.—A pleasant county town; the county buildings; Monnow Bridge or Western Gate; church, modern except tower.

Symond's Yat.—Beautiful scenery on the Wye.

Goodrich Castle.—On the Wye; beautiful ruins of one of the earliest castles built in England.

Ross.—Picturesque little town; Wilton Castle and bridge; the market hall; the 'Man of Ross'; the church, good Early English work, with interesting monuments; the castle remains.

Dursley Cross.—The Long Hope; very fine views.

Gloucester.—Old-fashioned county town; a grand cathedral, with tomb of Edward II.; the Guildhall; the museum; Llanthony Abbey; the churches of St. Catherine, St. Mary de Lode, St. Mary de Crypt, and others; many old timbered houses; the New Inn.

(TRUNK) No. 9. ABERGAVENNY TO GLOUCESTER.

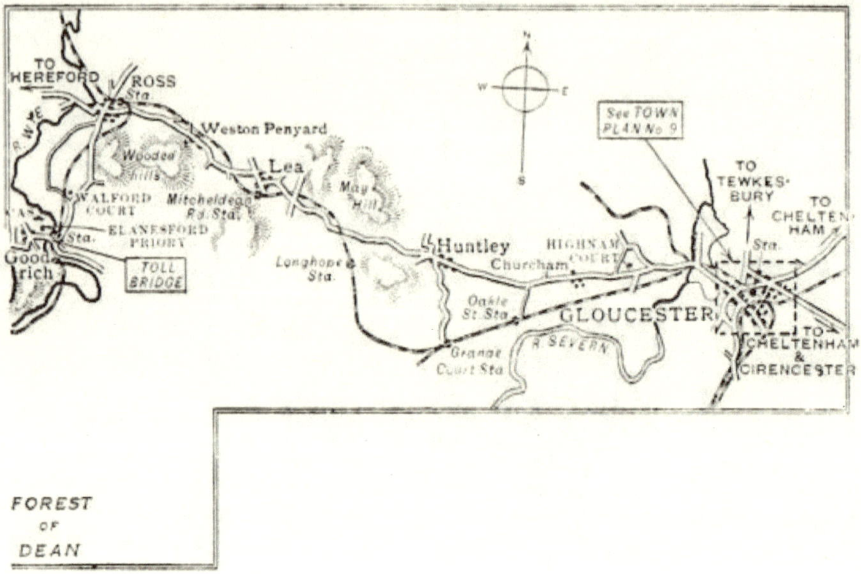

ABERGAVENNY TO GLOUCESTER.

Soon after leaving Abergavenny the classic portico of Coldbrook House, in its large park, is passed upon the left. Looking backwards over the route, the picturesque situation of Abergavenny is seen, with the Sugar Loaf, nearly 2,000 feet in height, towering up beyond. Upon the right Blorenge Hill stands out boldly, a great rounded mass clothed with plantations to the summit. It is a prominent feature in the landscape for some time.

Between Abergavenny and Llanvihangel-on-Usk the road follows the railway-line and the river, and at the latter place a pretty stretch of Usk scenery is met, while the fine church of Llangattock-juxta-Usk, where there are some awkward turnings in the road, is well worth a visit. Just beyond Llanvihangel the road to Raglan branches off to the left, and a glance backwards shows the great mass of the Brecknock Beacons silhouetted against the western sky. Clytha Castle, a building dating from 1790, stands near this parting of the ways. Although so near the border-line between England and Wales, the stereotyped whitewashed cottages of Wales are still to be seen.

RAGLAN

The road to the castle turns to the left in the middle of the village, and stops abruptly at a meadow in which are the entrance-gates. (*Admission to the castle 6d. at any reasonable time on weekdays; on Sundays from 2.30 to 5.*)

A description of Raglan Castle that will give an approximate idea of the exquisite beauty of this ruin has yet to be written; many have attempted it, but all have fallen short of the charming reality. It is a poem in stone; a crystallized ideal of all that was beautiful in medieval architecture; the embodiment of centuries of progressive emulation in castle-building, now mellowed by the hand of time, and with its corners and rough edges covered by clinging masses of creepers. It is eminently the most beautiful ruin to be met with in this western tour. The chief characteristic is undoubtedly the detached keep, which was built after the main structure; the element of romance and mystery haunts one while looking down upon the dark waters of the moat encircling this keep, and one feels a disinclination to leave the place, although other castles await one. No part of the building is of a date anterior to Henry V., and it was chiefly erected by Sir William ap Thomas and his son, William, Earl of Pembroke, who was beheaded in 1469.

Subsequent architecture, however, may be traced down to the time of Charles I. It came into the possession of the Beaufort family (the present owner is the Duke of that name) by the marriage of an ancestor. The Earl of Richmond, afterwards Henry VII., was a prisoner here for a time, and Charles I. sought refuge within these walls after Naseby, in 1645. It was besieged by Fairfax in 1646, and dismantled by Act of Parliament.

Raglan Church is not worthy of much attention if time is short. The tower was rebuilt, it is said, after having been demolished for strategic purposes by Cromwell's orders.

USK

Usk was formerly a Roman station, and in the immediate vicinity there are several encampments, both Roman and British, where excellent views are obtainable over the surrounding country, reaching to the mountains near Abergavenny and to the wooded summits about Monmouth.

The Castle, now dismantled and covered with ivy, stands upon a prominent hill to the north; the Parliamentarians were responsible for its destruction.

The Church is of Norman origin, with a tower rebuilt in recent years.

CAERLEON

'For Arthur on the Whitsuntide before

Held court at old Caerleon upon Usk.'

Idylls of the King.

The name of Caerleon brings vivid recollections to the mind of the Round Table and King Arthur, but its history commenced before the sixth century, when the great Pendragon flourished. The name Caerleon means 'The Camp of the Legion,' the Roman *Isca Silurum*, the capital city of the province of *Britannia Secunda*. After the Roman occupation it became a seat of learning. Remains of villas, Roman walls, and other traces of the conquerors of the world, abound, and the local museum is rich in treasures—chiefly of that period, but by no means confined to it. The building is upon the farther side of the churchyard. (*There is no fixed charge, but a box for contributions. Key at the schoolhouse opposite.*) The church is Early English, with traces of Norman work in it. To the right of the schoolhouse a lane leads for about a hundred yards to a field on the left, opposite a racecourse, where the amphitheatre, 220 feet by 190 feet, may be seen. Excavations have revealed the stone seats surrounding this concave site, known locally as 'King Arthur's Round Table.' In the main street of the sleepy little town some old timbered houses are found, and of the once famous castle nothing now remains except a small tower, which once protected the bridge over the river, behind the Hanbury Arms Inn. The few houses upon the other bank of the Usk are known as 'Ultra Pontem,' a most remarkable instance of persistence and survival. It is difficult when walking through the streets of Caerleon to realize that London, York, and this little place were once the three chief cities of Britain.

NEWPORT

Newport is an example of rapid growth from a small market town into a flourishing port, with extensive docks, wharves, and jetties. It, however, may claim a high antiquity, for it formed a post during the Roman period.

The Castle.—This was at one time an extensive building, and the river face of it is still of impressive proportions. For many years the ruin was occupied by a brewery, but the town has lately gained possession of the sadly-diminished fortress. A deep moat, filled at high tide, defended the walls of the bailey on the north, west, and south sides, but all this has vanished, leaving only the eastern side, with three imposing towers, washed by the muddy waters of the Usk. The Norman Fitzharon, who conquered Glamorgan, built a castle at Newport towards the close of the eleventh century; but the existing structure is three centuries later, and was, to some extent, remodelled in the fifteenth century. The town was protected by a wall as late as Leland's time, and he speaks of three gates. One of these was close to the inn, called the West Gate to this day. Conspicuous in the High Street is the house of the *murringer*, a person whose duties were in connection with the guarding of the wall.

The Church of St. Woollos has been restored, but preserves many of its Norman features, and contains interesting memorials, some of them of considerable antiquity. A remarkable feature is the separation of the tower from the church by a small building, the Chapel of St. Mary, believed by some ecclesiologists to be the primitive church founded *c.* 550, and, if so, the most ancient building still used for Christian worship in the United Kingdom. The two structures are divided by a good Norman arch, the columns of which appear to be of Roman origin, and were possibly brought from Caerleon.

During the Chartist riots the Mayor of Newport, backed by some soldiers, defended himself from a mob headed by Jack Frost. Bullet marks may be seen upon a wooden pillar in the West Gate Hotel, where the Mayor concentrated his defence, many of the rioters being killed and wounded.

The road from Newport to Caerwent gives wide views over the alluvial flats between it and the Estuary of the Severn, protected from inundations by extensive embankments, while to the north the great woods lying upon high land are a pleasing contrast. At first the road is nearly flat, but it becomes undulating near Caerwent. This road is part of the *Via Julia*, which commenced near the mouth of the Severn, passed through Caerwent and Caerleon, and terminated at Neath in Glamorganshire.

Cencoed Castle lies upon the right hand; the remains are not very extensive, consisting chiefly of a gateway flanked with turrets. A mansion was at one time incorporated with the main portion of the castle, but was subsequently abandoned, and now the whole of the buildings form a farmhouse.

Penhow Castle lies by the side of the road, near the village of the same name. A short time after the Norman Conquest this fortress was in the possession of the Seymours. It seems to have been at one period fairly extensive, but only an old square tower with battlements remains, and this also has been converted into a farmhouse.

CAERWENT

is a small village with no pretensions of importance, although the descendant of a strong Roman town. The walls stand from 10 to 12 feet thick, are well preserved, and are similar in many respects to those at Carnarvon. A good facing of stone is backed up by a solid mass of concrete, and then a supporting bank of earth is raised behind them. The church occupies a prominent position, but does not possess any noteworthy feature. Caldicott Castle, lying to the south of the route, has extensive remains of the foundation of the twelfth century, and at the same time some indications of Saxon work belonging to the previous fortalice built upon the site. Passing Crick, Mathern is perceived upon the right. The Bishops of

Llandaff had a palace here in medieval times, and portions of it are still in existence, incorporated with the modern farm-buildings.

CHEPSTOW

is a market town and river port occupying a slope on the western bank of the Wye, and surrounded by beautiful and sometimes imposing scenery.

COMING NIGHT, NEAR BEDDGELERT.
Beddgelert is one of the most romantically situated villages in North Wales.

The Castle is the dominating feature in the town, and is one of the finest examples of a Norman fortress that has been preserved. It stands upon a rocky eminence, and occupies nearly three acres. Founded by Fitz-Osborn, Earl of Hereford, in the eleventh century, it was almost rebuilt in the thirteenth. It was garrisoned by the King during the Civil War, but surrendered in 1645 to the Parliamentarians. The castle was divided into four great courts, and a number of round towers defended the exterior walls, while a deep ditch upon the land side, now used as a public resort, completed the defences.

The Church of St. Mary is built near the river, and is coeval with the castle. A priory stood here in the time of King Stephen, and the nave of the present church is the nave of the priory chapel. The larger part of the building is Norman, while the western doorway is an exceptionally fine example of the period. The tombs of Somerset, second Earl of Worcester, and Elizabeth, his Countess, are worthy of special notice.

The road to Tintern gives at first a view of the remains of an ancient bridge opposite Chepstow Castle, which, when in use, rose and fell with the tide. Piercefield Park lies upon the right hand, with an early camp amongst the trees. At St. Arvans the road bears to the right, and a number of S turns are met. Near here is the well-known 'Lovers' Leap.' Moss Cottage stands by the road farther on, with the Windcliff, famous for its glorious view of the Wye, above it. Upon the opposite bank of the river, and beyond the railway, is a lengthy section of Offa's Dyke, and probably a glimpse may be obtained from the road of the Devil's Pulpit.

TINTERN ABBEY

Tintern Abbey occupies a beautiful site upon one of the loveliest rivers in England, and the ruins have been claimed by many as the most picturesque in existence; but many other roofless abbey churches, placed in the same exquisite surroundings, would appear to equal advantage, and one is inclined to attribute Tintern's fame to its scenery rather than to its architecture. The abbey owes much to Roger Bigod, Earl of Norfolk, and a descendant of the De Clares, who, according to the records, provided for extensive building in the middle of the thirteenth century; but much of the architecture, especially that in the south wall of the chapter-house, speaks of an earlier date. The cloisters are late Perpendicular (1469), and were undoubtedly of great magnificence. The abbey was dissolved in 1537, and since then the buildings have gradually fallen into decay. The structural parts which may be recognized are: the church, with north and south transepts; cloisters, on the north side of the nave; sacristy and monks' library, adjoining the north wall of the north transept; chapter-house and monks' parlour, monks' dayroom, parlour, refectory and almoner's room, all to the north; together with the kitchen, buttery, lavatory, and other small rooms.

The road from Tintern accompanies the Wye in conjunction with the railway-line, and beautiful hanging woods, broken up with grey cliffs, form lovely backgrounds to every view.

Tintern Parva is a small hamlet with a church erected in the Early English period, but not of great interest. At Bigsweir Bridge the river is crossed and the turning to the left taken. Offa's Dyke now lies upon the right hand.

Redbrook is a village placed in a small combe of great beauty. The church, with its Perpendicular tower, is worth seeing. The monuments to John Joce and his wife, *temp.* Edward III., are preserved there, together with two priests and a brass showing a 'free miner.'

MONMOUTH

The situation of Monmouth is an ideal one, as it is surrounded by hills, through which the Wye, the Monnow, and the Trothy flow. It was at one time fortified by a surrounding wall pierced by four gates; but the Monnow, or Western Gate, dating from 1270, is regarded by some writers as a toll-gate rather than one of those belonging to the wall. This gate stands upon the Monnow Bridge, and is a strikingly picturesque feature of the town. Of the Roman origin of Monmouth (the *Blestium* of Antoninus) there are at present no traces, but it was a fortified station as early as the Saxon period.

The Church of St. Mary was rebuilt from the designs of Street in 1881, with the exception of the tower and the tall and very slender spire. Near it, in Priory Street, is a building called 'Geoffrey's Study,' possessing a Perpendicular window corbelled out on brackets. It cannot possibly have been used by Geoffrey of Monmouth, after whom it is named, as he died in 1154. The building, or, more correctly, the old portion of it, is a remnant of the domestic buildings of the Benedictine Priory.

St. Thomas's Church, in Overmonnow, contains some Norman architecture. Near the door of the church stands an elaborate cross.

The Shire Hall, built in 1724, has a solemn façade bearing in the centre a niche filled with a metal statue of Henry V., the hero of Agincourt. One cannot be long in Monmouth without being reminded of Harry of that ilk, for the square in front of the Shire Hall, formerly the bull-ring, is now called Agincourt Square. Many quaint old houses and inns still exist in the town, the Robin Hood in Monnow Street and the Queen's Head in Wyebridge Street being good examples of the picturesque hostelry, so attractive after journeying for many miles in Wales, where every town is uniformly dreary in its architecture. Monmouth Castle stood on a raised site close to the church. It was a ruin at the beginning of the seventeenth century, and where the keep stood there is a house of that period. There are still, however, some sections of walls, and one window of the great hall survives.

On leaving Monmouth by the Ross Road, the little parish church of Dixton is soon encountered, and farther on the beautiful level height called King Arthur's Plain is seen across the river. At times it presents the appearance of towers belonging to a castle.

(It is advisable not to take cars down the road marked 'To Symond's Yat and the Hotel,' between Kerne Bridge and Whitchurch, as it is very narrow and rough. The road from Whitchurch is better.)

Symond's Yat is a rock which towers up to 800 feet above the surface of the river. The ascent is quite easy, and from the upper part a magnificent view is to be obtained. The scenery at this part of the Wye is of quite exceptional beauty. Between the road and Symond's Yat two hills—the Great and Little Dowards—occur. Upon the top of the latter is a fine British camp, reputed to have once been occupied by Caractacus.

Whitchurch is a pretty little village possessing an Early English church dedicated to St. Dubricius, Archbishop of Caerleon in the sixth century. The remains of a stone cross have been restored. After leaving Whitchurch, the roads become somewhat confusing, and care should be taken at the turns. At the foot of the bridge carrying the main road over the river stands Flanesford Priory, which was erected in 1347. From Kerne Bridge a magnificent prospect of the Wye is obtained.

Goodrich Castle was an early residence of the Earls of Shrewsbury (the Talbots) and there is little doubt that the ruins now seen upon these rocky heights are all that is left of one of the first castles built in England, dating well back into the Saxon period. The keep was built in the time of Stephen, and it will be noticed that no windows look away from the castle. In the Civil War it was taken by the Parliamentarians, with the inevitable result. It is a noble and imposing ruin, and a journey up the Wye Valley should not omit a visit to Goodrich Castle.

Goodrich Court lies half a mile north of the castle. It was built in the early part of the last century by Sir Samuel Meyrick, the well-known authority upon, and collector of, ancient arms and armour, and also the author of valuable works upon the same subject. The fine collection was sold some time since, and the house purchased in 1870 by Mr. George Moffatt.

Goodrich Church stands in the little village of that name near the Court, and should be visited, as the stained-glass windows are good. The ancestors of Dean Swift resided in the parish, and one of them was the Vicar and a notable Royalist.

The main road to Ross now leaves the Wye, but in order to see Wilton Castle, that passing near the river should be taken.

Wilton Castle was built soon after the Norman Conquest. It stands near the river upon ground which is not elevated, and was erected to protect the Welsh marches. It has been held by various families—the Longchamps, the De Greys, and that of Chandos. It suffered from the Parliamentary army in 1645. The remains consist of the outer walls only. A footpath will be found running between the walls and the river.

Wilton Bridge is a well-known landmark near Ross. It was built in the reign of Elizabeth, and consists of six arches. One of them—that near Wilton—is more recent than the others, having been rebuilt since its destruction by the Roundheads during the Civil War.

ROSS,

a picturesque little town with the steepest of streets, is perched upon uneven rocky ground high above the left bank of the Wye, and is surrounded by hills on three sides. It was a town at the time of Domesday.

The Market Hall stands prominently in the centre of the town, and its quaintness adds much to the attractiveness of the place. It was built in the time of Charles II., and the upper part is now used for the County Court and Petty Sessions. On the exterior of the south wall one notices a curious carving of the letters F and C, with a heart, reputed to be 'faithful to Charles in heart.' The 'Man of Ross,' who was famed for his good deeds, and is alluded to by Pope, lived opposite the Market Hall. The lower part of the house is now a stationer's shop. The good man's name was John Kyrle, and his portrait, by Sir Godfrey Kneller, can be seen in the upper room of the Market Hall, together with his will and an autograph letter, dated 1695.

TINTERN ABBEY.
Showing the beautiful reach of the Wye which flows between steep wooded scarps.

The Church stands on higher ground than the rest of the town, on the south-west side. It is chiefly Early English, and has a nave with aisles, chancel, and three chapels. One of the chapels on the south side has a parvise over it. Probably the feature which the average visitor finds most interesting is the presence of two elm-trees growing out of the wall inside the church. Both saplings are now dead, but some creepers running over them afford sufficient foliage to simulate vitality.

There is an Easter sepulchre in the chancel, and a tablet opposite the organ contains sage reflections upon man's life and destiny. Of the monuments remaining in the church, one, dated 1637, of a knight and lady, is probably one of the most perfect memorials of contemporary costume to be found in any church. The 'Man of Ross,' who follows the visitor wherever he goes in this town, lies interred under a flat slab, and against the wall is preserved a splendid marble monument to his memory, erected in 1766 by a relative. A door leading to the vanished rood-loft is on the north side of the chancel arch. The loft apparently contained a piscina similar to Eastbourne Old Church.

Of Ross Castle but little remains at the present time to give an idea of its former importance and extent. A tower, which may be entered, stands near the church, and in the High Street another portion is seen. From the first-mentioned there is a beautiful view, including Symond's Yat, the Great and Little Dowards, with a fine range of hills upon the horizon, and a splendid loop of the Wye lying at one's feet, with Wilton Castle and the bridge in the foreground. Ross is in many ways a capital centre for exploring the Wye Valley.

The road between Ross and Gloucester for about half the distance lies in a picturesque piece of country on the northern confines of the Forest of Dean, chiefly covered with coppices, grown for the sale of the bark, the manufacture of charcoal, and the distillation of wood-spirit. It is one of the wildest portions of Gloucestershire.

Weston-under-Penyard is a small village near the ruins of Penyard Castle and the conspicuous hill of that name. The church was restored in 1870, and is not of great interest. Near this village is the site of the ancient *Ariconium*. The rise to Lea affords a view of considerable interest backwards, extending as far as Graig Serrerthin in Monmouthshire.

Lea Church stands beside the road, and possesses a remarkable font of Indian workmanship inlaid with mosaic. The base represents an elephant, from which springs a twisted, snake-like column supporting the basin. Nearly two miles to the south of the road lies the village of Mitcheldean. The Early English spire of the church is occasionally seen through the trees, as it stands upon high ground.

A number of sharp turns now occur, and the rise to Dursley Cross is a steady one. The road is good, and a splendid view may be obtained from the summit, which is 500 feet above sea-level. A long descent eventually leads to

Huntley, lying upon the lowlands which surround Gloucester. After crossing the Severn, the ruins of Llanthony Abbey can be seen to the south. The whole of this comparatively level country is of the most beautiful description, covered with English homesteads nestling among orchards, which are quite exquisite in spring-time.

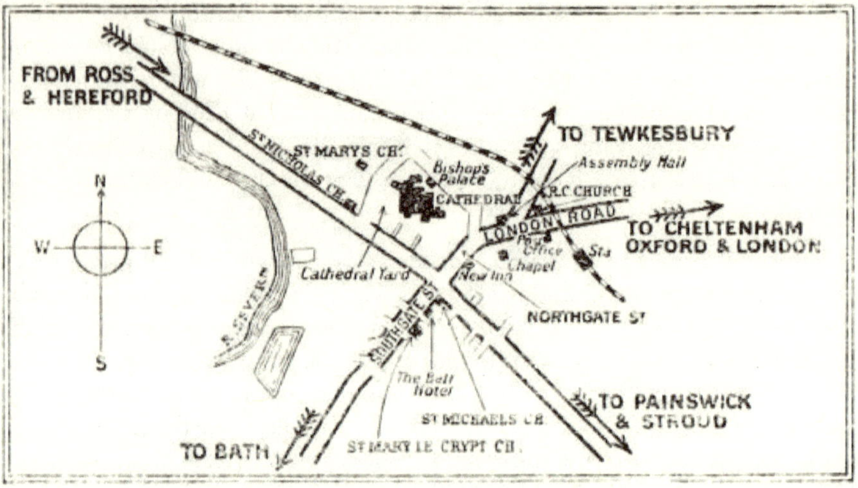

TOWN PLAN NO. 9—GLOUCESTER.

GLOUCESTER

Gloucester, the *Glevum* of the Romans and the *Glow Ceaster* of the Saxons, lies in the centre of a broad valley, and possesses a history of no mean order. The Saxon kings made the place their residence, and in 681 founded a nunnery, which subsequently became a monastery and the nucleus of the present cathedral. Parliaments have been summoned in this city, and its connection with the Empress Matilda in the time of Stephen is well known. In the Civil War, Gloucester was on the side of the Parliament, and resisted a Royalist army in 1643—a regrettable fact, to which must be attributed the demolition of the city walls at the Restoration.

The Cathedral has dignified surroundings, and velvety turf runs up to the weather-stained masonry. The most prominent architecture to arrest the eye is the Perpendicular, of which, from the exterior, the cathedral appears mainly to consist, although Norman, Early English, and Decorated are all represented. The Perpendicular south porch is richly decorated, and possesses a parvise. Upon entering, the enormous Norman columns of the nave, standing closely together and towering upwards, at once fix the attention. The semicircular arches upon them appear small when compared with other cathedrals, while the triforium and clerestory are dwarfed and rendered comparatively unimportant. The zigzag and chevron work in the bays is of excellent character. The choir is pure Perpendicular and probably unsurpassed, and the glass in the large window is old and a grand example of medieval work. The bold and original idea of ornamenting comparatively plain Norman work with the delicate beauty of the Perpendicular has been carried out to the fullest perfection. The vaulting of the roof should be especially noted. The monument on the north of the choir, of Osric, King of Mercia, 729, was probably made about 1520. Next to it is the splendid monument of the unhappy Edward II., whose wasted career was terminated at Berkeley Castle, where he was murdered in 1377. Above the altar-tomb is a beautifully sculptured effigy of the King in alabaster, resting under a gorgeously elaborate canopy. It is interesting to remember that this tomb—one of the finest of the royal monuments in England—was put up to a vain and worthless King by his son and successor, whose reign helped to make the country prosperous, while the man whose memory is perpetuated in richly carved alabaster allowed his father (Edward I.), a great and courageous King, to rest under the five plain slabs of marble to be seen in Westminster Abbey. The recumbent effigy of Abbot Parker, last Abbot of Gloucester, should be noticed. The chantry, however, is a cenotaph.

The North and South Transepts are Norman, enriched with Perpendicular work. From these points the flying arches, added to relieve the strain on the piers supporting the central tower arches, are features of grace and beauty. The north and south choir aisles each possess a side-chapel, in one of which Robert, Duke of Normandy, lies. He died in 1134 in Cardiff Castle, after an imprisonment of twenty-six years. The Lady Chapel is of magnificent Perpendicular work. There are chapels also leading from the choir triforium, superimposed upon those below. The Crypt is Early Norman work. The Cloisters are the finest in England, the roof being vaulted with fan-tracery, said to be the earliest example. In the north walk of the cloisters is the lavatory, with a long trough at which the monks washed, still in a perfect state, while in the wall opposite is a place for the towels. In the south walk are twenty recesses where the monks studied or wrote. The whole of the windows in these cloisters are filled with stained glass. The Chapter-house is of plain Norman work, with the exception of one small portion. By its side is the abbot's cloister, over which is the chapter library, containing some manuscripts of great value.

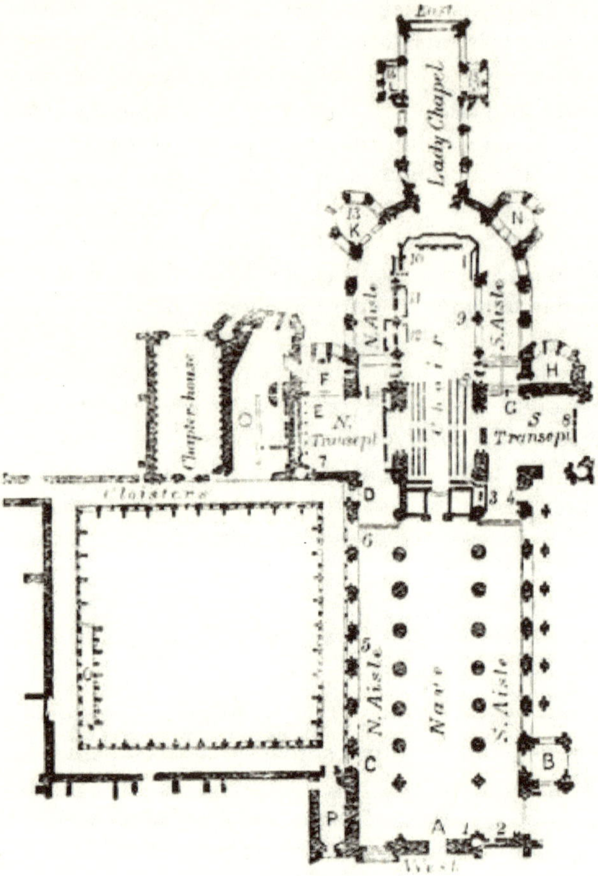

PLAN OF GLOUCESTER CATHEDRAL.

Parts of Building.

- A. West door.
- B. South porch.
- C. Monks' door to Cloisters.
- D. Abbot's door to Cloisters.
- E. Reliquary.
- F. Chapel.
- G. Doorway to Crypt.

- **H. Chapel of St. Andrew.**
- **I. Sedilia.**
- **K. Chapel of Duke of Normandy.**
- **L. Abbot Hanley's Chantry.**
- **M. Abbot Farley's Chantry.**
- **N. Chapel.**
- **O. Lavatory.**
- **P. Passage to Cloisters.**
- **Q. Slype and Sacristy.**

Monuments.

- **1. Dr. Jenner.**
- **2. Alderman Jones.**
- **3. Abbot Seabroke.**
- **4. Brydges.**
- **5. Sarah Morley (by Flaxman).**
- **6. Alderman Machen.**
- **7. Bower.**
- **8. Alderman Blackleech.**
- **9. Abbot Foliot.**
- **10. Osric.**
- **11. Edward II.**
- **12. Bishop Parker.**
- **13. Courtehouse.**
- **14. Bishop Godfrey.**
- **15. Thomas Fitzwilliams.**

The cathedral has a number of interesting ruins on the northern side. These include the remains of a Dominican monastery, founded in the ninth century and rebuilt in 1115, of which some arches and pillars remain. There are other buildings partially adapted for modern purposes.

Gloucester also possesses some churches of considerable interest, such as St. Mary de Lode, said to be the oldest in the city, with the Norman chancel and tower of the original building. In the churchyard stands a monument to Bishop Hooper, burnt alive on the spot in 1555. St. Mary de Crypt is of Early English workmanship, and derives its name from two large crypts beneath it. It stands in Southgate Street, and has a beautiful and lofty tower. St. Michael the Cross was rebuilt in 1815, but incorporates original Decorated work. It is said to have a connection with the ancient Abbey of St. Peter. The curfew bell is still rung from the tower every evening. St. Nicholas, in Westgate Street, also contains Norman and Early English work.

One of the greatest charms of Gloucester lies in the multiplicity of houses to be found which range in date from the fourteenth to the seventeenth century, and a ramble through the streets will disclose many besides those seen with a hurried glance. The New Inn, for example, despite its unpromising name, possesses a courtyard with surrounding gallery eminently medieval in every respect, and the feeling is not lessened by a descent into the adjoining vaults. It was built in 1450 by John Twining, a monk, for the accommodation of pilgrims to the shrine of Edward II. It may be of interest to note that the wood employed is chestnut. A fine old timbered house stands in Northgate Street, but has been refronted. A passage, however, affords a view at the side. There are many other examples of old domestic architecture to be found at the junctions of the four principal streets in the centre of the town, where, it may be mentioned, the Town Hall stands upon the site of the ancient Courts of Justice.

In selecting a motoring centre in this part of England, the writer has found Gloucester to be a very suitable one in every way. The Bell and County Hotel has a large garage, and combines in a very exceptional manner the charm of the old-fashioned English hostelry with the needs of the present day. Apart from the long routes described in these pages, there are many short runs from Gloucester to pretty villages in the Cotswolds and to historic spots, such as Berkeley Castle, Llanthony Abbey, Deerhurst Priory, and a dozen other places, which a local handbook will point out. Nearly all the important places in the neighbourhood are described in this book.

LOOP No. 6

FIRST PORTION: HEREFORD TO SHREWSBURY—**SECOND PORTION**: SHREWSBURY TO WORCESTER, LEDBURY, AND HEREFORD

HEREFORD TO SHREWSBURY, 54¾ MILES

DISTANCES ALONG THE ROUTE

	Miles.	
Hereford to Moreton-on-Lug	4	
Moreton-on-Lug to Bodenham Moor	3	¾
Bodenham Moor to Leominster	7	
Leominster to Wooferton	7	¼
Wooferton to Ludlow	4	
Ludlow to Craven Arms	7	¾
Craven Arms to Church Stretton	7	¾
Church Stretton to Dorrington	6	½
Dorrington to Shrewsbury	6	¾

NOTES FOR DRIVERS

To **Shrewsbury** a first-class road; a hill of 1 in 12 at **Ludlow** and 1 in 15 at **Bodenham Hill**.

PLACES OF INTEREST ON THE ROUTE

Sutton Walls.—Remains of Offa's castle.

Bodenham.—A village with a large and handsome church.

Hampton Court.—A house dating from the time of Henry IV.

Leominster.—A very picturesque town; the Town Hall; the church, with the nave of a former Priory; the Butter Cross.

Ludlow.—An old and very interesting town; the church, one of the finest in England; the Guildhall; an excellent museum; Richard's Castle near the town.

Stokesay Castle.—One of the most perfect fortified houses of the thirteenth century in the kingdom; strikingly picturesque.

Craven Arms.—The camp of Caer Caradoc; the Long Mynd district; extremely picturesque hills of exceptional interest to geologists.

Church Stretton.—A pretty village in charming surroundings of wooded hills and valleys; Norman and Transitional cruciform church.

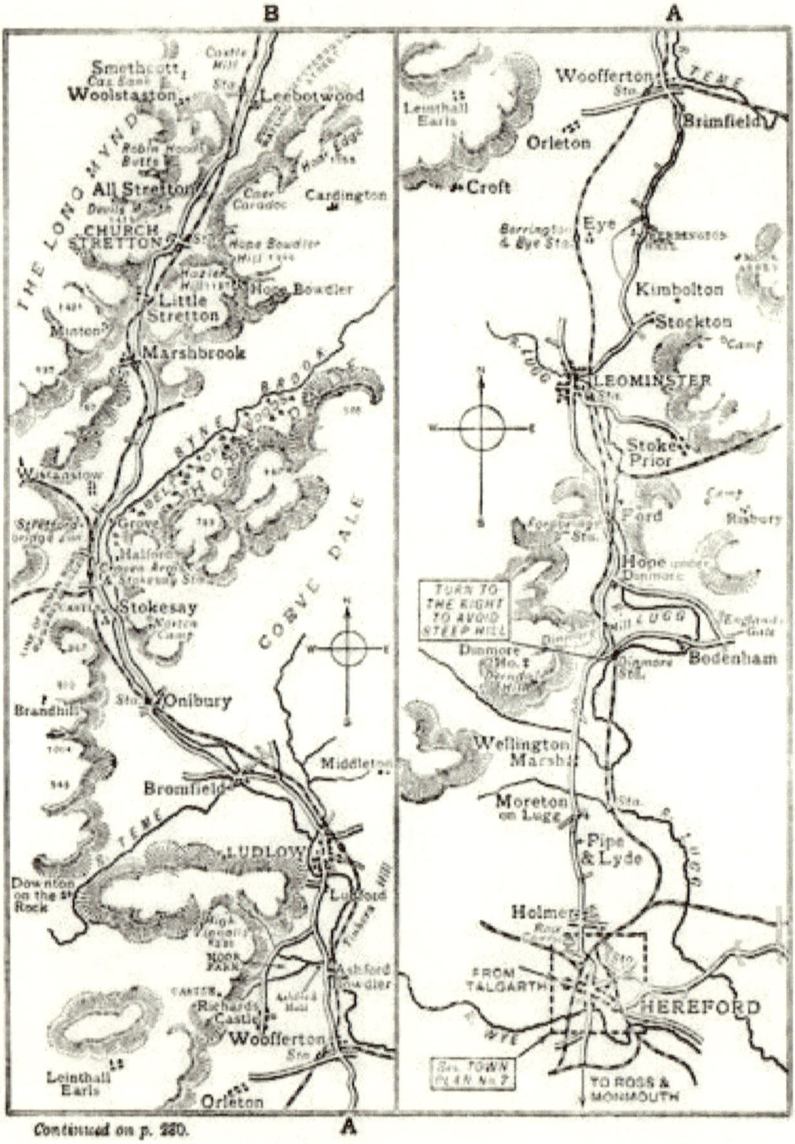

LOOP 6 (FIRST PORTION). HEREFORD TO CHURCH STRETTON.

Continued on p. 230.

(*For description and plan of* Hereford, *see pp. 176-179.*)

The road to Leominster passes due north out of Hereford by, or rather through, the racecourse, and directly afterwards Holmer Church is seen upon the left side of the road. It belongs to Early English times, and has a detached tower.

Moreton-on-Lug has a church which has recently been restored, but it contains some altar-tombs of the Dauncer family. From this point onwards Robin Hood's Butts and the Sugar Loaf Hills become prominent objects in the landscape on the left, their rugged summits of sandstone resisting the action of the weather better than the soft marls through which they protrude.

Sutton Walls lie to the right upon a wooded hill, and are of great historical interest. Offa, king of Mercia, had a palace there, and to it Ethelbert, king of the East Angles, was invited, the ostensible object being his marriage to the daughter of the Mercian king. The young prince was foully murdered by the connivance of Quendrida, Offa's queen, and East Anglia annexed to Mercia in A.D. 782. In expiation of this deed Offa founded the great monastery at St. Albans. There is a large encampment upon the hill, with four entrances, apparently of Roman origin, and containing an area of about thirty acres.

Entering a low-lying district, upon which stands Wellington Marsh, Marden Church is seen upon the right, the place of Ethelbert's first interment, the original building having been erected by Offa. Wellington Church, lying to the left of the road, is chiefly of modern construction. Two miles farther on a bifurcation occurs, and the road to the right may be taken if one wishes to avoid the rather steep way leading over Dinmore Hill. Bodenham is the next village on the route. It possesses a large church of the Early English and Decorated Periods, containing an alabaster tomb of Sir Walter Devereux, 1401. In the village will be seen the remains of a large cross and a well. A sharp turn to the left at England's Gate leads back in a few miles to the junction with the main road near Hope-under-Dinmore, crossing the River Lug just before the junction. Hope Church, standing on the hill-side, contains many tablets to the Coningsby family. About two miles to the right of Ford lies Risbury Camp, of an oval form, with deep ditches surrounding it, and containing an area of about eight acres. Hampton Court was built by Sir Roland Lenthall in the time of Henry IV., and much enlarged by ransoms subsequently obtained from prisoners at the Battle of Agincourt. It was once the home of the Earl of Coningsby. Mr. J. H. Arkwright, a descendant of Richard Arkwright, is now the owner. The Court has been partially rebuilt.

LEOMINSTER

This town presents an exceedingly picturesque aspect, a number of medieval or Renaissance buildings having survived. It was a place of importance in the days of the Heptarchy, and a monastery was instituted by Merewald, king of the West Mercians, in the seventh century, which, however, disappeared subsequently in the Danish invasions. A residence of the Saxon kings, together with a stronghold, was also raised here, only to be destroyed in a Welsh raid in 1088. In 1125 Henry I. established a Benedictine cell under the rule of Reading Priory, and the buildings now form part of the workhouse!

The Church includes examples of almost every style of architecture. The nave is Norman, and originally formed part of the Priory Church standing upon this site. The monuments are very numerous, and some of the finest window tracery in any ecclesiastical building in the British Isles exists here. A fire in the eastern parts of the church in 1699 led to a restoration in a very debased style. The Butter Cross is an object of interest, and in the Bargates are Georgian almshouses dating back to 1736. They have an effigy with an inscription containing an admonition against the exercise of charity without discrimination. The road to Ludlow lies upon the eastern side of the railway, and a sharp turn to the right occurs in the town. Ivington Camp is a British earthwork, but was considerably strengthened by Owen Glendower when he retreated from Leominster and was vigorously pursued by Prince Henry. One mile to the right lies Eaton Hall, now a farmhouse. It was erected in the time of Henry V., and was once occupied by the old family of Hakluyt.[1]

Eye lies to the left of the road, and has a church with some fine alabaster monuments in it—one figure with the collar of SS. Berrington Hall and Park, the seat of Lord Rodney, are close by. The country passed through for some miles past is a cider district, and numerous orchards can be seen on every side. Near Woofferton is a fine open stretch of country, in which the highlands upon the left, wooded to their summits, form a welcome break. Richard's Castle, of the motte and bailey type, lies under the hills. It was erected in the reign of Edward the Confessor, and stands upon a mound 60 feet in height, with some peculiar earthworks adjoining. It is a matter for remark that this stronghold was erected and occupied by a Norman, Richard, the son of Scrop, *before* the Conquest, and thus is one of a little group of castles of peculiar interest. An old church at the town of Richard's Castle has a detached belfry.

[1] A Welsh family, of whom Richard Hakluyt (1552?-1616), the famous geographer, is the best known.

LUDLOW

This is an ancient British town lying in an amphitheatre of high ground, but no reliable history relating to the place is extant until after the Conquest, when Roger de Montgomery founded the Castle, which for a considerable time was the residence of Royalty, more particularly of Edward IV. and his children. Ludlow was also the seat of the Grand Council entrusted with the jurisdiction of the Marches. The keep of the castle was erected between 1086 and 1096. In the Civil War the castle surrendered to the Parliamentary forces in 1646, at the same time as Bridgnorth. The appearance of the dismantled fortress on an eminence above the River Teme is imposing and impressive, as the Norman towers and bastions, together with a considerable portion of the curtain walls, are still standing.

The Church stands upon elevated ground near the castle, and is of Decorated Gothic, dating from the time of Edward III., although originally built in the twelfth century. It is dedicated to St. Lawrence, and is a cruciform building with a lofty tower, and one of the finest churches in England. There is also a guildhall, a town-hall, and the museum, chiefly confined to natural history, has a grand collection of Silurian fossils. A very fine timbered house, the Lane Asylum, dates from 1672.

From the district round Bromfield a fine view is obtained of Clee Hill lying to the right, with Titterstone Camp, 1,749 feet above the sea, on it. Farther to the north is Brown Clee Hill, 1,792 feet high, with Corne Dale to the left. Near Onibury the route is well wooded, and the valley becomes contracted as the road leads through a break in Wenlock Edge. Upon the right Norton Camp, a horseshoe-shaped entrenchment, occupies the summit of a knoll.

STOKESAY CASTLE

is reached just before coming to Craven Arms Station. It is, without exaggeration, one of the most picturesque and also one of the earliest fortified houses in the kingdom. From almost any point of view it thrills the artist, the architect, the archæologist, and the ordinary visitor who has any capacity to read sermons in stones. The very name 'Stokesay' tells the story of Norman owner superseding Saxon, the Says or Sayes being descendants of Picot de Sai, who came over with the Conqueror, a similar instance being found in Stoke d'Abernon in Surrey, where the Saxon 'Stoke' is again tacked on to the name of the new Norman owner. The gatehouse of the castle, although a highly picturesque timber-framed building of Elizabethan times, with a carving of Adam and Eve and the Serpent over the door, is not the most interesting feature, for the rest of the building belongs to the thirteenth century, and is quite one of the best examples of a fortified house of the Early English period. The moat is now dry, but otherwise one can see in Stokesay the type of house close to the Welsh Marches which was occupied by a lesser feudal lord in the days when Wales was still the home of unconquered tribesmen, who might at any time make a sudden descent into English territory. Facing the gateway is the hall, 51 feet by 31 feet (internal measurements), lighted with four tall lancet windows looking on to the moat on the west side. The open timber roof is blackened with smoke, for there was no fireplace, and the smoke from the central brazier escaped through an outlet in the roof. The builder of this hall is given by the late Mr. Augustus Hare as John de Verdun, who died in 1279, while the curious and picturesque polygonal tower at the south corner was no doubt built by Verdun's successor, that Lawrence de Ludlow who received permission from Edward I. to fortify his house of Stokesay. It would be a pleasant task to describe every room and every architectural detail of this fascinating castle, but space unfortunately does not permit.

The Church at Stokesay was rebuilt after the Civil War. Beautiful views of the Long Mynd, of Wenlock Edge, and the ridge lying between them, now open up. The church at the little village of Wistanstow has been restored, and during the alterations a carved oak roof of the Perpendicular period came to light.

CHURCH STRETTON

is a village in an exceedingly pleasant situation, with the Long Mynd ridge of hills to the west, and with Hope Bowdler, Caer Caradoc, and the Lawley nearly opposite. The name Stretton, like Streatham, indicates the presence of a Roman road—one of those leading southwards from the great Roman city of *Uriconium.*

The interesting cruciform church has a Norman nave with Transitional central tower and transepts. Several Perpendicular windows have been inserted. Mr. Hare mentions a stone in the churchyard, near the sundial, bearing this inscription to Ann Cook, who died in 1814:

'On a Thursday she was born,

On a Thursday made a bride,

On a Thursday broke her leg,

And on a Thursday died.'

'Hesba Stretton,' the novelist, took her pen-name from this village, where she lived for many years.

Near Church Stretton the site of Brockhurst Castle is passed over. Bodbury Ring, to the left beyond Church Stretton, is said to have been occupied by Ostorius Scapula previous to his great battle with Caractacus. The site of the engagement is on the right, and a mile farther on the road leads under Caer Caradoc Hill, 1,506 feet high, with a perfect camp, vallum, and ditches upon the summit, wherein Caradoc entrenched himself previous to the fight. The district under the Long Mynd is extremely picturesque, with deep gullies and cross valleys running into the great ridge, whose elevation in places reaches to 1,600 feet. It is a paradise for geologists, deposits emerging from underneath the Silurian which are of more than ordinary interest. The Caradoc Range is an old volcanic outburst. The line of the Roman road traversing the valley already mentioned may be noted running parallel with the railway.

(*For description and plan of S h r e w s b u r y , see pp. 76-79.*)

LOOP No. 6—SECOND PORTION

SHREWSBURY TO HEREFORD, 81¼ MILES

DISTANCES ALONG THE ROUTE

	Miles.	
Shrewsbury to Buildwas	11	¾
Buildwas to Ironbridge	2	
Ironbridge to Bridgnorth	7	¾
Bridgnorth to Birdsgreen	7	
Birdsgreen to Kidderminster	7	¼
Kidderminster to Worcester	14	½
Worcester to Malvern	8	¼
Malvern to Ledbury	8	
Ledbury to Hereford	14	¾

NOTES FOR DRIVERS

Shrewsbury to Worcester.—A few hills only to Bridgnorth; thence to Kidderminster some steep hills, but otherwise an excellent road. One of the hills is 1 in 12 after Shatterford; after that good.

Worcester to Hereford.—To Malvern splendid; between Malvern and Ledbury ascent 1 in 9, descent 1 in 11 in crossing the Malvern Hills, then very good road to Hereford, with only trifling hills.

PLACES OF INTEREST ON THE ROUTE

Buildwas Abbey.—A beautiful ruin.

Bridgnorth.—A picturesque town, with a church and the remains of a castle; the bridge.

Kidderminster.—A town famed for its manufacture of carpets; church, Perpendicular.

Stourport.—An uninteresting town.

Ombersley.—A picturesque village; The Court, the residence of Lord Sandys.

Worcester.—A busy city; the cathedral and tomb of King John; the Edgar Tower; the Guildhall; the famous porcelain works.

Great Malvern.—A finely-situated watering-place; the abbey gateway; a Norman church, originally a priory church.

Ledbury.—Picturesque market town, with old market hall and several quaint houses; church, Norman, Early English, and Perpendicular; tower detached.

Hereford.—(See p. 176.)

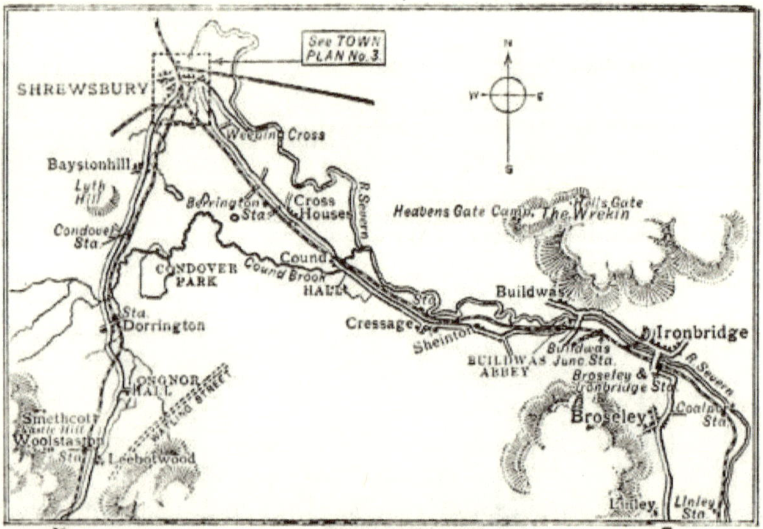

B *Continued on p. 239.* C

LOOP 6. (NORTHERN PART INCLUDING SHREWSBURY).

The route from Shrewsbury follows that to *Uriconium* for nearly a mile, when a bifurcation occurs, and the road to the right is chosen, passing through Sutton and Cound. The church at the latter place is chiefly of Early English architecture; it contains a carved early Norman font of great interest. The Wrekin, with Heaven's Gate Camp upon it, is a prominent feature in the distance, while the Severn indulges in sinuous windings by the side of the road. B u i l d w a s A b b e y is quite close to the road; it presents a beautiful aspect, and is one of the finest ruins in the county. The abbey was founded by Roger de Clinton, Bishop of Chester, in 1135, for Cistercians. Parts of it still remain roofed. Coalbrookdale is historically interesting as the cradle of the iron trade. It sprang into prominence when the Sussex ironfields had to be abandoned, owing to the shrinkage of the forests there. In 1700 members of the Darby family experimented upon iron ore smelted with coal and coke, and since then it has been a centre of the iron industry.

I r o n b r i d g e contains nothing of any particular interest. It is a town of foundries, forges, and furnaces, while hideous tiers of dirty cottages cluster on the steep hill-side. In the town is the iron bridge from which the place gains its name; it is a bridge of a single span, stretching 120 feet, and is the first on record. Its presence is due to the energy of Abraham Darby, of the Coalbrookdale Works, in 1779. From Ironbridge the road trends away from the Severn, passing through a well-wooded country, and eventually reaches

BRIDGNORTH

This picturesque town is reputed to have been founded by a daughter of Alfred the Great, and was fortified with walls and a castle by Robert de Belesme, Earl of Shrewsbury. Henry I. besieged it in 1102, and in the time of Henry II. it was dismantled. The walls suffered the same fate at the hands of the Parliamentary forces after a long siege in 1646. The upper town is built upon a steep rocky plateau, which rises abruptly from the river, crowned by the remains of the old castle, which deviate remarkably from the vertical. A bridge of fine design joins the upper to the lower town.

A t Q u a t f o r d a fortress was built by Ethelfleda, and subsequently a college by the wife of Roger de Montgomery, from a romantic remembrance of having first met her husband upon that spot. Slight indications of a keep still remain upon a rock overlooking the Severn. The church has the chancel arch and font of the Norman period, and the remainder is Decorated work of the fourteenth century.

The Forest of Morfe at one time covered the whole of this district. Dudmaston Castle is passed immediately before Quatt is reached, and then an undulating run eventually leads to

KIDDERMINSTER

The name of the town means the 'minster on the brow of the hill.' From the time of William the Conqueror down to *c.* 1135 it was a manor in possession of the Crown.

T h e   C h u r c h . —This is dedicated to St. Mary, and is chiefly of the Perpendicular period. It contains a number of ancient monuments, and has recently undergone a restoration. The town is celebrated for its manufacture of carpets; a peculiar property of the River Stour is reputed to add to the brilliancy of the colouring. Dyeing, worsted-spinning, together with iron manufactures, are carried on in the town.

On leaving Kidderminster the road lies almost due south to S t o u r p o r t , a rather uninteresting town, possessing, however, an iron bridge over the Severn. The church is of modern construction.

O m b e r s l e y is a village of uncommonly neat appearance, with many timbered houses effectively rendered in black and white. The Court was erected in the time of Queen Anne, and is the country residence of Lord Sandys. The church in the village is new.

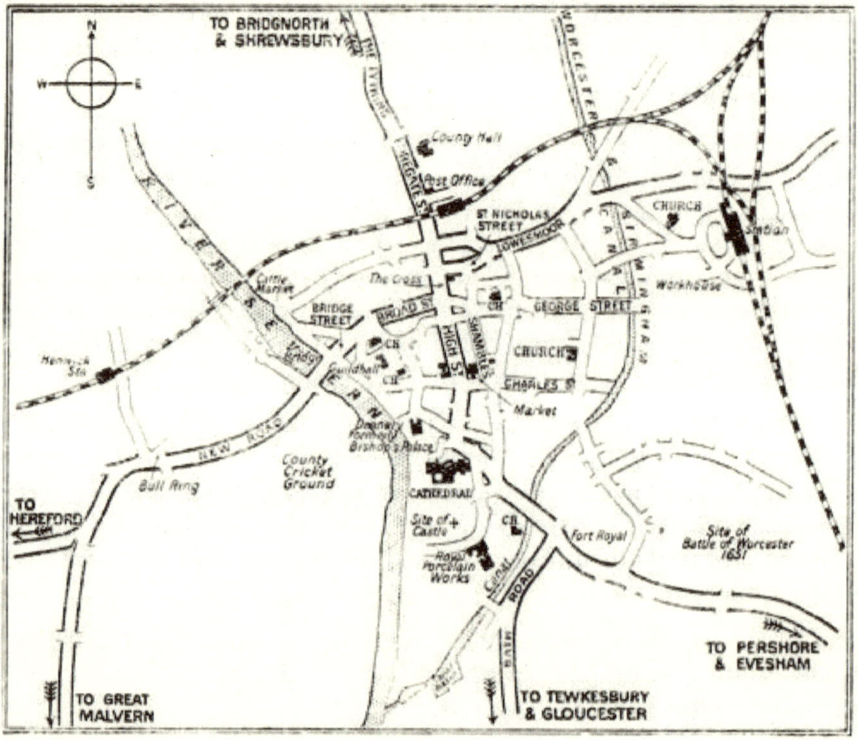

Town Plan No. 8—Worcester.

WORCESTER

is sheltered by the Malvern Hills on the south-west, and by other picturesque eminences. A Roman road originally traversed the city, and as early as the year 680 Worcester was surrounded by lofty walls and fortifications, which, by existing records, appear to have compared favourably with other towns.

The Cathedral.—(*Open on weekdays 9.30 to 6, but closed at 5.30 between October and March 31 [or dusk]. 6d. each charged for entering the Choir, Lady Chapel, and other special portions.*) When Mercia became an independent kingdom a church was raised, and subsequently another built by Oswald in the tenth century a little north-east of the present building. Wulfstan found Oswald's church in ruins, the handiwork of Hardicanute's soldiers. He began a new cathedral in 1084, but two fires subsequently ruined it. Re-erected, it was reconsecrated in 1218. The cathedral suffered but little at the Reformation, but very much during the Civil War. It is not a grand building so far as massiveness is concerned, but possesses a variety of styles which harmonize in a remarkable degree, and a sense of unity pervades the whole building. The tower is a beautiful specimen of Perpendicular work, and has recently been thoroughly renovated. The chief objects of interest in the interior are the stalls, with their miserere seats, dating from 1397, formerly in Worcester Priory; the cloisters, chapterhouse, and remarkable Norman crypt, with King John's tomb in the choir. There are picturesque remains of the old Guesten Hall, the refectory and dormitory.

The Edgar Tower stands near the entrance to the cathedral cloisters. It was originally the entrance to Worcester Castle, but the monks converted it into a monastery gateway.

The Guildhall dates from 1721, and is an impressive building, containing some objects of interest from the battlefield of Worcester.

The Commandery.—This is a hospital founded in 1085; the great refectory and Guesten Hall, with beautiful roofs and stained glass, should be seen.

There are a number of old timbered houses remaining in the city, especially in Friar Street, near the city gaol, and in Lich Street. In the Corn Market is King Charles's House, built 1577, in which Charles II. took refuge in 1651 after the Battle of Worcester. It has the inscription, 'Fear God; honour the King,' over the doorway. In the Trinity, not far off, is an interesting Elizabethan house with an open gallery. The Royal Porcelain Works, founded in 1751, are in Severn Street, near the cathedral. (*Open 9.30 to 12.30, 2.15 to 5. Admission 6d.*)

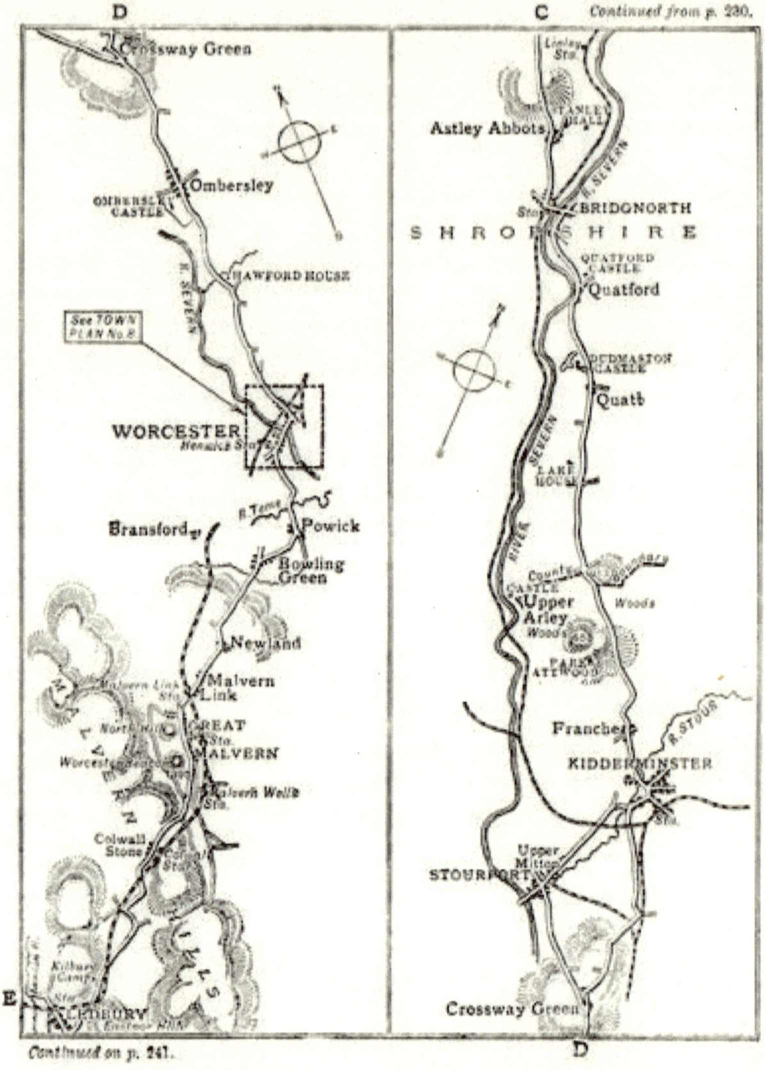

LOOP 6 (PART OF SECOND PORTION).
SHREWSBURY TO HEREFORD.

GREAT MALVERN

Malvern is a watering-place, situated in a beautiful district on the eastern slope of the hills of the same name, and is much frequented by reason of its fine air, its healthy surroundings, and its mineral springs. A Benedictine priory was founded here shortly after the Conquest, and one of the buildings, the Abbey Gateway, dating from 1083, still remains.

The Church is of Norman work, with Perpendicular additions, dating from the time of Henry VII.; it originally formed the Priory Church, and was purchased by the inhabitants at the Dissolution, and made parochial. The recumbent effigies in it are of considerable interest.

Between Malvern and Ledbury lie the Malvern Hills; in crossing them one has to negotiate a hill of 1 in 11. One is reminded of Touraine in the quantities of mistletoe growing on the trees as the quaint old town of Ledbury is neared.

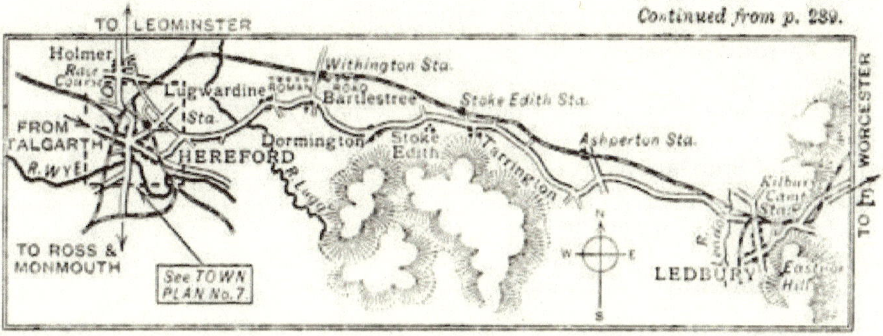

LOOP 6 (LAST PORTION). LEDBURY TO HEREFORD.

LEDBURY

The main street is full of charm in its possession of several old houses and a market-house standing on chestnut pillars. The upper portion has been much restored, but the wooden supports are those of the building believed to have been put up by John Abell in Elizabethan times.

The most notable feature of the church is the detached Early English tower, now crowned with a modern spire. Of the original Norman church the western doorway remains in the Perpendicular nave. Besides the tombs of the Biddulphs the stained glass in the north chapel should be examined. These windows are of the Decorated period, and the chapel is dedicated to the local St. Catherine, who lived at the beginning of the fourteenth century. During the Civil War there was a hot fight in Ledbury in the year 1645 between Prince Rupert and a body of Roundheads. Marks of bullets can be seen on the church doors and elsewhere in the town.

(*For* Hereford, *see p. 176*.)

LOOP No. 7

GLOUCESTER TO BATH, MALMESBURY, EVESHAM, TEWKESBURY, AND GLOUCESTER, 153 MILES

DISTANCES ALONG THE ROUTE

Miles.		
Gloucester to Stroud	12	1/4
Stroud to Nailsworth	4	1/4
Nailsworth to Old Sodbury	13	1/4
Old Sodbury to Bath	11	
Bath to Chippenham	13	
Chippenham to Malmesbury	10	
Malmesbury to Minety	7	1/4
Minety to Cricklade	4	3/4
Cricklade to Highworth	7	1/2
Highworth to Lechlade	4	1/2
Lechlade to Burford	8	3/4
Burford to Shipton-under-Wychwood	4	1/4
Shipton to Chipping Norton	6	3/4
Chipping Norton to Moreton-in-the-Marsh	8	
Moreton to Broadway	8	1/2
Broadway to Evesham	5	3/4
Evesham to Tewkesbury	13	1/4
Tewkesbury to Gloucester	10	

NOTES FOR DRIVERS

Gloucester to Nailsworth.—The road is fairly level, with a good surface.

Nailsworth to Bath.—The road climbs for the first 2 miles (1 in 15), and then is undulating along a ridge of downs until about 3 miles from Bath, where the long descent is 1 in 15.

Bath to Highworth.—An excellent road, with a steep hill soon after Cricklade (1 in 12), and an abrupt descent after Highworth (1 in 12).

The road becomes hilly near **Chipping Norton**, with a very stiff descent at Fish Hill (1 in 11), after which the road is excellent all the way to **Tewkesbury** and **Gloucester**.

PLACES OF INTEREST ON THE ROUTE

Painswick.—Exceptionally picturesque little Cotswold town. Fine church and churchyard, with clipped yews; Painswick Court, a fine old Tudor house near the church.

Stroud.—A small town with cloth manufactures. Town Hall of fifteenth century; church modern, except tower.

Nailsworth.—A cloth manufacturing place scattered in the valley south of Stroud.

Bath.—The famous Georgian watering-place. A large stone town. Roman baths in splendid preservation; the Abbey Church, Perpendicular; Pulteney Bridge lined with shops; good eighteenth-century houses.

Bradford-on-Avon.—An old village with a famous Saxon church. (On a short loop from Bath. See Map.)

Box.—A small village near long tunnel on G.W.R. Church of various periods.

Corsham (*just off the road to the right*).—An old village with interesting Norman church. Corsham Court, partially Elizabethan house, the seat of Lord Methuen.

Chippenham.—Old town on Avon with manufactures. Church spoiled by restoration; Maud Heath's Causeway.

Malmesbury.—Picturesque old town on the Avon. Abbey Church Trans-Norman; tower of old parish church; Elizabethan houses; fine market cross; old almshouses.

Cricklade.—A pleasant little town on the uppermost windings of the Thames. St. Sampson's Church, with fine Perpendicular tower; St. Mary's, Norman; early crosses in both churchyards.

Lechlade.—Another little town on the Thames. Old bridge; Perpendicular church.

Shipton-under-Wychwood.—Village with a fine church, close to Wychwood Forest.

Chipping Norton.—Highest town in Oxfordshire; picturesque street.

Moreton-in-the-Marsh.—A pleasant little market town.

Bourton-on-the-Hill.—A very picturesque Cotswold village.

Broadway.—A beautifully-situated and strikingly attractive Cotswold village. Many old houses, including manor-house of Abbots of Pershore Abbey. Old church 1 mile from village, interesting.

Evesham.—A small town on Avon; picturesque. Booth Hall, Bell Tower, and various remains of the extensive abbey. Churches of (1) St. Lawrence, not very interesting; (2) All Saints, Early English and later. Battle fought in 1265.

Tewkesbury.—Very picturesque old town on Avon and Severn. Abbey Church, splendid Norman; many old timber-framed houses. Battle of Tewkesbury, 1471.

Deerhurst Priory (*off road to west*).—Pre-Norman buildings lately well restored.

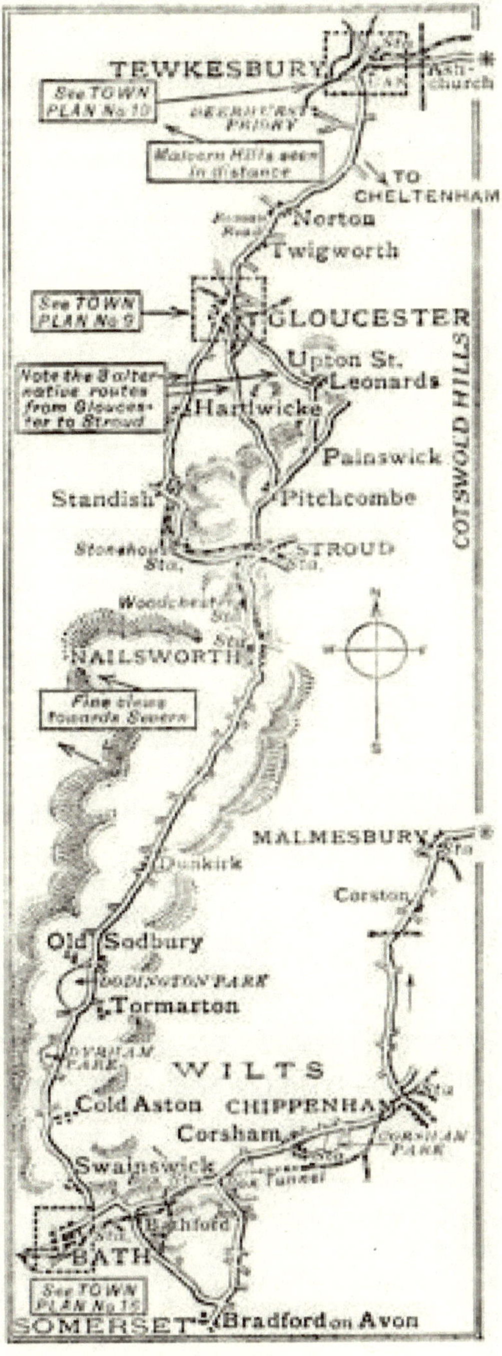

Loop 7. GLOUCESTER TO BATH.

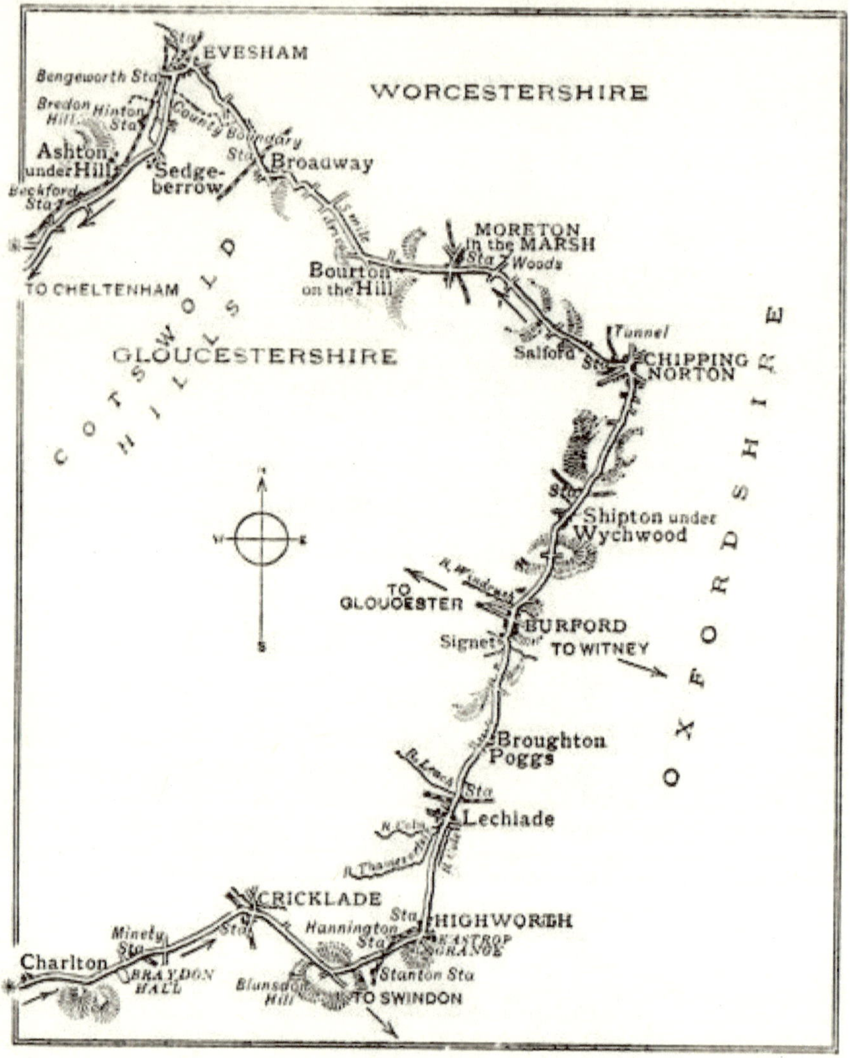

LOOP 7. GLOUCESTER TO BATH AND EVESHAM.

The extensive loop described briefly in this chapter takes one to many interesting towns in Gloucestershire and the neighbouring counties, and as there is much to see, it is advisable to break the journey at Bath, and possibly again at Broadway or Evesham, in order not to be obliged to hurry through beautiful scenery and romantic towns.

Although the level road from Gloucester to Stroud by Hardwicke is to be recommended to those who would avoid a long, stiff climb, the way through the Cotswolds is so much more interesting and so vastly more picturesque that it should by all means be taken if the hill is of no consequence.

The easiest ascent of the face of the Cotswolds is by the road through the village of Brookthorpe, descending into the Painswick valley near the secluded and quite typical Cotswold hamlet of Pitchcombe.

A still more beautiful road goes through Sneedham's Green, near Upton St. Leonards, and winds up a long steady ascent among beeches. This road is well engineered, and the views from it, first over the Vale of Severn and then into the Painswick and Sheepscombe valleys, are full of exquisite charm at all times of the year.

PAINSWICK

is one of those little stone towns with that peculiarly foreign flavour so frequently experienced in the Cotswolds. Perched on a steep hill-side and dominated by the tall tower and spire of its stately church, the place is the centre of the life of a lovely valley. Every other house in the town is a picture by itself, and when grouped with others and backed by the emeralds and blues of the opposite side of the valley, the stranger can hardly be prevented from exclaiming aloud as each corner brings some new composition before him.

In the centre of the town stands the fine church, with a unique churchyard, wherein a wonderful array of richly carved altar-tombs of delicate classic design are scattered in picturesque irregularity under the sombre shade of rows of closely trimmed yews. The stems of these trees are kept clear of twigs and branches, and the masses of green are shaped into great round-topped cylindrical forms. Just below the church, beyond a group of magnificent elms, stands Painswick Court, a stone, many-gabled house of such reposeful dignity that one seems to find in it as nearly as possible the ideal English manor-house of modest proportions. The title 'Court' came to the house, not in connection with the manor, but through a visit paid to it by Charles I. in 1643. The King slept in the house, and issued a proclamation 'given at our Court at Paynewicke.'

Whether one decides to go through Painswick or Pitchcombe, or even if one keeps below the hills, all the roads meet at

STROUD

This is a hilly town abounding in very steep streets, and possessing, as all Cotswold towns do, a number of good old stone houses of the sixteenth, seventeenth, and eighteenth centuries. It is, nevertheless, a place without much appeal to the passing motorist, for the church has been rebuilt in recent times, with the exception of the tower, which is Early English. The Town

Hall, formerly the market-house, was built in the fifteenth century by John Throckmorton of Lypiatt.

Stroud still maintains its woollen industry, and thousands of people are employed in the mills in the town and in the valley to the east.

Leaving Stroud for Bath, one ascends the valley towards Nailsworth, a busy locality, where the weaving of broadcloth is the chief industry. There are also flock factories and workshops where beech—'the weed of the oolite'—is used in making beds, gunstocks, and umbrella-sticks.

A little beyond Nailsworth the road comes out on the ridge of wind-swept hills, and continues a slightly undulating course southwards to Bath, a distance of over twenty miles, without a village and scarcely a hamlet on the whole journey. There are wide views in both directions, and some grand panoramas across the Severn.

After dropping down from the level of the downs, one turns to the right and enters the ancient city of

BATH

This wealthy, picturesque, and still popular watering-place, is described at some length in another volume of this series—the Southern Section of England—and it must therefore be dealt with in the briefest fashion here. The thermal springs attracted the Romans to the spot, and of their city *Aquæ Solis* there are probably very considerable remains beneath the present city. The Baths themselves have been excavated, and several feet below the street-level one can now see the Roman tanks filled, as they were some sixteen centuries ago, with the steaming waters which still bring many ailing folk to the town. Besides the baths there is the Abbey Church, a magnificent example of late Perpendicular work, crowded with memorials to distinguished visitors and residents of Bath, whose virtues and achievements are not overlooked on the marble tablets.

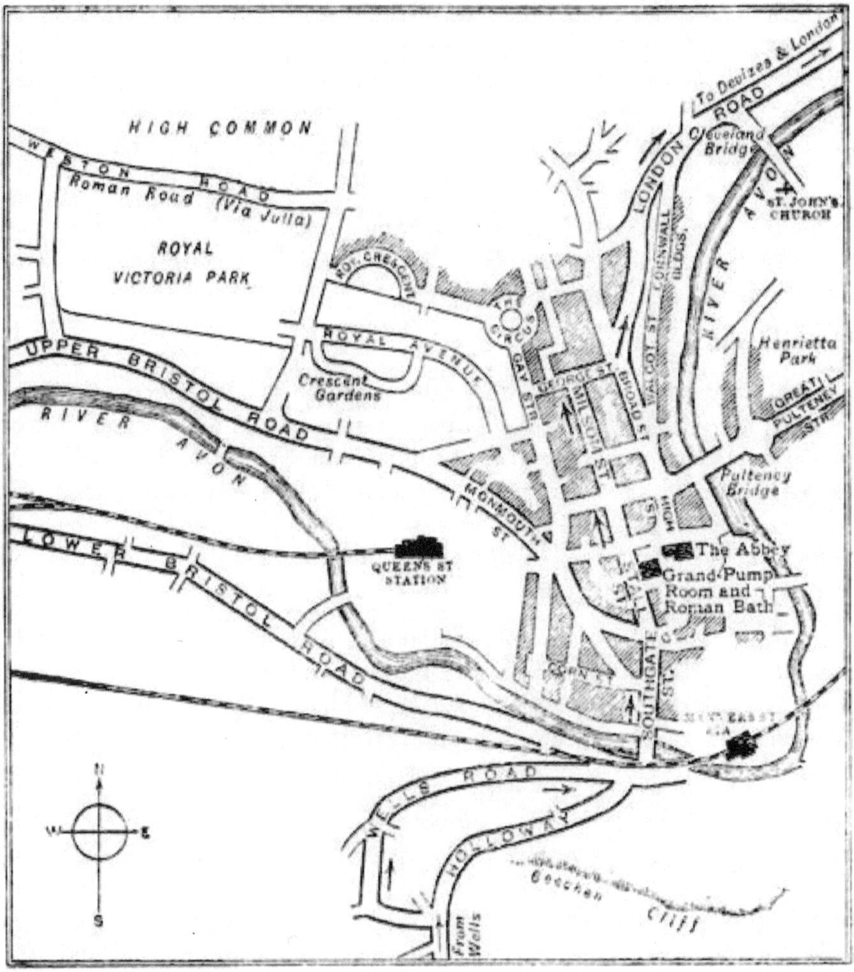

TOWN PLAN NO. 16—BATH.

P u l t e n e y B r i d g e , like the Ponte Vecchio, is lined with shops, but the famous bridge at Florence quite eclipses this structure of a much later and less artistic age. In walking through the streets of Bath one cannot fail to be struck by several of the Georgian façades, whose dignity and classic perfection reflect the formal manners of the latter part of the eighteenth century, when Beau Nash drew admiring and envious eyes upon his elaborately-attired person as he passed along the stone-built streets of the great centre of smart society when George was King.

From Bath to Chippenham the road goes through Batheaston, and keeping to the north side of the railway for a couple of miles, passes under it to reach the village of B o x , which has given its name to one of the longest tunnels on the Great Western Railway. It is one and three-quarter miles in length, and cost more than half a million pounds to build. Box village has a church belonging to the three great periods of Gothic, with a Perpendicular tower.

Going to the left in the village, the road to Chippenham rises from the valley of the By Brook, crosses the ridge of oolite and fuller's earth pierced by the famous tunnel, and drops down to

CORSHAM

The little town lies chiefly to the right, towards the railway and Corsham Court, Lord Methuen's stately Elizabethan house. It is quite desirable to run through the place, returning to the Chippenham road by the road that skirts the park, north of the church. There are some old houses in the street, and among them one dating back as far as the fifteenth century. Corsham Court contains a magnificent collection of paintings, mostly brought here by Sir Paul Methuen, who was at one time Ambassador to Madrid, and died in 1757.

The beautiful cruciform church was shorn of its central tower during the restoration by Street, who built a new tower and spire in a rather unusual position south of the south transept. The Norman nave and a north door of the same period are the earliest portions of the building, and the Methuen Chapel, built in 1879, is the most recent.

From Corsham the road falls continuously to

CHIPPENHAM,

an old manufacturing town on the Avon. As its name suggests, it has been a market town from a very remote age. It was a place of importance in Saxon times, and one or two events are recorded as happening there before the year 878, when the Danes took the place and made it their headquarters, while, with fire and sword, they spread ruin and desolation over the neighbourhood. After Alfred reappeared from his hiding-place in marsh-bordered Athelney to the south-west, and gained his famous victory over the marauding Danes at Ethandune, he regained possession of Chippenham, and gave it to his daughter Ælfrith for life. For objects to connect the Chippenham of to-day with these thrilling times of half-civilized Britain one looks in vain, for the church, the most hopeful link, reveals no Saxon work, and what is Norman has been so cruelly handled that its interest has vanished. The richly-carved Norman chancel arch, dating from about half a century after the Conquest, has been recut and removed to the north side of the chancel.

The modern church of St. Paul was built in 1853 by Sir Gilbert Scott. A new Town Hall belongs to this period, but the old one is still standing.

MAUD HEATH'S CAUSEWAY

A very remarkable feature of Chippenham is a paved track some four and a half miles in length, and still bearing curious inscriptions, leading northeastwards from the town to the ridge of Bremhill Wick. This path owes its existence to a bequest made by a certain Maud Heath, who lived as long ago as the fifteenth century, and the cost of the maintenance of the path at the present day is defrayed by the property she bequeathed for the purpose. Tradition says that Maud Heath was a market-woman of Langley Burrell, a village on the causeway; and if this is correct one imagines that the good dame left her money to save those that came after her the toil and discomfort of trudging with a heavy basket in the deep mire of the heavy clay of the valley. On the ridge where the path terminates stands a column bearing a statue of the woman, put up in 1838 by the Lord Lansdowne of that time—Bowood, the ancestral home of the Lansdownes, from which Rembrandt's 'Mill' has lately been sold and removed to America, being only two miles distant.

An undulating road goes almost due north to Malmesbury, passing through the hamlet of Corston, which has a small church with a curious Perpendicular bell-turret at the west end.

MALMESBURY

This interesting and historic town is comparatively unknown to the ordinary tourist. Its situation on a spur of raised ground, with two branches of the Avon almost surrounding it with a natural moat, made the place of importance in early days, when such things were eagerly sought after. One is not surprised, therefore, to find that the site was a stronghold of the British, known as *Caer Bladon*, and in Saxon times was a frontier town of Wessex. According to Murray, the present name is derived from Maidulph or Maldulph, an Irish missionary who, about the beginning of the seventh century, established a hermitage under the protecting proximity of the castle, and there began educational work among the semi-barbarous Saxons. One of his scholars was the learned Ealdhelm, who became the first abbot of the monastery of Malmesbury, founded in 680. Of the great religious house which eventually grew up at Malmesbury only the church remains, now, alas! sadly diminished and curtailed. Both the central and the western towers collapsed somewhere about the sixteenth century, crushing the adjoining parts of the nave and chancel in their fall. The existing church is therefore only a portion of the nave of the magnificent abbey church which dominated the little town in pre-Reformation times. The arcades are Transitional Norman with massive cylindrical pillars, but above the arches rises a

Decorated clerestory, supporting a richly vaulted roof of the same period. If it had not been for Master Humpe, whom Leland describes as 'an exceeding riche Clothiar,' there would quite possibly have been nothing left at all of the abbey church after the suppression of the monasteries; but this worthy man bought the buildings from the Crown and presented the church to the parish. The old parish church was utilized as a town hall, but nothing remains of that structure except the tower, with a spire.

The beautiful Elizabethan house to the north-east of the abbey church is built on a portion of the monastic buildings in which Master Humpe had set up his looms. The famous historian, William of Malmesbury, who lived in the twelfth century, was librarian and precentor of the abbey. Before leaving the town the lovely Perpendicular market cross should be seen, and also the almshouses near St. John's Bridge.

Leaving Malmesbury by the Cirencester road, one soon goes to the right for Cricklade, skirting Charlton Park, with its dignified Jacobean house built by Sir Thomas Knyvet, with a west front designed, it is said, by Inigo Jones. It is the seat of the Earls of Suffolk and Berkshire. The present holder of the title was extra A.D.C. to Lord Curzon of Kedleston, and married, in 1904, a sister of the late Lady Curzon. The interior of the house has been modernized, but it contains a remarkably fine collection of old masters.

CRICKLADE

This prettily-situated little town is on the Thames, about ten miles from Thames Head, close to the Foss Way, St. Sampson's Church, with its pinnacled tower, rising picturesquely over the roofs half hidden among trees. It is a cruciform building, and the interior of the tower, which is enriched with armorial shields, contains a clock possessing no face on the exterior! In the churchyard there is a fine cross with niches in the head, and another is to be found in the churchyard of the little St. Mary's. Cricklade is one of those really ancient places whose beginnings are far off in British times, the origin of the name being the two British words *cerrig* (stone) and *lád* (ford).

From Cricklade one goes south-west as straight as an arrow for about four miles on the Roman Ermine Way leading from Cirencester (*Corinium*) to Speen (*Spinæ*), near Newbury. Then one goes to the left to H i g h w o r t h , where the route turns due north and meets the Thames again at

LECHLADE

The Lech and the Coln meet the Thames at the town, and the united streams suddenly assume an air of dignity, having reached a width of some 20 yards and a depth sufficient for vessels of 80 tons. Across the 'stripling Thames' there stands the first stone bridge, whose core is the medieval structure built somewhere about the beginning of the thirteenth century, or possibly earlier, in the days when bridge-building was regarded as a pious enterprise. In its prosperous days Lechlade sent great quantities of cheese down the river to London. The church is mainly Perpendicular, dating, according to Bigland, from about 1470.

Continuing northwards, the road climbs among the eastern slopes of the Cotswolds, and reaches picturesque old Burford (see p. 276). The next place to the north is

SHIPTON-UNDER-WYCHWOOD,

an interesting and attractive old village on the east side of Wychwood Forest. The spacious church is chiefly an Early English building, with alterations in Perpendicular times, and no indications at all of Decorated work. The spire, like that of Witney, is Early English, while the font and stone pulpit are Perpendicular. Adding immensely to the picturesqueness of the church, there is on the east side a group of timeworn buildings of ecclesiastical origin dating back to the time when Shipton was a prebend of Salisbury Cathedral. One should also notice the sixteenth-century work of the Crown Inn, standing near the centre of the village.

Going on towards Chipping Norton, one comes after two miles to some tumuli, called Lyneham Barrows, and not far beyond these there is a standing stone about 6 feet high.

CHIPPING NORTON,

another of the towns with the distinctive term revealing an old-time importance as a market, is the highest town in Oxfordshire, being nearly 700 feet above the sea. The place consists chiefly of one long and picturesque street, and what there is to tell of its history is almost exclusively in relation to its cloth manufactures, its breweries, or its glove factories. The conspicuous church is mainly Decorated and Perpendicular, with the tower above the obviously Early English work, rebuilt in 1825.

There is a story of Bishop Juxon having been the cause of a complaint to Cromwell because once, when the prelate was hunting, the hare, closely followed by the hounds, ran through the churchyard. The Protector's reply, however, took the form of a question: 'Do you think the Bishop prevailed on the hare to run through the churchyard?'

Nothing whatever is left of the castle formerly standing to the east of the church, but the almshouses, built in 1640, still survive.

Chipping Norton is left by the road to Evesham, and a run of eight miles brings one into the long, wide street of Moreton-in-the-Marsh, a little market town without any exceptional features needing special reference here. The next place, however, is Bourton-on-the-Hill, a lovely village, with its old cottages perched either above or below the steeply ascending road. Of the gardens gaily decked with flowers one could write many pages; but not far off is Broadway, one of those delightful villages of the always lovely Cotswolds, full of pleasing stone architecture, in spite of the evil tendencies which have marred, if not destroyed, the beauty of so many pleasant old-world haunts. At the picturesque Lygon Arms, at the lower end of the village, Charles I. is said to have stayed on more than one occasion, and near it is a house called the 'Abbot's Grange,' where Mr. Millet, the artist, has his studio. This was the manor-house of the Abbots of Pershore, a Benedictine abbey possessing much property at Broadway. There is a large hall open to the roof, a solar, and a small chapel chiefly dating from Decorated times. The old church of Broadway, dedicated to St. Eadburgh, is three-quarters of a mile away, in the Snowshill Valley. It contains a plain Norman font, a painted wooden pulpit of the fourteenth century, and some good brasses. From the tower, built in 1797, above the village one can see a wide panoramic view over the beautiful rounded hills, broken up by belts of beech and larch.

If there is no need to economize time, it would certainly be unwise to pass so near the picturesque old town of Chipping Camden without having a peep at its fine market hall, its church, and beautiful array of stone-built houses. After this the hills are left behind, and Evesham, on the river which flows past Shakespeare's birthplace, is reached.

EVESHAM

This picturesque little town owed its importance to the great Benedictine abbey, which up to the Dissolution had, according to Grose, such a great assemblage of religious buildings that its equal was not to be found out of Oxford and Cambridge. Of these, however, there remain to-day only the beautiful Perpendicular bell-tower, the almonry, the mutilated Norman gatehouse, and the archway leading to the chapter-house, now the entrance to allotments. Many houses in the town are built of stones from the destroyed abbey. The Booth Hall, in the market-place, is a charming old building, and in the High Street and in Bridge Street there are many fine old houses.

The two churches of Evesham stand in one churchyard, and both were founded by the monks of the abbey as secular chapels for the town. The Church of St. Lawrence was practically rebuilt a century ago, but All Saints, which existed in 1223, has an Early English north aisle and chancel, and examples of the succeeding periods in the other parts of the building. The Battle of Evesham was fought on August 4, 1265, rather less than a mile from the town, on high ground to the north, marked by an obelisk. Simon de

Montfort, who held Henry III. prisoner, was crushingly defeated by Prince Edward, and both he and his son Henry were killed, their bodies being buried in Evesham Abbey Church before the high-altar.

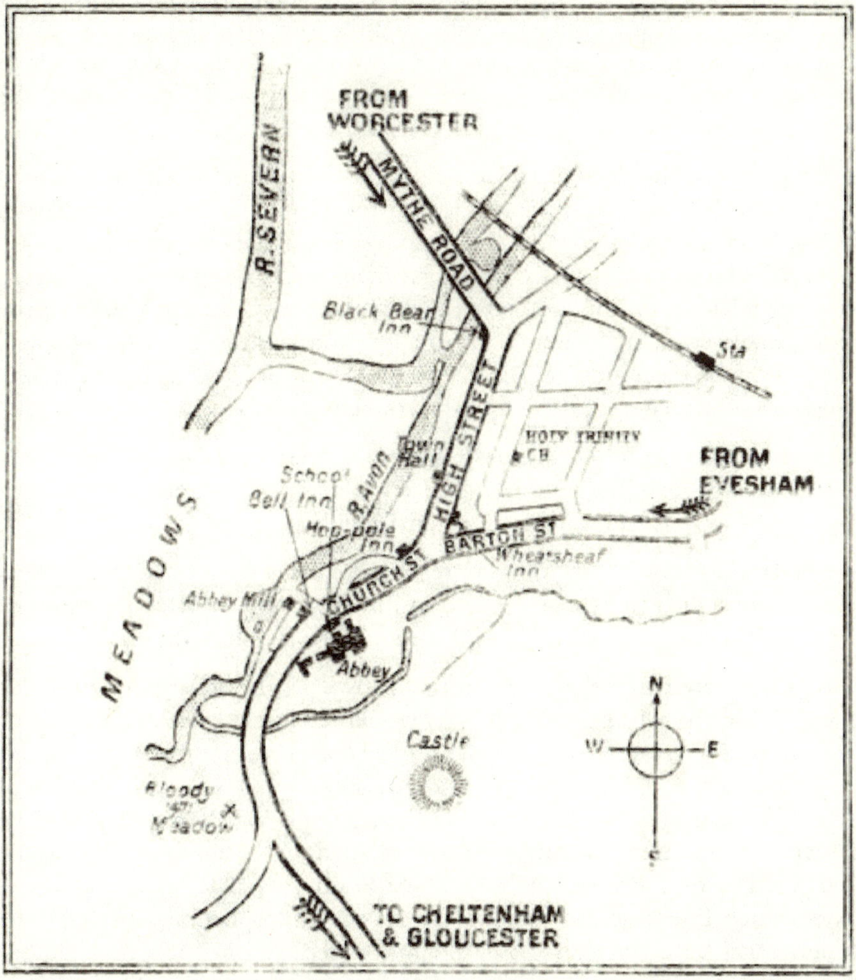

TOWN PLAN NO. 10—TEWKESBURY.

TEWKESBURY

is the last place passed through on this extensive loop, and going in this direction one finds the best wine reserved to the last, for this exceptionally picturesque old town, with its solemn abbey church, surrounded by tall ancient trees, and the sweet green meadows, where Severn and Avon are only separated by a belt of level greensward, is one of those places that have a way of fixing themselves in the memory, even if one has never read Miss Mulock's 'John Halifax, Gentleman.' If one has done so, and remembers the descriptions of 'Norton Bury,' the old town will never be forgotten. One can hardly think of Tewkesbury without the dominating presence of its great Norman abbey church, but even without it the long street contains so many delightful sixteenth-century houses, each possessing individual charms, that the town would still make an irresistible appeal to all for whom the architecture of the vanished centuries has some message.

The founder of the present abbey was Robert FitzHamon, who was related to William the Conqueror, and received the Honour of Gloucester from Rufus. Having decided to rebuild the modest Saxon abbey, FitzHamon soon removed all traces of the early buildings when, in 1102, the work was begun. Five years later the founder died of a wound received during a siege of the impregnable castle of Falaise in Normandy, and was buried in the chapter-house. The consecration took place in 1123, and in 1178 a fire occurred, which was fortunately restricted to the conventual buildings.

Gilbert de Clare, one of the barons who had signed Magna Charta, was buried in the abbey, and after him, for two and a half centuries, every one of his successors was laid to rest in the same building.

When Tewkesbury Abbey was suppressed, the nave, which had always been secular, continued to be a possession of the town, and the other portions of the great fabric were bought from the Crown for the sum of £453.

It is often stated that the great Norman tower is the most perfect in this country, but the people of St. Albans would no doubt question this claim. The tall wooden spire, covered with lead, fell during service on Easter Sunday in 1559, and was never replaced. Inside the church one sees little that is not pure Norman, and for solemnity and vast, imposing dignity it would be difficult to find any building able to overshadow Tewkesbury. It may be compared with Durham, Selby, and Christchurch. The west end has a wonderfully fine recessed window of immense proportions. In 1661 the window was blown in during a gale, and was replaced in 1686. Surely those who were attached to the Commonwealth must have thought there was something significant in this parallel to the rending of the veil of the Temple, for the seventeenth century was a superstitious age.

The Battle of Tewkesbury, one of the decisive encounters of the Wars of the Roses, was fought, in 1471, on the south side of the town (its position is shown in the accompanying plan). Edward IV. crushingly defeated the Lancastrians under Edward, the youthful Prince of Wales, whose army fought with Tewkesbury in their rear. The defeated army took refuge in the town, and the slaughter continued in the abbey church in hideous fashion, until the abbot, bearing in his hands the consecrated elements, brought the fighting to a close. Prince Edward, who had been struck in the mouth by the gauntleted hand of the King, was killed in a house in Church Street.

With the rooks cawing high overhead in the tree-tops, and a sweet solemnity pervading the whole abbey precincts, it is almost impossible to picture the ghastly scene of civil war which, four and a half centuries ago, soaked the meadows in human blood and turned the noble church into a shambles. For a month no services were held in the building while every blood-stain was removed.

On the way back to Gloucester one could make a very profitable detour of a few miles to Deerhurst Priory, a highly interesting pre-Norman building, until recently used as part of a farm, but lately restored in a most efficient manner.

SECTION X
(TRUNK ROUTE)

GLOUCESTER TO OXFORD, 50 MILES

DISTANCES ALONG THE ROUTE

Miles.		
Gloucester to Cheltenham	8	¾
Cheltenham to Andoversford	6	
Andoversford to Northleach	7	
Northleach to Burford	9	
Burford to Witney	7	½
Witney to Eynsham	5	¾
Eynsham to Oxford	6	

NOTES FOR DRIVERS

Gloucester to Cheltenham.—Level; excellent surface.

There are no hills of any importance all the way to Oxford, but the surface is rather rough between **Andoversford** and **Burford**. The road falls nearly all the way from **Northleach to Oxford**.

PLACES OF INTEREST ON THE ROUTE

Cheltenham.—A watering-place dating from the eighteenth century. Spa; promenades; St. Mary's Church, Decorated.

Northleach.—Picturesque Cotswold village-town. Perpendicular church, with famous brasses of wool-merchants and remarkably fine porch.

Burford.—A very interesting and picturesque old town; several old houses; market hall; church, large and irregular, Norman, Early English, and Perpendicular; Priory ruins.

Asthall Barrow.—A prominent prehistoric mound.

Witney.—A pleasant and unusually charming old town, famous for blankets. Church very picturesque, chiefly Early English; old market house.

Eynsham.—A quaint old village with old market house, church, and picturesque houses. Red Lion Inn with quaint sign.

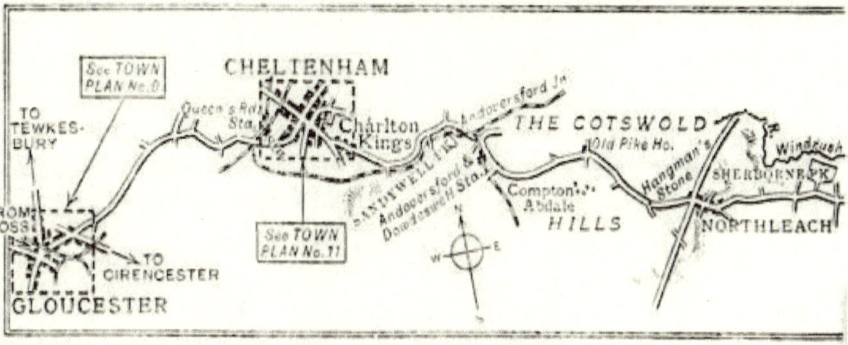

(TRUNK) No. 10. GLOUCESTER TO OXFORD.

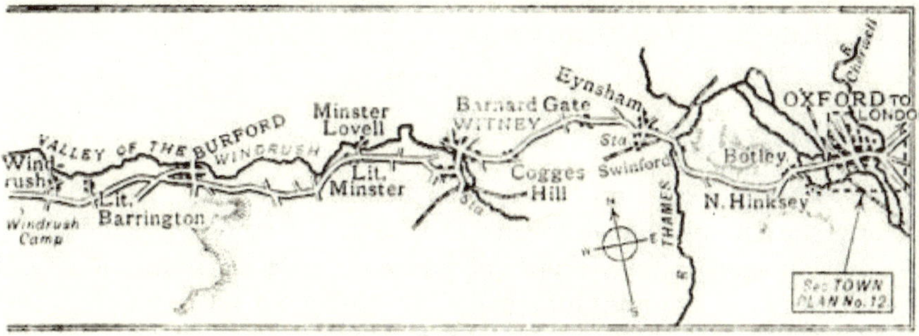

(TRUNK) No. 10. GLOUCESTER TO OXFORD.

At W o t t o n S t . M a r y , Churchdown Hill is a prominent feature on the right. Some picturesque old cottages stand beside the road, while the general aspect of the country is pastoral, broken up by large orchards, a delightful feature of the county. The road rises slightly as Cheltenham is approached.

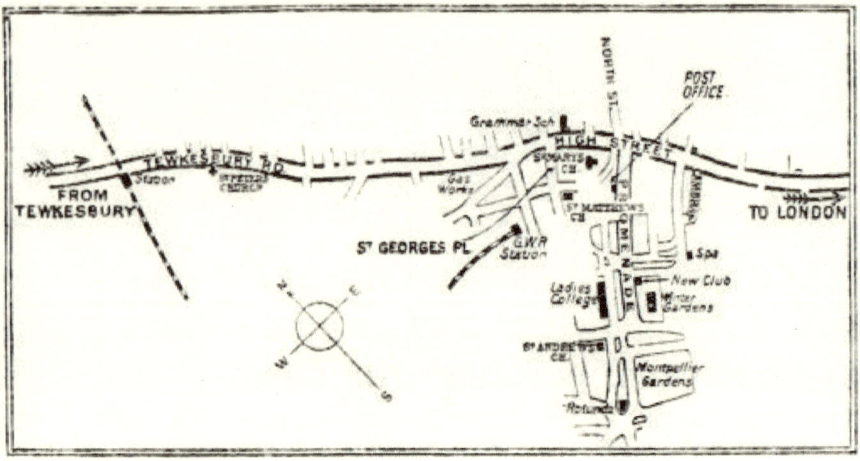

TOWN PLAN NO. 11—CHELTENHAM.

CHELTENHAM

Cheltenham stands close to the steep, north-west face of the Cotswold Hills, and until the springs were discovered in 1716 it was but a struggling hamlet. It is now an aggregation of imposing squares, crescents, promenades, and villas, interspersed with beautiful parks. As may be expected, there are few antiquities to be found in a town of such mushroom growth, the only exception being the Parish Church of St. Màry, standing just off the High Street. The prevailing style of the building is early Decorated, and it contains a piscina believed to be one of the largest and most perfect in England. To those interested in modern architecture the Church of St. Stephen may be mentioned, but All Saints', the parish church of Pittville, is the best modern expression of architectural ideals in Cheltenham, although the Roman Catholic Church of St. Gregory is a formidable rival. The public buildings are on a level with the importance of the town. The merits and uses of the chalybeate and other waters are easily discovered locally, and no one who remembers the oft-repeated epitaph of the individual who with three daughters 'died from drinking the Cheltenham waters' should be prejudiced against their good properties, which for certain ailments are not to be despised. Cheltenham is a famous educational centre for girls, and Gloucestershire, as a whole, has been in the van in educational matters from quite early times.

Cheltenham is the 'Coltham' in 'John Halifax, Gentleman,' where John and Phineas saw Mrs. Siddons act.

The road to Oxford from Cheltenham crosses the beautiful Cotswolds, climbing up to 800 feet at the Puesdown Inn. From this point there are wide expanses visible in nearly every direction; but such views do not give one the real charm of the Cotswolds. To become intimate with the exquisite valleys and secluded upland villages, one must be in a mood to potter and loiter, and be content to desert the car at intervals in order to plunge into some beautiful beech-wood, falling steeply down a declivity, and revealing glimpses between the tall smooth trunks of the Vale of Severn, or some sleepy hollow wherein a silver-grey village nestles. The beautiful architecture of the Cotswolds, in conjunction with its lovely scenery, is a joy to all who know these oolite hills. Cottages, farms, mills, and manor-houses, all with steep roofs of grey stone like the walls, stately gables, mullioned windows, and picturesque chimneys, are all one can desire.

Even if there is no time to wander from the direct road, one cannot avoid seeing an exceedingly pleasing little Cotswold town. This is

NORTHLEACH,

a place of some importance when the woollen industry of these hills was flourishing. There is a subtle charm in the greyness of the old houses, relieved by the dark green of yew and the lighter tones of deciduous trees and grass banks here and there. The quaint little shops add other touches of colour, and wherever one turns there are pictures of simple Cotswold life, not much altered by the rapid changes of recent years. The old fellow standing meditatively by the churchyard gate may talk of the great changes since his youth, when the cloth industry had not ebbed away from the hills, but to outward appearances Northleach is, one suspects, little altered since the days of our great-grandparents, if, indeed, anything has materially changed the town since the beautiful Perpendicular church was put up. The date of its building was about the year 1489, when Cotswold wool was one of the chief industries of England. One may admire the embattled spire and the graceful delicacy of the whole building, but it is by its porch that one remembers Northleach Church. It is illustrated here; but, good as the drawing is, it does not do justice to the wonderful beauty of that noble piece of Perpendicular craftsmanship surmounted by its parvise.

On the floor of the nave are a series of brasses to the memory of some of the most successful of the wool-merchants of the town. They belong to the fifteenth century, and are exceptionally fine examples of brasses of the period, giving the details of costume with the greatest faithfulness. It is pleasant to find that the wealthy men of the Cotswold wool industry seem to have devoted their surplus riches to such public works as schools, almshouses, and churches.

At Northleach the Roman Foss Way is crossed coming from Cirencester in a north-easterly direction.

A few miles beyond Northleach, S h e r b o r n e P a r k, the residence of Lord Sherborne, is passed on the left. It is a dignified house, situated in open country, many portions of which are well wooded.

From this point all the way to Witney the road falls steadily, with the shallow, but always pleasing, valley of the Windrush just below on the left. This pretty stream coming out of the heart of the Cotswolds is one of the chief feeders of the Thames, which it meets a dozen miles above Oxford. Actually on the road there are no villages except Little Minster between Northleach and Witney, but just below the highway, on the banks of the little river, there are several. The first three—Windrush and Great and Little Barrington—are in Gloucestershire, and the rest are in Oxfordshire. It is tempting to describe all these places, but one must be content with pointing out the particular charm of

BURFORD,

one of the most delightful of the old-world towns of the county. There is a town hall, probably of the fifteenth century, and adjoining it are some of the best of the old houses in the town. Close to the stream stands the splendid cruciform church, with its tower and west door dating back to the Norman period. In Early English times nearly the whole building appears to have been changed into the Gothic style, and another transformation took place in the fifteenth century, when the Perpendicular phase had set in. Owing to the Sylvester aisle and several chapels, the church is of curious shape, and this helps to give that indescribable atmosphere of pre-Reformation days entirely vanished from so many old churches in this country.

Both the school and the almshouses are old foundations, and the Priory, now a partial ruin, although preserving no ecclesiastical remains, is a picturesque Elizabethan building to some extent rebuilt in 1808.

A mile or two beyond Burford one passes Asthall Barrow on the right-hand side of the road, and only a few yards away across a field. It is a prehistoric mound of earth, now kept in position by a circular retaining wall of stone, thus preventing degradation. The trees surmounting it form a prominent landmark. About three miles farther on is the fine old manor-house of M i n s t e r L o v e l l, about a mile to the left, on the Windrush.

WITNEY

Soon after turning to the right the road enters the main street of picturesque old Witney at right angles. Extending away some distance to the right is the pleasant elongated belt of green, giving much charm and distinction to the place, and at the end of the grassy perspective, rising in stately dignity from old trees, appears the tower and spire of the cruciform church. This is one of those peculiarly fascinating buildings one finds it hard to leave. It is mainly an Early English church, but there are features of other periods, and among them a Decorated window on the north side, which is the finest in the whole county. The spire is an Early English masterpiece. In the middle of the little town stands the quaint Butter Cross, dated 1683. On the west side of the green is the Grammar School (1663), with an avenue of elms.

The blanket industry is still in existence, for in spite of modern competition the little place holds its own on account of some particular benefit the wool derives from the water of the neighbourhood.

EYNSHAM

is the last village passed on the way to Oxford. It is a sleepy and picturesque little place with a small market hall, the shaft of a fifteenth-century cross, and an inn-sign of the drollest order. This sign hangs outside the Red Lion, and the King of Beasts is painted on one side, but the draughtsman had difficulty in accommodating the tail, and he solved it by the original plan of painting the caudal appendage on the opposite face of the sign!

Just below Eynsham the road crosses the Thames at Swinford Bridge, where the beautiful hanging woods of Wytham Hill are on the left, and a couple of miles farther on the spires and towers of Oxford are in sight.

THE CHURCH PORCH AT NORTHLEACH.
A rare example of the stateliness of Perpendicular architecture in a village church.

LOOP No. 8

OXFORD TO STRATFORD-ON-AVON, COVENTRY, BANBURY, AND OXFORD, 110 MILES

DISTANCES ALONG THE ROUTE

	Miles.	
Oxford to Woodstock	8	
Woodstock to Enstone	6	¾
Enstone to Long Compton	8	
Long Compton to Shipstone-on-Stour	5	¾
Shipstone-on-Stour to Stratford-on-Avon	10	½
Stratford-on-Avon to Leamington	10	½
Leamington to Warwick	2	¼
Warwick to Kenilworth	4	¾
Kenilworth to Coventry	5	¾
Coventry to Princethorpe	7	
Princethorpe to Southam	6	
Southam to Fenny Compton	5	½
Fenny Compton to Banbury	8	¼
Banbury to Deddington	6	
Deddington to Sturdy's Castle Inn	7	¾
Sturdy's Castle Inn to Kidlington	2	
Kidlington to Oxford, Carfax	5	¼

NOTES FOR DRIVERS

Oxford to Stratford.—Splendid surface; steep drop down to Long Compton.

Stratford to Coventry.—Surface on the whole excellent; not so good near Stratford.

Coventry to Banbury.—An excellent road, but a few rather steep hills are encountered.

Banbury to Oxford.—Excellent.

PLACES OF INTEREST ON THE ROUTE

Woodstock.—A little town, with a church containing several styles of architecture; Blenheim, the residence of the Dukes of Marlborough; the Column of Victory.

Long Compton.—The Rollright Stones, a prehistoric circle of importance.

Stratford-on-Avon.—Shakespeare's birthplace; the memorial; the church and its interesting monuments; New Place, the residence of the poet; the Grammar School; Guild Chapel; and Anne Hathaway's Cottage, 1 mile west.

Warwick.—A picturesque town, famous for its castle; St. Mary's Church and the Beauchamp Chapel and monuments; Lord Leycester's Hospital; the West Gate and various old houses.

Leamington.—A beautiful spa; the Jephson Gardens.

Guy's Cliffe.—An exquisitely-situated country house.

Kenilworth.—A little town, containing half-timbered houses; the ruins of the famous castle; the church, chiefly Decorated; the remains of the Priory.

Coventry.—A fairly large town; St. Michael's, an exceedingly fine parish church; Holy Trinity Church; St. Mary's Hall, a fourteenth-century guild-hall; St. John's Church; the Bablake Hospital; Peeping Tom; Ford's Hospital.

Long Itchington.—Interesting fourteenth-century church.

Southam.—A town without much interest.

Banbury.—A little Oxfordshire town, famed for its cross and its cakes; but the cross is modern, and so is the church.

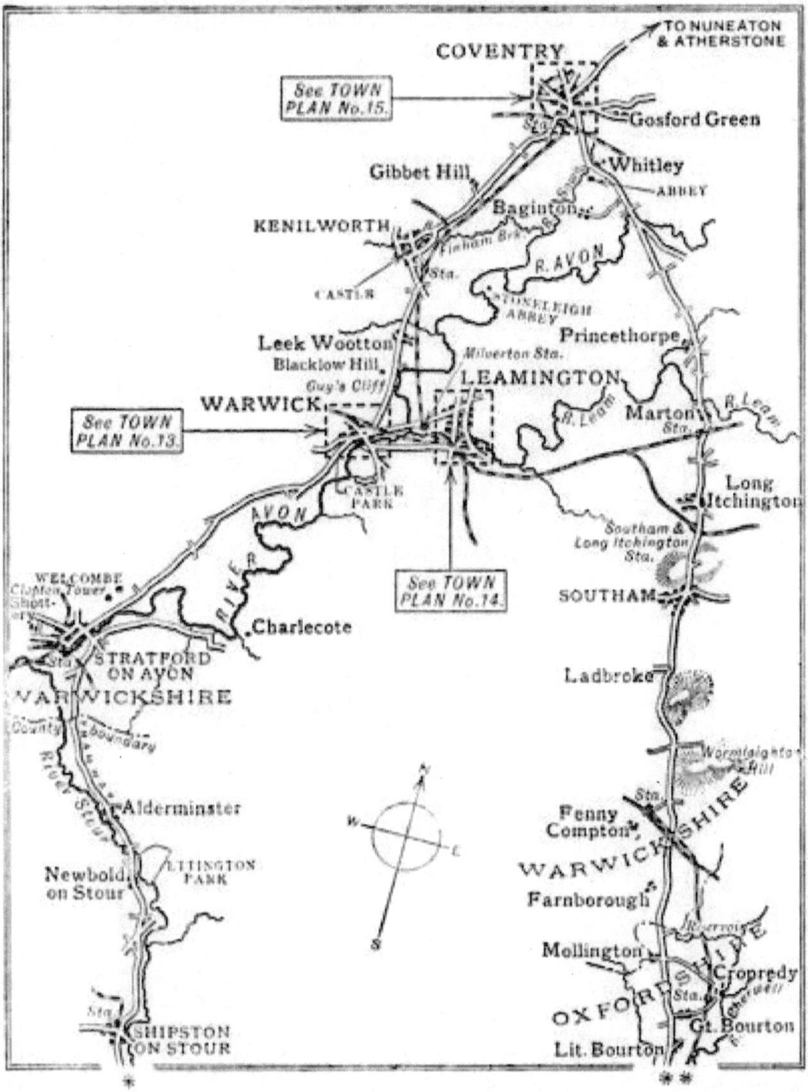
TO NUNEATON & ATHERSTONE
COVENTRY
See TOWN PLAN No.15.
Gosford Green
Whitley
Gibbet Hill
Baginton
KENILWORTH
R. AVON
Sta.
CASTLE
STONELEIGH ABBEY
Princethorpe
Leek Wootton
Blacklow Hill
Milverton Sta.
Guy's Cliff
LEAMINGTON
WARWICK
See TOWN PLAN No.13.
R. Leam
Marton
Sta.
R. Leam
CASTLE PARK
AVON
Long Itchington
Southam & Long Itchington Sta.
WELCOMBE
Clopton Tower
RIVER
See TOWN PLAN No.14.
SOUTHAM
Charlecote
STRATFORD ON AVON
WARWICKSHIRE
Ladbroke
County Boundary
River Stour
Wormleighton Hill
Alderminster
Fenny Compton
WARWICKSHIRE
Newbold on Stour
ETTINGTON PARK
Farnborough
Mollington
Cropredy
OXFORDSHIRE
Sta.
SHIPSTON ON STOUR
Gt. Bourton
Lit. Bourton
N
W
E
S

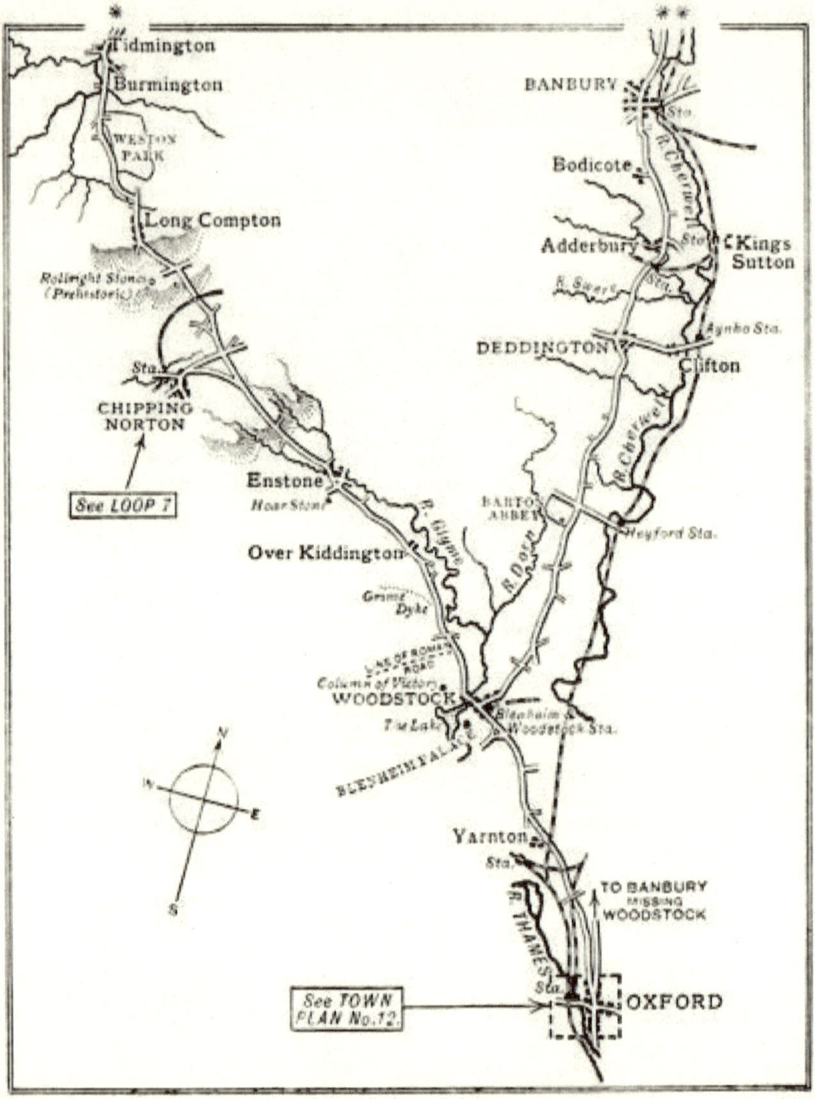

LOOP 8. OXFORD TO COVENTRY.

There are two main roads running to Woodstock from Oxford, lying parallel to each other; the western one should be selected. It passes through a well-wooded country, part of the valleys of the Thames and Evenlode rivers. Upon reaching Woodstock, B l e n h e i m P a l a c e claims attention, with the entrance to the park lying upon the left. The house was built at the public expense in 1715 as a national recognition of the services of the Duke of Marlborough. It was designed by Vanbrugh, and is of a heavy Renaissance character. The interior decorations and the treasures preserved in it are of an exceedingly interesting nature. (*It is open to the public every day, except Saturdays and Sundays, between 11 and 1, and the gardens from 11 to 2. Tickets 1s. each.*) The park contains the site of the old Manor-house of Woodstock, which is supposed to have stood upon the foundations of a Roman villa; it was a royal residence of the Saxon kings. Here Alfred the Great translated Boethius, and King Ethelred published his code of laws. Woodstock was the scene of the courtship of Henry II. and Rosamund Clifford, whose birthplace was Clifford Castle (see p. 175). Queen Elizabeth was a prisoner for a time in the old manor-house, and it endured a siege from the Parliamentarians, finally disappearing in 1723.

WOODSTOCK

This little town sprang into existence solely in consequence of the proximity of the royal seat. The Church of St. Mary Magdalene is of Norman date, but much restoration has taken place. The south aisle is Early English, and contains part of a Norman doorway. The chancel and north aisle are Decorated, while the west porch and west tower are Perpendicular. There are many monuments of interest in the church.

Soon after leaving Woodstock the Column of Victory is prominent on the left, where the ancient course of the Akeman Street, coming from Cirencester, is crossed, and shortly afterwards Grim's Dyke occurs, one of the many Grim's Dykes that are found in England.

Near Enstone is a cromlech, called the 'Hoarstone,' and soon afterwards a turning to the left leads to

CHIPPING NORTON

This is a quiet little town, devoted to the manufacture of woollen goods, and especially horse-cloths. The 'Chipping' is derived from the same root as 'Chepe,' a market. In the church the chief objects of interest are some fourteenth-century brasses, which, however, suffered very much in a restoration some forty years since, when they were wrenched from their matrices and thrown into the parvise. Of the castle which once stood here nothing remains.

Between Chipping Norton and Long Compton, at Great Rollright, are the well-known Rollright Stones, consisting of a prehistoric circle of standing stones and a cromlech. They are sixty in number, and lie about 500 yards to the left of the main road. After passing the stiff descent into Long Compton, a good surface is found to Shipstone-on-Stour, although the road is second class; but beyond that town a first-class road lies up the valley of the Stour to Stratford-on-Avon. At Alderminster tram-lines commence, which reach to Stratford, and a short distance beyond, Atherstone-on-Stour is passed, where formerly stood a monastery of mendicant friars. The scenery, meanwhile, has been gradually assuming the characteristics which distinguish the beautiful county of Warwick—luxurious hedgerows, gently-flowing streams, red loam in the fields contrasting with the varying shades of green. The half-timbered houses and cottages introduce another pleasant feature into the landscape.

STRATFORD-ON-AVON

This far-famed country town on the banks of the Avon presents a general appearance of prosperity, the well-built houses, wide streets, and prevailing aspect of cleanliness giving this impression. Everything in the town, however, lapses into insignificance in face of the paramount interest attaching to the town as the birthplace of Shakespeare. Whether the 'Bard of Avon' was nothing more than an Elizabethan play-actor or the author of the plays now so widely attributed to the great scholar and statesman, Francis Bacon, is a question which now cools the spirit of devotion of many a pilgrim; but however keen a Baconian may be the visitor to Stratford, he cannot fail to appreciate the charm of the carefully-restored Elizabethan houses associated with Shakespeare.

Shakespeare's Birthplace is in Henley Street, a half-timbered, unpretentious house of two rooms and a kitchen on the ground-floor, with the room overhead in which he was born. The adjoining cottage has been converted into a museum, in which documents and relics bearing in a direct or remote manner with the poet—and some, it must be confessed, are very remote—are preserved. The birthplace was in possession of the members of the family for two centuries after the death of Shakespeare in 1616; in 1847 it was purchased by subscription for £3,000 and carefully restored. (*Admission 1s.—6d. for the birthroom and 6d. for the museum.*)

The Town Hall is in the High Street; on the front is a statue of Shakespeare, presented by Garrick.

New Place stood close by, but of the house occupied by the poet during the last nineteen years of his life there is nothing left but the site. In it lived Dr. Hall, who married Shakespeare's daughter Susannah. The house was pulled down in 1702 by Sir John Clopton, and the new building on its site, together with the famous mulberry-tree, were destroyed by the Rev. Francis Gastrell in 1759, 'because he was pestered by visitors'! In 1861 the site of New Place and its gardens were purchased by public subscription. A Shakespeare Library and Museum have been established there, *open daily except Saturday and Sunday; admission 6d. On Saturday the Gardens are free.*

STRATFORD-ON-AVON.
Holy Trinity Church contains the tomb of Shakespeare.

At the opposite corner, Chapel Lane, stands the Grammar School, founded in 1553, where the poet is reputed to have been educated. It is a delightful old timber-framed house standing near the Guild Chapel, a Perpendicular building which is conspicuous in the High Street.

The Shakespeare Memorial Theatre occupies a pleasant position on the banks of the Avon. The old theatre was demolished in 1872, and the present building erected at a cost of £30,000.

The Parish Church, of Early English and Perpendicular architecture, is a fine cruciform building standing on the site of an early Saxon monastery. In Edward III.'s reign John de Stratford rebuilt the south aisle and erected a chantry for priests. In 1351 Ralph de Stratford built a chapel for the latter, now known as the College. The beautiful choir dates from the time of Dean Balshall (1465). Shakespeare's monument is on the left side of the chancel; the door there formerly led to the charnel-house, and the grave is near the monument under a flat stone, upon which is the oft-quoted verse said to have been written by Shakespeare. Between this spot and the north wall is buried his widow, who died in 1623, while those of relatives lie near, such as Susannah, the eldest daughter, and her husband, Dr. Hall, and Thomas Nashe, who married Shakespeare's only granddaughter. (*Admission to the church 6d.*)

Anne Hathaway's Cottage is at Shottery, a mile west of Stratford, divided since the poet's time into three tenements. The room where Anne was born is shown.

Charlecote Park lies about four miles north-east of Stratford. It is famous for its hall, erected in 1547 by Sir Thomas Lucy upon the capital E plan, and was visited by Queen Elizabeth. Here also is the reputed site of Shakespeare's deer-shooting escapades.

The main road to Warwick lies through a beautifully-wooded country, rich in pleasant views of hill and dale. Clopton Tower is on the left shortly after leaving.

The tower of Barford Church can be seen two miles off to the right of the main road; it was rebuilt in the last century, except the tower, which retains the marks of Cromwellian cannon-balls.

Sherbourne is near at hand. The church is modern, and of fine design.

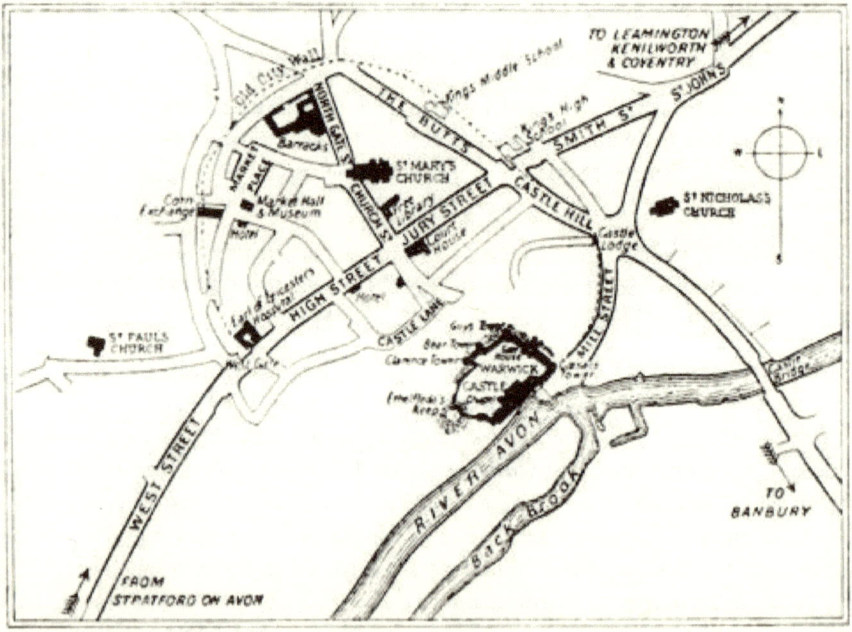

TOWN PLAN NO. 13—WARWICK.

WARWICK

It has been asserted that the history of Warwick is the history of England, and certain it is that the ancient town has been involved in the majority of the great events which have helped to make the national record. In those stirring events W a r w i c k C a s t l e has played no mean part, and is still the glory of the town and county. It is undoubtedly the most magnificent of the ancient feudal mansions still used as a residence, and its grand position upon a crag overlooking the Avon has accentuated its imposing grandeur in no mean degree. Its chief features are Cæsar's Tower and Guy's Tower, of the fourteenth century, and the Gateway Tower in the centre. The residential apartments and the Great Hall suffered in the fire of 1871, but have been rebuilt. Both the castle and the contents teem with interest. (*Open to visitors as a rule; no fixed fee. Tickets obtained at small cottage opposite Castle Lodge, Castle Hill.*)

S t. M a r y ' s C h u r c h is one of the most interesting ecclesiastical buildings in the country. A Saxon church stood upon the site, and a later building was made collegiate by Earl Roger de Newburgh. It was granted to the town as a parish church at the Dissolution. The central object of interest is the famous Beauchamp Chapel, 1443 to 1464, one of the best examples extant of Perpendicular architecture bordering upon the Tudor, and showing occasionally traces of incipient Renaissance. Richard Beauchamp, Earl of Warwick, Regent of France, and guardian of Edward VI., lies buried here, and his effigy in bronze, the finest in existence of that nature, lies in the centre of the chapel. Against the north wall is the magnificent monument of the famous Robert Dudley, Earl of Leicester—splendid in life and sumptuous in death. Two small ante-chapels are seen—one is probably a chantry. In the chancel lie Thomas Beauchamp, Earl of Warwick, and his second Countess, both of whom died in 1370; their effigies of white marble, with many 'weepers' round the pedestal, are of great interest.

L o r d L e y c e s t e r ' s H o s p i t a l.—There are but few places in England where such a picturesque and impressive grouping of old timbered houses may be seen; antique gables and eaves, richly-carved beams and mysterious recesses; overhanging stories and twisted chimneys, with an old gateway and a church tower thrown in—it forms a gem of which any city might be proud. The Hospital was originally a hall of the Guilds; in 1571 the Earl founded it for the reception of twelve poor men, who still wear the bear and ragged staff as a cognizance. Many half-timbered houses and quaint old-world nooks remain in Warwick to delight the eye of the artist and the antiquary, especially near the castle.

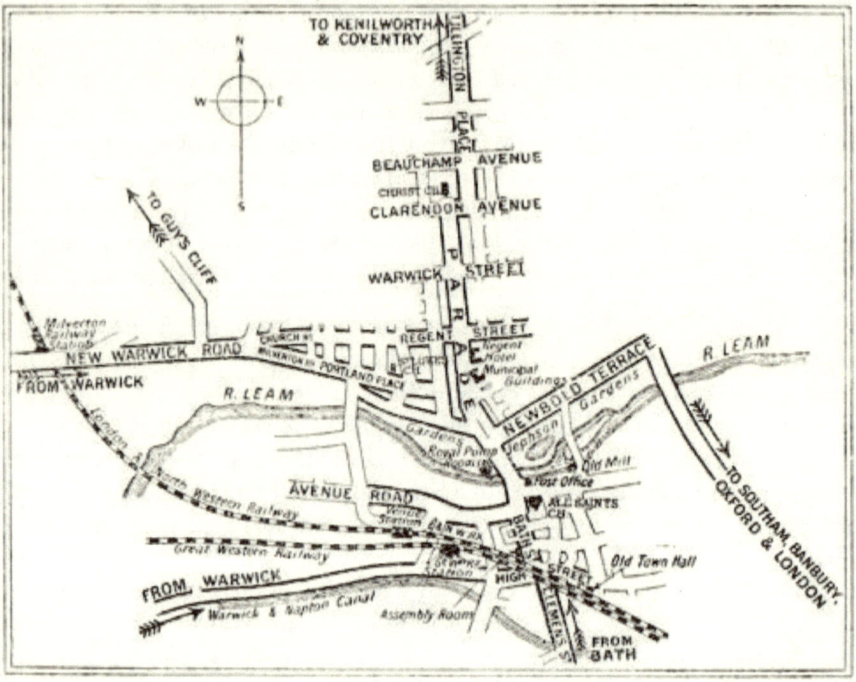

TOWN PLAN NO. 14—LEAMINGTON.

LEAMINGTON

A little over a mile separates Warwick from the Royal Leamington Spa, a beautiful garden city, which has sprung into existence by reason of the discovery of the efficacy possessed by the mineral waters in 1784. Until that period it was a small village called Leamington Priors. The chief springs are saline and sulphuretted saline.

The J e p h s o n   G a r d e n s are beautifully placed on the north bank of the River Leam, and form one of the chief centres of attraction, and the Royal Pump Room Gardens face the river on the other side of the bridge. As might be expected from such a modern town, there are no objects of antiquity to describe. Returning to Warwick, the road to Guy's Cliff is taken, running due north, and the entrance-lodge occurs in about a mile. A fine view of the house is obtained from this point on looking up the avenue of majestic firs; it was built in 1822, succeeding a small country mansion, and is in the possession of Lord Algernon Percy. Situated upon a cliff with a wide part of the river beneath, it forms a singularly beautiful picture. (*It is only shown to visitors when the family is absent.*)

T h e C h a p e l adjoins the mansion on the east, and contains a figure of Guy, Earl of Warwick, dating from the fourteenth century. Guy's Lane is near the chapel.

T h e M i l l was built in 1821, and occupies the site of one dating as far back as Saxon times.

Guy of Warwick is a mythical personage, and the romance mentioning his deeds dates from the thirteenth century. In the fifteenth century, when the age of chivalry and romance was at its zenith, Guy was treated in the same manner as King Arthur, and all kinds of doughty deeds were attributed to him by the romancers.

B l a c k l o w H i l l stands half a mile farther on to the left of the road. It is surmounted by a cross, erected in 1821 to commemorate the execution in 1312 of Piers Gaveston. At Gloucester, the tomb of Edward II., who, like his favourite, came to a tragic end, has been mentioned.

KENILWORTH

T h e C a s t l e is the centre of attraction, although there are some good examples of half-timbered cottages to be seen in the long street of the little town. The fortress was in ancient times one of the strongest in England, as it afforded accommodation for a large garrison, and by reason of the lake and broad moats filled with water—now disappeared—it was almost impregnable. Numerous roads converged towards it as the centre of England, and for many years it was a royal residence. T h e K e e p was built about 1170, and is a splendid example of military architecture of the late Norman period. It is square, with a projecting rectangle, and turrets at the corners. The walls at the base are 14 feet thick. T h e G a r d e n , celebrated in Scott's novel, lay upon the north side of the keep. South of the keep occur Leicester's Buildings, with fourteenth-century kitchens and other offices between. By the side of the Great Hall was the Strong Tower, called Mervyn's Tower by Scott. Mortimer's Tower is isolated to the south-east; the cutting through the great dam which restrained the waters of the lake occurred here. The tilt-yard lay upon the top of the dam. Beyond the Great Lake was the C h a s e , and the circuit of the castle, manor, parks and other lands, was about twenty miles. Many historical names are associated with Kenilworth—the Clintons, Simon de Montfort, John of Gaunt, and Robert Dudley, who entertained Queen Elizabeth for seventeen days, and spent a fortune in doing so. The castle was dismantled and the lake drained in the time of the Commonwealth.

FORD'S HOSPITAL, COVENTRY.
A late fifteenth century almshouse enriched with much elaborate carving.

The Church lies east of the castle. The tower and nave are of Decorated work, but a Norman doorway has been inserted in the west side of the tower, taken, probably, from the Priory.

The Priory stood close to the church; it was founded about 1122 by Geoffrey de Clinton, and richly endowed. The remains of a gatehouse may be seen, and also some exposed foundations of the walls of the church.

On leaving Kenilworth for Coventry a stretch of moorland extends upon the right hand, on which are two mounds with the usual fosses around the summits, denoting British hill-forts. Beyond this the road begins to assume that characteristic which has made the way from Kenilworth to Coventry renowned as 'one of the two finest roads in England'—needless to say, the other road is from Coventry to Kenilworth—a magnificent avenue with broad strips of greensward lying on either side, and glimpses of splendid Warwickshire scenery between the boles, justify the foregoing descriptions.

Two miles from Kenilworth is Gibbet Hill, the erection upon which has now gone, but was used last in 1765 for the execution of two murderers. Crossing Stivichall Common, with its triple array of oak-trees on either side the road, the Coventry Grammar School buildings are passed upon the left, and the 'City of the Three Spires' is entered.

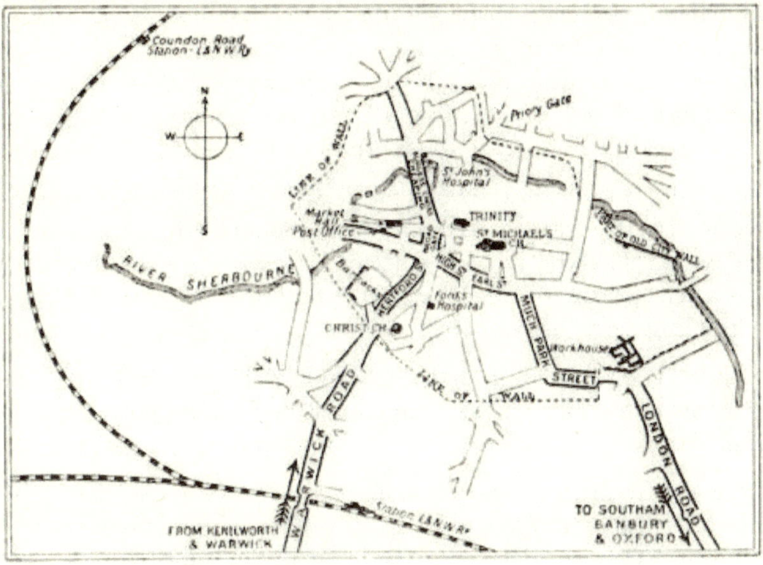

TOWN PLAN NO. 15—COVENTRY.

COVENTRY

The city derives its name from Conventre, or Convent Town, in recognition of the Benedictine monastery erected by Leofric and Godiva in 1043. The well-known legend connected with these famous personages need only be referred to here. Gosford Green, outside the town, was the scene of the historical encounter between the Dukes of Hereford and Norfolk in the reign of Richard II., which had such momentous results. Many Parliaments have been held in the town, and it was famous for the great number of religious communities which during the medieval period were lodged in the town. The ancient fortifications were dismantled in the time of Charles II. as a punishment for the Commonwealth tendencies of the citizens.

St. Michael's Church, a 'masterpiece of art,' and one of the finest parish churches in England, stands in the centre of the city. It is in the Perpendicular style, and has been recently restored. The spire is 303 feet high, and was begun in 1372; flying buttresses of great elegance support the tower. The oldest part of the church is the south porch, with a parvise over it. The chapels belonging to the various guilds in the town still retain their old names. There are many effigies, but none of great antiquity.

Holy Trinity Church is adjacent to St. Michael's. The date of foundation is unknown; the style is late Early English, and the work by the north porch dates from *c.* 1259. The porch has a domus, or priest's chamber, over it. There are several chapels in the church devoted to the city guilds. The foundations and remains noticed on the north side of the church are those of the west front of the cathedral, built about 1260 upon a preceding Norman foundation. It was the Priory Church of the monastery founded by Leofric, and was demolished at the Reformation.

St. Mary's Hall, near St. Michael's, was begun in 1394, and belonged to three guilds. It is of very great interest, and should on no account be passed by. The great hall, crypt, tapestry, ancient glass windows, and knaves' post, are all objects worthy of attention, while the building generally is a vivid reminder of medieval life and feeling.

Bablake Hospital, founded in 1560, is close to St. John's Church, and presents some picturesque examples of half-timber construction with quaint gables.

Peeping Tom is a prominent feature of the King's Head Hotel in Smithford Street, and Ford's Hospital, down Greyfriar's Lane, possesses an extremely fine façade and a charming timbered court rich in carved oak and diamond-paned windows.

The road to Southam and Banbury leaves Coventry as the London Road, and about two miles to the south Whitley Abbey is reached, formerly the seat of Lord Hood, son of the famous Admiral. In Whitley Abbey Charles I. resided while conducting operations against Coventry in 1622. On Whitley Common are traces of earthworks thrown up by the Royalists. Baginton, lying about two miles to the right, contains the remains of an ancient castle. Shortly after Whitley the road divides, the one going to Southam being that upon the right. A turning shortly afterwards at the cross-roads leads to the well-known Stoneleigh Abbey, lying five miles to the west, the site of a former castle and of a subsequent foundation for Cistercian monks, which was dispossessed at the Reformation. Some remains of the castle exist, but the present building is an imposing range of buildings in the classic style, and forms, with the grounds, one of the most splendid country homes in the kingdom. It is the seat of Lord Leigh.

Long Itchington has some fine half-timbered houses, and is a picturesque village. The Church was rebuilt in the fourteenth century by the Priors of Maxstoke. In the eighteenth century the spire was damaged by lightning; hence its present truncated appearance. The aisle is part of the original church, and is Early English except the doorway, which dates from the Norman period. There are some very interesting details to be found in the interior, notably the chancel screen, which is an extremely rare example of early fourteenth-century woodwork. St. Wolstan, the last of the Saxon Bishops, was a native of this place. Long Itchington was honoured by two visits from Queen Elizabeth during her progresses to Kenilworth. Two miles farther on is S o u t h a m , of no particular interest, although the church may perhaps repay a casual inspection. The road lies through a pleasant district, essentially Midland in its general aspects, but near the road turning off to Fenny Compton higher ground is reached. C r o p r e d y , where the battle was fought in 1644, is one and a half miles to the east by the turning close to Mollington.

BANBURY

Banbury is chiefly known by reason of its cross and its cakes. The former has been destroyed, but a replica exists upon the site. It is a small borough of about 4,000 inhabitants, and was formerly a notable place for the manufacture of plush, but now produces agricultural implements and portable engines. A castle was built here in 1125, but it was entirely destroyed in the C i v i l W a r . The moat, however, may still be traced. In 1469 the common men of Yorkshire, to the number of about 16,000, marched to Banbury under the leadership of 'Robin of Redesdale,' and captured the Earl of Pembroke, after inflicting a defeat upon him on the borders of Oxford. A college and hospital formerly existed in the town. The church is of comparatively modern construction, having been thoroughly rebuilt about a century ago.

Leaving Banbury, the little village of A d d e r b u r y possesses a church the chancel of which was built by William of Wykeham. Passing the Astons, North, Mid, and Steeple, we come to the junction of roads leading respectively to Woodstock and Oxford, and at this point a Roman road—the Akeman Street—crosses the route, running between Cirencester and Bicester. In the course of a few miles the outlying portions of Oxford appear in view.

MAGDALEN TOWER AND BRIDGE, OXFORD.

SECTION XI
(TRUNK ROUTE)

OXFORD TO LONDON, 67½ MILES

DISTANCES ALONG THE ROUTE

	Miles.	
Oxford to Dorchester	9	¼
Dorchester to Nettlebed	9	½
Nettlebed to Henley	4	½
Henley to Maidenhead	9	¼
Maidenhead to Windsor	6	½
Windsor to Staines	6	¼
Staines to Hampton	7	
Hampton to Hampton Court	1	
Hampton Court to Kingston	1	¾
Kingston to the G.P.O., London	12	½

NOTES FOR DRIVERS

Between **Oxford and Maidenhead** the road is somewhat hilly, but the surface is generally good; there is a steep hill (1 in 13) **after leaving Henley**.

From **Maidenhead to London** the road is level, with an excellent surface, except **between Maidenhead and Windsor**, where the road is sometimes flooded.

PLACES OF INTEREST ON THE ROUTE

Sandford-on-Thames.—Small village; church not interesting; remains of preceptory of Knights Templars.

Nuneham Courtney.—Eighteenth-century village, very unusual; Manor-house of Harcourts.

Dorchester.—Old village, with many picturesque cottages; Abbey Church of considerable interest.

Henley.—Picturesque little town; the church, Early English and Tudor; splendid river views; the Town Hall.

Maidenhead.—Large modern town; fine boating centre.

Eton.—The college and War Memorial Hall.

Windsor.—The castle, dating from the Norman period, with many subsequent additions; Town Hall, finished by Wren; a few old houses.

Hampton.—Hampton Court, magnificent palace of Henry VIII.

Kingston.—The church and Coronation Stone; almshouses and Lovekyn Chapel.

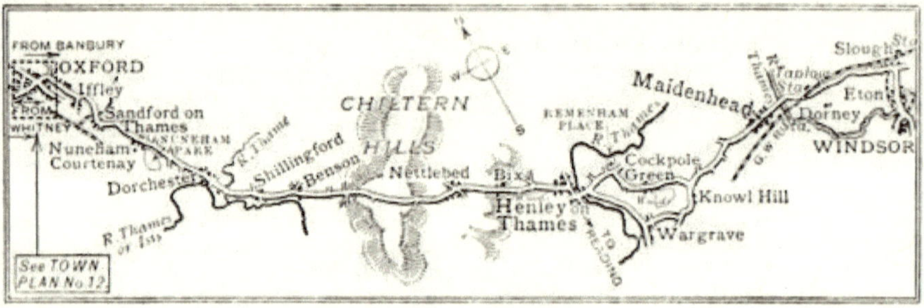

(TRUNK) No. 11. OXFORD TO WINDSOR.

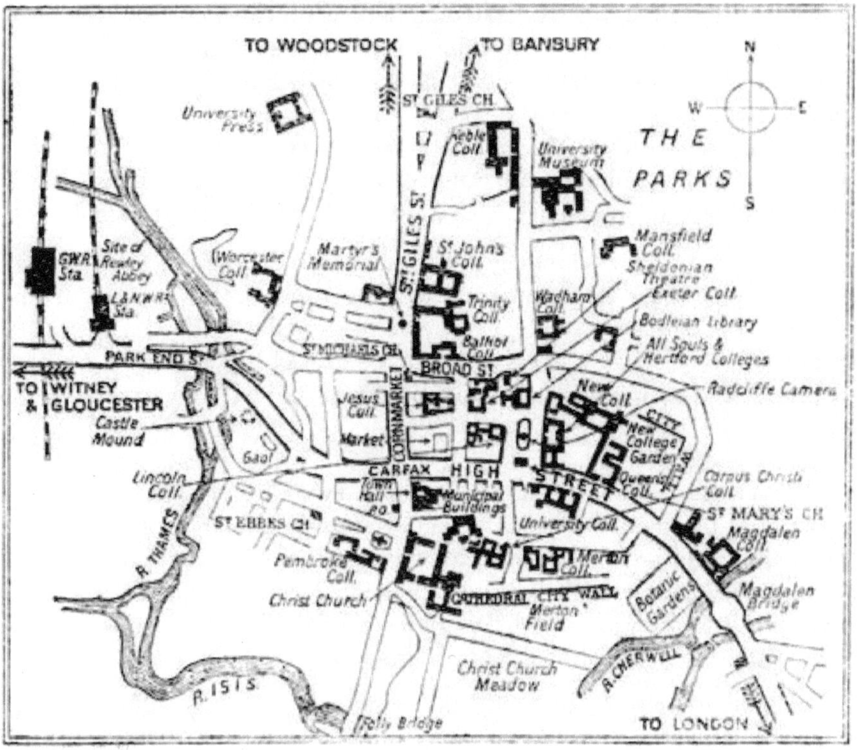

TOWN PLAN NO. 12—OXFORD.

OXFORD

The entrance to the 'city of palaces' is through suburbs of a commonplace, uninteresting, or even ugly character, the builders having apparently gained no inspiration from the magnificent examples of architecture which they are gradually hemming in. That such squalid, or, at the best, perky and meretricious streets of houses should have been allowed to encompass the architectural splendours of the great University is a public scandal, and it is to be hoped that before many years have passed some steps will be taken to wipe out the worst of these new abominations. To adequately describe Oxford within the limits of this work is impossible, and it will be sufficient to indicate the salient features which should not be passed over. The city lies upon a low ridge between the Thames and the Cherwell, and is surrounded by a fine range of hills. The imposing array of towers and spires, the many colleges with their historic quadrangles, the avenues and groves and secluded college gardens, the marvellous profusion of carved stonework, all combine to render the nucleus of this ancient seat of learning one of the most beautiful in the British Empire. The Bodleian Library is the hub round which the colleges cluster, and after it has been seen the church of St. Mary the Virgin should be visited, from its long connection with the seat of learning. Near it are the New Schools, the Botanic Garden, and the Clarendon Press, while the Taylor building contains many interesting pictures. Of the colleges, All Souls, Balliol, Brasenose, Christ Church, Magdalen, Merton, and New College, are among the most interesting.

The Cathedral belonging to Christ Church dates from 1160, and is a noble example of Norman architecture. The nave is pure Norman, the chancel Transitional, the chapter-house Early English. The shrine of St. Frideswide, the Bishop's throne, and the grand modern reredos, are particularly notable.

The first village passed after leaving Oxford is Sandford-on-Thames, but the flatness of the country and the presence of a paper-mill with a tall chimney deprive the place of any particular charm beyond what is found in the quietest reaches of the Upper Thames. Sandford Church is not interesting, but there are remains of a preceptory of Knights Templars at the farm by the brook a little to the north-west.

The road continues parallel with the river, and soon passes through the curiously uniform village of Nuneham Courtney. The two lines of picturesque cottages facing one another across the road were built by the first Earl Harcourt, who, disliking the proximity of the village to the manor-house, razed the cottages to the ground after constructing the new ones, which have now been sufficiently toned down by the weather to give a pleasing effect. This same building Earl demolished the old church and erected another near the house, now abandoned for a new one lately put up near the village. He also rebuilt the house (*not shown to visitors*) in the severely classic style in vogue at the close of the eighteenth century. The grounds and gardens were laid out in part by the popular 'Capability' Brown, and these may be seen on Tuesdays and Thursdays in the summer. *It is advisable, however, if one particularly wishes to see them, to write in advance to Mr. H. Gale, Nuneham Courtney.*

About a mile beyond the village, at the cross-roads, there formerly stood a little hostelry called the Golden Ball. It acquired a bad reputation through the murder of a guest by his servant. The landlord, having been found with a knife in his hand in the dead man's bedroom, was condemned to death and hanged, but later on the servant confessed that he had committed the murder which the landlord had intended.

DORCHESTER

is a dreamy old village, beautifully placed upon the River Thames. It contains many quaint timbered houses, some with thatched roofs, and nearly all with some attractive features which make it hard to tear oneself away from the place. The chief object of interest, apart from the cottage architecture, is the huge church, so strangely out of place in such a hamlet. Dorchester, however, has a history stretching right back to the British period. During the Roman occupation the camp here was supposed to be called *Dourcastrum*, altered into Dorchester in the Saxon period, but this Roman name is uncertain. When Dorchester was the seat of the Saxon bishopric of Wessex, the see included about twenty English counties, but Remigius, the first Norman Bishop, transferred it to Lincoln in 1085. The Saxon church, built in 1036, was occupied as a monastic church in 1140, when a monastery of the Augustinians was founded. In 1200, and also in 1350, extensive additions were made. In the church the Jesse window on the north side is unique, for the figures are carved in stone. The east window is a remarkable example of Decorated work; there is a massive buttress in the centre, and the whole of the spaces are occupied by reticulated tracery. The recumbent effigies, dating from 1200 to 1410, are very interesting, while a brass of the Henry V. period lies in the floor. The furnishing of the interior savours so much of the Roman church that one might easily imagine oneself on the other side of the Channel. One notices a bell conspicuous on the altar steps, and 'sacred' pictures, with candles and half-withered floral offerings in front of them, are placed on the pillars and elsewhere! Is the Bishop of Oxford aware of these strange reversions to the practices condemned by the Protestant Church of England for the last four centuries? The leaden font is of Norman workmanship, and is a comparatively rare object. In the churchyard stands a cross with a restored head.

The ascent of the Chilterns is very gradual, becoming steeper, however, in places, and delightful views are obtained over the surrounding country. The quaint little village of Nettlebed stands upon the summit (1,650 feet above sea-level), and thence the descent to Henley commences. Near Nettlebed many cultivated downs are to be seen, their rounded summits crowned as a rule with plantations—a contrast in this respect with the bare South Downs. These rounded knolls are all that denudation has left of the tertiary sand deposits on the chalk. In many parts beeches flourish, and occasionally brick and timber cottages of quaint aspect are passed.

HENLEY-ON-THAMES

is a charming old town, apart altogether from the prominent position it holds in the boating world, owing to the magnificent reach of the Thames which occurs here. There are many picturesque old houses in the wide, sunny street, and, as at Dorchester, the artist and architect will find much to attract their attention. The Church, standing out boldly near the bridge, possesses an Early English chancel, and the oldest part of the nave is of the same date. Nearly everything else, including the flint tower, is Tudor. A monument to Lady Elizabeth Periam, a sister of Lord Bacon and the mistress of Greenlands (died 1621), is under the tower. There are two hagioscopes and a priest's entrance to the vanished rood-loft. The bridge, with open stone parapets, was built in 1786, after the old one had been carried away by a flood. It is, therefore, much older than the regatta, which was first held in 1839.

The road between Henley-on-Thames and Maidenhead crosses the ground lying in a loop of the Thames, gradually rising from Henley and falling towards Maidenhead. The numerous turnings should be taken with care. About two miles before reaching Maidenhead the Bath road is joined.

MAIDENHEAD

is more a centre for river excursions and boating-parties than a place of any attractiveness in itself. It might easily be mistaken for one of the better suburbs of London, and contains practically nothing of interest. The great railway-bridge, with spans of 128 feet, was designed by Brunel.

ETON

On the left of the High Street, leading to the bridge facing Windsor, are the picturesque Tudor buildings and the huge chapel of Eton College. The great courtyard, surrounded by beautifully mellowed ranges of red-brick buildings on three sides and the chapel on the south, is delightfully picturesque; and the chapel itself, with its enormous buttresses and lovely Perpendicular details, is a noble work within and without. A statue of Henry VI., the founder, stands in the centre of the large courtyard. The famous playing-fields, where it is generally understood that those qualities which won the Battle of Waterloo were developed, extend down to the Thames.

WINDSOR

As one crosses the bridge, the long, imposing line of the castle walls and towers frowns above the red roofs of the little town, generally described as the Royal Borough of Windsor. A steep street winds up to the castle gateway, and as one approaches nearer, the work of Wyatville on the huge pile becomes painfully apparent. In vain does one look for the slightest indication that the whole of the great fortress, including the conspicuous Round Tower, was not built yesterday. This is the tragedy of Windsor, and after the first general glance one learns to expect nothing that tells its age by its masonry or its weathering. Everything, except the timber and brick Horseshoe Cloisters, is encased in harsh grey stone of a drearily uniform grey.

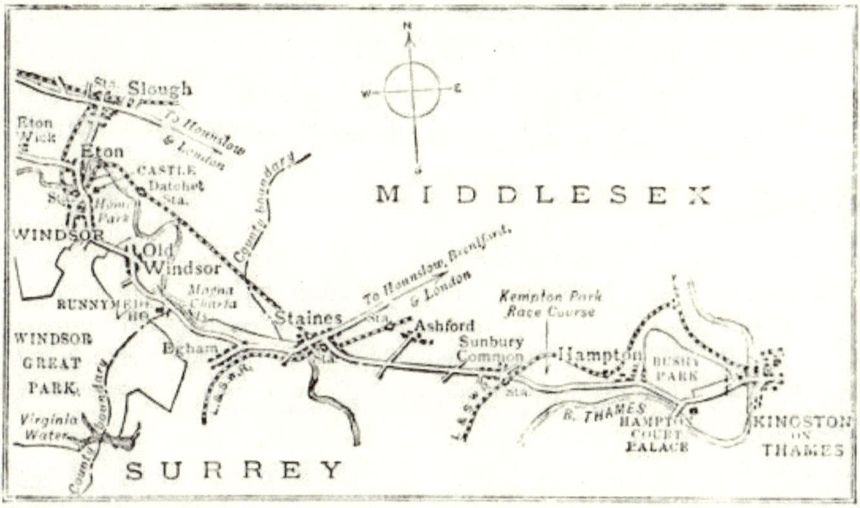

(TRUNK) No. 11. WINDSOR TO LONDON.

The way into London from Kingston-on-Thames is over Putney Heath and across Putney Bridge, where it is only necessary to follow the motor omnibuses to reach Hyde Park Corner or any other central point.]

It was probably William the Conqueror who built the first fortress on the wonderfully defensive site raised above the Thames, but Henry III., the builder of Westminster Abbey and much of the Tower of London, who planned the castle on its present vast scale. Edward III., having instituted the Order of the Garter, gave up the lower ward to that distinguished body of knights, and it was he who employed William of Wykeham as his architect or surveyor. The third, and practically the last, great builder was George IV., who gave up the historic buildings, then in bad repair, to the tender mercies of Sir Jeffry Wyatville, with the results already deplored.

(*The State apartments may be seen during the absence of the Court, but about a week elapses after the Royal departure before the public are admitted.*)

The magnificent Chapel of St. George—one of the three finest Perpendicular chapels in the kingdom—was mainly built by Edward IV., and finished by Henry VII. and VIII. In the choir are the stalls of the Knights of the Garter, twenty-six in number, with their banners above. Edward IV., Henry VI., Henry VIII., and Jane Seymour and Charles I., were all buried in the chapel.

Windsor Park is famous for the Long Walk—three straight miles of elms, planted by Charles II.; for the beautiful artificial lake, known as Virginia Water; and for the mausoleum in the grounds of Frogmore House, where

Queen Victoria and the good Prince Consort lie buried. (*On one day only—December 14—every year is this open to the public.*)

The road keeps near the river, and passes close to historic Magna Charta Island, where the unwilling John Lackland signed the great charter of English liberty in 1215.

STAINES

possesses an important bridge, the descendant of a wooden one which stood there in 1262. The stone bridge, put up in 1792, gave way, and its successor, built in 1803, was a bold engineering feat in the form of a single iron span of 180 feet; but this, too, had to be replaced, and in 1829 the present stone bridge was planned. It was opened in 1832 by William IV. and Queen Adelaide.

After passing the picturesque Hampton Court Green, one reaches Wolsey's magnificent red-brick palace—

HAMPTON COURT

The site had been in the possession of the Knights of St. John of Jerusalem, and it was from the Prior that Cardinal Wolsey obtained a lease in 1514. He demolished the manor-house, then standing, and in its place planned the stately palace, with its several courtyards entered by great gateways of red brick and stone. Here the princely ecclesiastic entertained in a manner so sumptuous that the Court of Henry VIII. was outshone by its brilliance. In 1526, the King having commented on this fact, Wolsey promptly handed over his palace to his royal master, who did not hesitate to accept a gift so pleasing. After Wolsey's death, Henry spent much time at Hampton Court, and rebuilt a large part of the palace.

To chronicle a bare summary of historic events which took place in the castle is not possible here, but in the early period of its existence Edward VI. was born there, and within these old red walls Jane Seymour died, Catherine Howard was disgraced, and Catherine Parr was married. Here, too, Charles I. spent his honeymoon, and afterwards was confined as a prisoner for three months.

KINGSTON-ON-THAMES

on the other side of the river, is a busy little town of some picturesqueness, possessing at one end of its narrowing market-place the famous Coronation Stone from which the place derives its name. The Perpendicular church, which is large and contains a monument by Chantrey, used to have a quaint custom of cracking nuts during the services on the Sunday preceding Michaelmas Eve. So great was the noise of crunching nuts that it was almost impossible to hear the voice of the clergyman.

After ascending Kingston Hill the road crosses Putney Heath, and enters the Metropolis through the now uninteresting suburb of Putney. After crossing Putney Bridge, the motor omnibuses are the best guide to follow.

A SHORT TABLE, SHOWING THE KINGS AND QUEENS OF ENGLAND SINCE ALFRED THE GREAT, THE CHIEF EVENTS OF THEIR REIGNS, AND THE STYLE OF ARCHITECTURE PREVAILING IN EACH PERIOD

ARCHITECTURAL PERIOD.	SOVEREIGNS.	IMPORTANT EVENTS.
Saxon or Pre-Norman	*Saxon Kings from Alfred the Great.*	
	Alfred, 871	Danish invasions
	Edward the Elder, 901	
	Athelstane, 925	
	Edmund, 941	
	Edred, 946	
	Edwy, 955	
	Edgar, 959	
	Edward the Martyr, 975	
	Ethelred the Unready, 978	
	Edmund Ironside, 1016	
	Danish Kings.	
	Cnut, 1017	
	Harold Harefoot, 1036	
	Hardicanute, 1040	
	Saxon Kings.	
	Edward the Confessor, 1042	

	Harold II. 1066	Norman Conquest
Norman and Transitional, 1066-1190	William I., 1066	Domesday compilation
	William II., 1087	First Crusade, 1096
	Henry I., 1100	
	Stephen, 1135	Civil war with Matilda throughout reign
	Henry II., 1154	Murder of Becket, 1170
Early English, 1190-1280	Richard I., 1189	Third Crusade, 1189
	John, 1199	The Interdict, 1208 Magna Charta, 1215 Invasion of Louis the Dauphin, 1215
	Henry III., 1216	Battle of Lewes, 1264 First Parliament, 1265
Decorated, 1280-1360	Edward I., 1272	War with Scotland
	Edward II., 1307	
	Edward III., 1327	The Black Death, 1349
Perpendicular, 1360-1500	Richard II., 1377	Wat Tyler's Rebellion
	Henry IV., 1399	
	Henry V., 1413	Battle of Agincourt
	Henry VI., 1422	Wars of the Roses
	Edward IV., 1461	Wars of the Roses Printing introduced
	Edward V., 1483	Murdered in the Tower
	Richard III., 1483	Killed at Bosworth
Tudor, 1500-1600	Henry VII., 1485	Discovery of America, 1492
	Henry VIII., 1509	Field of the Cloth of Gold, 1520 Cardinal Wolsey, 1471-1530

		Dissolution of the Monasteries, 1536
	Edward VI., 1547	Copy of the Bible ordered to be placed in every church
	Mary, 1553	Persecution of Protestants
	Elizabeth, 1558	Execution of Mary Queen of Scots, 1587 Spanish Armada, 1588
Jacobean	James I., 1603	Gunpowder Plot, 1605
	Charles I., 1625	Civil War began, 1642
	The Commonwealth, 1649	
	Charles II., 1660	The Great Plague, 1665
	James II., 1685	Monmouth's Rebellion, 1685 Revolution and landing of William of Orange, 1688
Queen Anne	William and Mary, 1689	
	Anne, 1702	Union of England and Scotland
Georgian	George I., 1714	South Sea Bubble, 1720
	George II., 1727	Rebellion of 1745 Taking of Canada, 1759
	George III., 1760	American War of Independence, 1775 French Revolution, 1789
	George IV., 1820	
	William IV., 1830	The first railway opened Reform Act, 1832

Victorian	Victoria, 1837	The Chartists, 1848 Great Exhibition, 1851 Crimean War, 1854 Indian Mutiny, 1857
	Edward VII., 1901	
	George V., 1910	

MOTOR-CAR SIGNS

A	London
AA	Southampton (C.C.)
AB	Worcestershire
AC	Warwickshire
AD	Gloucestershire
AE	Bristol
AF	Cornwall
AH	Norfolk
AI	Meath
AJ	Yorkshire (N.R.)
AK	Bradford (Yorks)
AL	Nottinghamshire
AM	Wiltshire
AN	West Ham
AO	Cumberland
AP	Sussex, East
AR	Hertfordshire
AS	Nairn
AT	Kingston-on-Hull
AU	Nottingham
AW	Salop
AX	Monmouthshire
AY	Leicestershire

B	Lancashire
BA	Salford
BB	Newcastle-on-Tyne
BC	Leicester
BD	Northamptonshire
BE	Lindsey, Lincs
BF	Dorsetshire
BH	Buckinghamshire
BI	Monaghan
BJ	Suffolk, East
BK	Portsmouth
BL	Berkshire
BM	Bedfordshire
BN	Bolton
BO	Cardiff
BP	Sussex, West
BR	Sunderland
BS	Orkney
BT	Yorkshire (E.R.)
BU	Oldham
BW	Oxfordshire
BX	Carmarthenshire
BY	Croydon

C	Yorkshire (W.R.)
CA	Denbighshire
CB	Blackburn
CC	Carnarvonshire
CD	Brighton
CE	Cambridgeshire
CF	Suffolk, West
CH	Derby
CI	Queen's County
CJ	Herefordshire
CK	Preston
CL	Norwich
CM	Birkenhead
CN	Gateshead
CO	Plymouth
CP	Halifax
CR	Southampton
CT	Kesteven, Lincs
CU	South Shields
CW	Burney
CX	Huddersfield
CY	Swansea
D	Kent

DA	Wolverhampton
DB	Stockport
DC	Middlesbrough
DE	Pembrokeshire
DF	Northampton
DH	Walsall
DI	Roscommon
DJ	St. Helens
DK	Rochdale
DL	Isle of Wight
DM	Flintshire
DN	York
DO	Holland, Lincs
DP	Reading
DR	Devonport
DS	Peebles
DU	Coventry
DW	Newport (Mon.)
DX	Ipswich
DY	Hastings
E	Staffordshire
EA	West Bromwich
EB	Isle of Ely
EC	Westmorland

ED	Warrington
EE	Grimsby
EF	West Hartlepool
EH	Hanley
EI	Sligo
EJ	Cardiganshire
EK	Wigan
EL	Bournemouth
EM	Bootle
EN	Bury
EO	Barrow-in-Furness
EP	Montgomeryshire
ES	Perth
ET	Rotherham
EU	Breconshire
EW	Huntingdonshire
EX	Great Yarmouth
EY	Anglesea

F	Essex
FA	Burton-on-Trent
FB	Bath
FC	Oxford
FD	Dudley
FE	Lincoln

FF	Merionethshire
FH	Gloucester
FI	Tipperary (N.R.)
FJ	Exeter
FK	Worcester
FL	Peterborough
FM	Chester
FN	Canterbury
FO	Radnorshire
FP	Rutlandshire
G	Glasgow
H	Middlesex
HI	Tipperary
HS	Renfrew
IA	Antrim
IB	Armagh
IC	Carlow
ID	Cavan
IE	Clare
IF	Cork (County)
IH	Donegal
IJ	Down

IK	Dublin
IL	Fermanagh
IM	Galway
IN	Kerry
IO	Kildare
IP	Kilkenny
IR	King's County
IT	Leitrim
IU	Limerick
IW	Londonderry
IX	Longford
IY	Louth
IZ	Mayo
J	Durham
JI	Tyrone
JS	Ross and Cromarty
K	Liverpool
KI	Waterford
KS	Roxburgh
L	Glamorganshire
LB	London
LC	London

LI	West Meath
LN	London
LS	Selkirk
M	Cheshire
MI	Wexford
MS	Stirling
N	Manchester
NI	Wicklow
NS	Sutherland
O	Birmingham
OI	Belfast
OS	Wigtown
P	Surrey
PI	Cork
PS	Shetland
R	Derbyshire
RI	Dublin
RS	Aberdeen

S	Edinburgh
SA	Aberdeen (County)
SB	Argyll
SD	Ayr
SE	Banff
SH	Berwick
SJ	Bute
SK	Caithness
SL	Clackmannan
SM	Dumfries
SN	Dumbarton
SO	Elgin
SP	Fife
SR	Forfar
SS	Haddington
ST	Inverness
SU	Kincardine
SV	Kinross
SW	Kirkcudbright
SX	Linlithgow
SY	Midlothian
T	Devonshire
TI	Limerick

TS	Dundee
U	Leeds
UI	Londonderry
US	Govan
V	Lanark
VS	Greenock
W	Sheffield
WI	Waterford
WS	Leith
X	Northumberland
XS	Paisley
Y	Somersetshire
YS	Partick

www.ingramcontent.com/pod-product-compliance
Lightning Source LLC
LaVergne TN
LVHW100729061126
851857LV00011B/453